ADVANCE PRAISE FOR
HOW TO MANAGE COMPLEX PROGRAMS

This book offers a wealth of advice on program management, describing
how to scale up project management for large endeavors and avoid
common pitfalls along the way.

**—Rhonda Hostetler, PMP, Project Manager,
UC Berkeley Energy Biosciences Institute**

At long last we have a definitive work on program management. *How to
Manage Complex Programs* brings together a comprehensive view of
programs and how to manage them. Tom Kendrick has added new
research and insights to the fundamental knowledge about managing
complexity in the project/program arena. His insights and powerful
examples provide learning that can be applied immediately to even the
most complex program. Kendrick's style is easy and enjoyable to read.
How to Manage features nuggets for very experienced program managers
and an excellent approach for those new to managing complexity. This
is one of those books I have needed in my own attempts at managing
complex programs. This book will become a prominent and oft used part
of my project management bookshelf, and it should be required reading
for anyone asked to manage a complex program or project.

**—Patrick Neal, Ph.D., PMP, Principal Consultant,
Project Synergistics**

I was particularly impressed by the emphasis in Tom Kendrick's book on program strategy alignment and on pragmatic decision-making. He not only clearly describes program management challenges throughout the book, but he offers the reader effective guidance for dealing with them.
—**Frances C. Bellows, J.D., PMP,**
Strategy Implementation
and Planning Consultant

HOW TO MANAGE COMPLEX PROGRAMS

HOW TO MANAGE COMPLEX PROGRAMS

High-Impact Techniques for Handling Project
Workflow, Deliverables, and Teams

TOM KENDRICK

HarperCollins Leadership

AN IMPRINT OF HARPERCOLLINS

CONTENTS

Contents

ACKNOWLEDGMENTS

This book is the result of many classes, workshops, discussions, debates, personal experiences, and much more. I am deeply grateful to many friends with whom I have interacted and worked over the years. There are far too many to name, but a partial list includes Elie Asmar, James T. Brown, Ray Ju, Virginia Greiman, Takeo Kimura, Chuck Bosler, Craig Peterson, Esteri Hinman, and many colleagues from in and around Hewlett-Packard such as Terry Ash, Wolfgang Blickle, Ted Slater, Swen Conrad, Tom MacDonald, Lou Combe, Cedric Bru, Art Greenberg, John Lambert, Peter Bruce, Chris Briggs, Martin Smith, Garry Gray, Charlie Elman, Patrick Neal, Randy Englund, Richard Bauhaus, Richard Simonds, Scott Beth, Kathy Meikle, Denis Lambert, Ron Benton, Rick Ellis, Cathy Tonne, and Bill Seidman.

I am particularly grateful to all the patient managers who provided the most valuable crucible for learning, the opportunity to strive on following mistakes, stumbles, and problems—which are all inevitable on large programs—to discover what works and ultimately to succeed.

While others have contributed enormously to the content of this book, all errors, omissions, or other problems are strictly my own. Should you find any, please let me know.

INTRODUCTION

Programs are complex—often extremely complex—collections of projects. Successful program management begins with a good command of project management processes, but that is never sufficient. Once a project exceeds a certain scale, project processes become unwieldy. To make the methods of project management effective for major programs, the work must be broken down and organized into a set of interdependent undertakings that can be autonomously executed. Program management challenges include dealing with complex hierarchies in three main domains: deliverables, workflow, and staffing.

System deliverables require up-front analysis to decompose them into a hierarchy of understandable components. Successfully developing complex systems requires that each part be sufficiently independent to permit parallel development, with the interconnections to other components sufficiently defined to warrant confidence that they can be successfully integrated and function as expected.

Major programs involve thousands (or many thousands) of activities, overwhelming the basic project planning techniques. Developing practical, effective schedules for the work begins with decomposing program work (often along similar boundaries as the component deliverables) to limit what each project plan must contend with. This process involves trade-offs and a goal of minimizing the number of linkages and handoffs where workflow transitions between the related projects.

Program management also requires developing an organizational chart hierarchy for staff, ensuring that it is clear where each high-performing project team fits in a large community of contributors. Developing an appropriate layered structure for programs involving multiple distributed (often global) teams and project leaders can be challenging. Leadership, including use of effective program management office (PMO) techniques, is essential for motivating and coordinating the large staffs required by major programs.

This book focuses on the processes required to effectively manage programs. What follows assumes a knowledge of the fundamentals for managing projects effectively. The book does not focus on or prescribe any particular project methodology or processes, but rather shows how to build on effective project-level practices. Good program management need not rely on a specific approach for handling projects, but it does require that processes that work well are in place and consistently (and competently) applied. Project planning techniques may range from practices such as Scrum for agile undertakings to network critical path analysis for conventional projects, but effective program management always relies on some consistent, effective means for understanding the projects that constitute a program. Other necessary project management practices include project risk analysis and management, application of software tools, and other basic techniques.

This book also assumes that the organization has well-established, functioning life cycles or iteration standards, clearly defined project metrics that are accepted and routinely used, and an analysis-based procedure for managing a portfolio of projects and programs. To thrive, the principles of effective program management require a firm organizational foundation to take care of both project details and the overall context. This book describes, using examples, how program management extends and builds on project management methods, and it explains techniques for organizing and controlling large, complex undertakings.

PMI (THE PROJECT MANAGEMENT INSTITUTE)

CHAPTER 1

Program Management

Make everything as simple as possible, but not simpler.
  —Albert Einstein

The size and scale of programs makes them complex and difficult to manage. As with any undertaking, the prospects for success diminish and uncertainty increases significantly with the magnitude of the work. Where small projects are almost always successful and carry low risk, long-duration programs with large staffs of contributors have a high probability of falling short of their goals, and many fail.

Program management techniques strive to simplify the work by breaking it down into more manageable pieces. By converting large undertakings into collections of smaller projects, we move the work into a context where things are more easily understood and project management methods can be effective. That's the good news.

Unfortunately, decomposing a major effort into a coherent set of projects that can be independently planned and managed is easier said than done. The act of converting a large program into a collection of smaller projects does not make the complexity go away. Overall program complexity affects the deliverables, the workflow, and organizing the people who will do the work. Creating a program plan that will serve as an effective foundation for execution can succeed only if it is done carefully and with an understanding that what remains, even using the best program management methods, will still be challenging. Simplicity is a worthy goal, but there are limits.

This chapter explores the organizational context for programs, describes a range of program types and sizes, discusses program origins and challenges, and explores the dimensions of complexity that programs must face.

PROJECTS, PROGRAMS, AND PORTFOLIOS

Projects are undertakings that are of finite duration and seek to deliver a specific result using limited assigned resources. Typical organizations have many projects underway in parallel, with a wide variety of goals. Some of these projects are autonomous, with little connection to other work, while others are chartered as a part of something larger, encompassing several or even many projects.

Program is a term that means different things in different contexts, but the Project Management Institute (PMI) defines a program as "a group of related projects, subprograms, and program activities that are managed in a coordinated way to obtain benefits not available from managing them individually." Subprograms may be part of larger programs, also containing multiple projects. Programs require a leader and generally a program staff, sometimes referred to as a program (or project) management office (PMO). Program activities often involve effort in the "white space" outside specific defined projects and subprograms, effort provided by support, marketing, legal, manufacturing, or other operational functions. Programs are generally larger than projects, but there may be some overlap in scale between large projects and small programs.

At any given time an organization may have multiple programs executing alongside independent projects. All of these undertakings taken together represent a portfolio of endeavors comprising projects, subprograms, programs, and other work. Graphically, such a portfolio might look something like Figure 1-1.

The relationship between portfolio management and project and program management is explored in some detail in Chapter 2.

PROGRAM DEFINITION

Programs are made up of related efforts, most of which will be projects staffed by a project leader and a team of contributors. Some clusters of projects may be complex enough to justify treatment as a program within a

Figure 1-1 A portfolio of projects and programs.

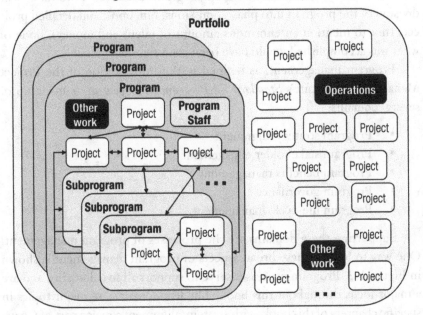

program, and the presence of these subprograms will result in a multiple-level program hierarchy.

The 20th-century NASA space program provides a good example of a multiple-level program hierarchy. Once President John F. Kennedy set the goal in 1961 of "landing a man on the moon and returning him safely to Earth," a massive manned space program took shape. Within the overall space program, three subprograms were outlined: the Mercury program with its one-astronaut missions, the subsequent Gemini program containing more complex two-astronaut launches, and finally the Apollo program supporting the three-astronaut flights capable of reaching and exploring the moon. Within these major subprograms, each was further subdivided into missions with specific goals to be achieved in order to support the objectives of later phases of the program. Further subprograms within each mission provided the systems, support, functions, and other needs for each launch. These were further broken down into increasingly detailed and specific efforts, ultimately delegated to project teams. Thousands of contributors worked on the projects that made the program successful. Without a clear division of the program into phases, missions, functions, and detailed projects (not to mention an enormous amount of talent and money), none of what was accomplished would have been even remotely possible.

Program management, as defined in the third edition of the Project Management Institute's *Standard for Program Management*, is made up of several domains:

- Program strategy alignment
- Program stakeholder engagement
- Program benefits management
- Program governance
- Program life-cycle management

Supporting these domains are the processes of program management. One way to look at these broad aspects of program management is shown in Figure 1-2. Program processes serve to support all five domains, and are a major focus throughout this book. The five domains are major topics in specific chapters of this book, with strategy alignment a major part of Chapter 2, and program governance addressed in both Chapters 2 and 5. Stakeholder engagement is central to Chapters 3, 5, and 6, and program benefits and results are a focus in Chapters 3 and 6. Details of the program life cycle are based on both the specifics of the work to be done and the outputs from

Figure 1-2 Program management domains.

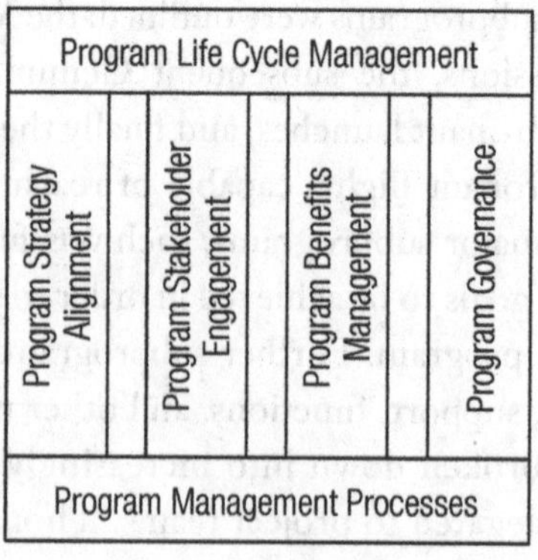

Program Life Cycle Management			
Program Strategy Alignment	Program Stakeholder Engagement	Program Benefits Management	Program Governance
Program Management Processes			

the other program management domains. Adopting and using an appropriate program life cycle is explored later in this chapter as well as in Chapter 4.

Ultimately programs are about getting results, generally results with substantial expected benefits and value. Program management requires a deep understanding of the synergies and strategies that underlie the objectives. Programs often carry long-term objectives that require a persistent, high-level focus on the main strategic priorities. These must be balanced with shorter-term tactical goals, but not so much that the things that are truly important can be undermined by what seems urgent at the moment. Program leaders must understand the overall organizational strategies and strive to remain aligned with them. The conflicting needs of dealing with detail-level complexity and high-level longer-term objectives are what make program management challenging.

HOW DO PROGRAMS ORIGINATE?

Successful programs generally require a lot of staff, money, time, and resources, so they tend to arise from the higher levels of an organization where there is sufficient authority to get them going. Some programs are aimed at solving significant problems, such as the following:

- Major customer or user difficulties
- Mandated legal, regulatory, or compliance changes
- Gaps and deficiencies in current offerings
- Significant competitive or external shifts
- Inefficient or expensive procedures
- Evolving organization needs
- Emerging risks

In addition to resolving shortfalls in the organization, programs also address strategic opportunities, including objectives such as these:

- Development of new products, platforms, solutions, or services
- Acquisitions of other companies or organizations

- Strategic partnerships, alliances, or collaborations
- New markets, users, or growth
- Long-term strategic plans
- Reorganization
- Executive fiat or initiatives

However programs arise, there is nearly always a lot of energy and enthusiasm, at least initially, because the program objectives tend to be important and come from people who have significant clout.

WHY ARE PROGRAMS DIFFICULT?

Programs are difficult to manage for quite a few reasons, most of them related to the scale and complexity of what is expected. Their size means that in most cases there are many diverse stakeholders. The deliverables (and there are almost always at least several) are generally complicated systems of interrelated components. Programs are also usually lengthy, far longer in duration than can be planned with much precision. The staffing for a large program involves more people than can be effectively coordinated as a single team, and the funding required is often both substantial and must cover future periods well beyond what is presently committed. The techniques of program management can help in each of these areas, but control of the work is never straightforward.

Stakeholders: The community of people involved with a large program can be both unruly and crowded. It is exceedingly unlikely that all those who can affect a program or will be affected by it will be in complete agreement on program objectives. Perspectives will differ and conflicts are common. Even when there is initial harmony, differences can arise in future program phases. Keeping a fix on expectations, desires, needs, and priorities, even among the most significant stakeholders, can be a full-time effort. Some ideas for establishing effective governance and managing stakeholder conflicts are explored in Chapters 2 and 3.

Deliverables: Program deliverables often involve complex hierarchies of interrelated systems and integrated components. To further complicate matters, definition of what is needed often lacks clarity, especially at the beginning. On lengthy programs, changes are inevitable. Controlling program scope effectively is never easy but can be made more tractable using systems analysis, iterative techniques, effective change control processes, and other tactics discussed in Chapter 3.

Planning: Programs often have long durations, and some (such as those aimed at long-term process improvement) may be initiated without a defined termination date. All project and program planning has a finite planning horizon, beyond which precise forecasts and estimates are not possible. The limits vary for different kinds of work, but very rarely will you be able to accurately plan for more than about 6 months of work (and for programs involving complex technology it will be considerably shorter). Program planning also must anticipate and manage workflow dependencies between the projects making up the program and external inputs and linkages. Developing credible, workable plans for program work and conducting periodic in-depth plan reviews are the focus of Chapters 4 and 6.

Leadership and staffing: The scale of programs involves many leadership, staffing, and financial challenges. The number of people involved is often very large, and coordinating their efforts is made even more difficult because of matrixed reporting relationships (where the connection to the program is "dotted line" for a significant number of program contributors). The effective authority and power of the program leader and staff is often weak, especially when dealing with distant, contract, or part-time program contributors. Programs with large staffs also must manage across a hierarchical organization chart having multiple levels, further diminishing relationships and teamwork. Across the program, projects and teams will rarely share common perspectives and backgrounds, so conflicts may be common and motivation may be low. Access to resources and budgets pose problems for many programs, particularly for major undertakings that will require renewal of funding each year to continue the work. Tactics that can help in these areas are explored in Chapter 5.

PROJECT/PROGRAM SIZE BOUNDARIES

As mentioned earlier, there may be some overlap in scale between a large project and a small program. In general, the size at which projects of a given type start to fail more often than not provides a reasonable limit for the utility of project management processes, and represents a good starting point for adopting program management techniques. Exactly where this threshold falls varies by program type, with predictable, routine projects having higher limits and "bleeding edge," novel, more uncertain projects having lower boundaries. That said, there are some general guidelines that broadly apply when determining when project management principles can be expected to falter.

Project leaders generally find that about 10 percent of their time is spent on activities associated with each contributor on a project team. This effort primarily involves communication (verbal and written, face to face, and electronic) and meetings, but also factors in general oversight, portions of work devoted to the team as a whole, and occasional interactions that are not strictly project oriented. Based on this, a project team should have roughly a dozen or so members. Teams of twenty or more people tend to interact too little, which interferes with teamwork and project progress.

Another perspective comes from the rough guidelines generally recommended for project planning. If a project plan has 100 to 200 lowest-level activities, it becomes difficult to understand and manage. At these levels, the utility of project scheduling tools decreases, and the logical workflow and interactions between parallel efforts become more difficult to see and control. Typical activity estimate guidelines fall into the range of 80 hours of effort or 2 to 20 workdays in duration (with an average of about 2 weeks). Both of these guidelines for work breakdown provide tasks that are small enough for fairly accurate estimating. This granularity also ensures a planned frequency for activity completion that will enable project leaders to detect problems quickly and respond to slippage while recovery remains straightforward.

If a hundred or so of these activities are scattered among about a dozen contributors, the project leader will have a manageable ten to twenty tasks ongoing at any one time, with five to ten completing in a typical weekly status interval. The overall project duration suggested by all of this (assuming all contributors are devoted to the work full-time) is about a half year, or perhaps a bit longer. This corresponds to the general guidelines for a maximum planning horizon, and tends to be about as far out as a project team will be able to schedule and to plan for risks.

An analysis from the cost perspective converges on similar numbers, with a project budget guideline of roughly $1 million (covering about 100 effort-months or so) being a typical maximum for normal projects. Once again, a project falls into the range of about a dozen people, with an approximate duration of a half year.

Simple projects can exceed these limits (although if they are truly simple, they rarely need to) and still be adequately controlled. For complicated projects, work that is not well defined, or environments anticipating a lot of change, much shorter, smaller, or less aggressive limits are more appropriate. Many such projects adopt agile methods, where iterations deliver results approximately monthly. They use feedback to adjust for future cycles and manage the unknowns, evolving requirements, and novelty.

Project management methods do work well, but only up to a point. Exactly where the threshold lies varies somewhat with the type of work, but the following are useful general limits for project parameters:

- Approximately ten to twelve full-time contributors
- Roughly 6 to 8 months of overall project duration
- About 100 to 200 lowest-level activities in the project work breakdown structure
- Around 100 effort-months of estimated work
- A budget nearing $1 million

Going beyond these limits creates project management challenges and difficulties. Program management techniques extend the usefulness of project management processes by breaking down larger undertakings into smaller projects. This can be effective, but only if the breakdown is done logically and the program leader applies program management techniques to understand and coordinate the resulting aggregation of projects.

PROGRAM LIFE CYCLES

Programs are, in general, much larger than projects. They have a start, an execution phase (containing multiple projects and other work) that can be quite lengthy, and may or may not have a planned close.

Program initiation requires significant effort, especially for major programs. It focuses on creating an overall business case and a roadmap laying out high-level expectations for the work. It also establishes the overall program governance, processes, staffing and funding required, and the infrastructure for the undertaking. Program initiation will be explored in some detail in Chapter 2.

Program execution focuses on delivering results. In this phase, the projects that make up the program will be defined, funded and planned, coordinated and synchronized, monitored, and brought to successful conclusion. The value and benefits expected from a program are delivered through the projects that constitute the majority of the program effort and expense. Program execution involves defining and controlling deliverables (discussed in Chapter 3), establishing coordinated plans (discussed in Chapter 4), leading the efforts (discussed in Chapter 5), and monitoring and controlling the overall work (discussed in Chapter 6).

Program closure winds down the work. Closure for some programs is planned from the beginning, but for others it may be left open-ended; the program will continue indefinitely as long as the benefits and value of the planned future phases justify program costs and overhead. Program closure is discussed in Chapter 7.

The structure of a program's execution phase varies depending on the needs of the sponsoring organization and the nature of the project breakdown. Some programs require large staffs and will include a collection of projects executing in parallel. Other programs will require a long duration and contain a series of projects in sequence. Still other programs will involve both, and contain a succession of multi-project phases. Each type of program carries some overhead for leadership, including a program staff or a PMO.

Programs Requiring Large Staffs

When the analysis of a large undertaking indicates the need for more contributors than can be managed effectively as a single project team, you can use program management techniques to break the effort down into a set of projects running in parallel, as in Figure 1-3. Defining the individual projects generally begins with system analysis to decompose program deliverables into components for development by the project teams. Such programs involve complex deliverable analysis, coordinated planning, and large hierarchical team leadership. Successful completion of such programs relies on the concepts in Chapters 3 through 5.

Programs with Long Durations

Programs that will require significant time to complete (or may be open-ended) can be decomposed into a succession of projects executed in sequence. This structure provides for shorter planning horizons and delivers a series of interim results, releases, or products. Figure 1-4 shows a multiphase program. Programs of this type generally have a staff small enough to

Figure 1-3 A program having a large staff and multiple project teams.

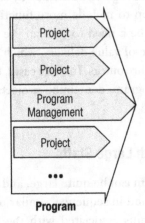

Project

Project

Program
Management

Project

•••

Program

Figure 1-4 A program made up of a sequence of projects.

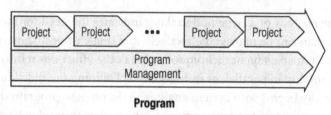

Program

work as a single team to address a sequence of related project objectives one after another. These programs do need some high-level overall analysis for the succession of deliverables required, along with a process for adjusting the specific scoping for each successive project. Planning and leadership for this sort of program differ little from that for basic project management. In fact, if the durations for each successive project are kept very short, in the range of several weeks, this type of program can be managed quite well using agile methods, such as Scrum (although for some programs you may need to be flexible with some of the guidelines and lengthen the "time boxes").

One aspect of such programs that can increase their complexity is a tendency for them to expand as the work progresses. Early work on such a program may be simple enough to be tackled by a single team, but eventually pressure may develop to include more functionality in future release phases. There may also be a need to overlap the work on succeeding releases to increase the rate of value delivery, which will also add complexity and require additional contributors. In these cases, the programs will morph into the next type of program, containing projects both in parallel and in sequence.

Lengthy Programs with Large Staffs

This final type of program can be quite large, and incorporates both projects running in parallel and in sequence, similar to Figure 1-5. Such programs are staffed by teams associated with the rows of the figure and organized around releases, phases, or iterations as defined by the columns.

Figure 1-5 A program with multiple phases staffed by several project teams.

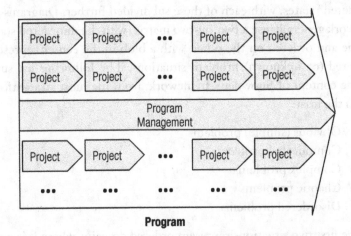

Program

Programs of this type may be small and contain only a few projects, or they can be massive, with many subprograms and hundreds of projects. Most multiphase programs with parallel projects tend to fall somewhere between these extremes.

Successful management of phased programs requiring parallel projects depends on effective planning, as discussed in Chapters 3 through 5.

DIMENSIONS OF PROGRAM COMPLEXITY

Managing a program requires dealing with complexity. Much has been written over the years about solving complex problems, but there has been a good deal of recent attention focused on this by Welsh academic and consultant David J. Snowden. He developed a framework for assessing the context of problems which he named "Cynefin" (a Welsh word roughly meaning "habitat"). He described Cynefin in a 2007 *Harvard Business Review* article he wrote with Mary E. Boone titled, "A Leader's Framework for Decision Making."

Snowden's framework divides problem situations into "ordered" and "unordered" states, with each of these subdivided further. Diagrams of the framework generally use a two-by-two matrix, with the unordered states on one side and ordered on the other, with a blob in the center representing disordered (or unknown) problem situations. The following list summarizes the content of Snowden's framework, from the most straightforward cases to the least:

1. Obvious (simple) problems
2. Complicated problems
3. Complex problems
4. Chaotic problems
5. Disordered problems

The first two situations represent ordered domains where it is possible to develop problem solutions through analysis. The remainder of the list contains cases where there is no obvious order or structure, and problem solutions, if they exist, must be developed using other means such as trial and error.

Obvious problems: Planning for a small project is generally a problem of the first type. There is a clear and apparent approach for achieving the objective, and developing a plan—if you even bother with one—is straightforward. The path forward is based on examining the goals, determining the work necessary, and then completing it using known methods and best practices.

Complicated problems: For larger projects and small programs, the picture becomes murkier. For these problems, the solution will not generally be immediately apparent. As with any situation containing many details, some of which may be incomplete or contradictory, the approach that makes the most sense begins with organizing what is known and then subjecting what you discover to analysis, seeking a way to proceed. This domain aligns well with the processes of basic project management. Project planning starts by defining the work, then analyzes the effort using techniques such as creating a work breakdown structure. Based on this analysis you can consider approaches, settle on a plan, and execute it. Resolving these problem cases requires expertise for dealing with unusual aspects and any inherent complications. In these cases you may find multiple approaches that could work, and there may be no clear "best" way forward. Overall, though, for these problems project leaders can develop reasonable confidence that their objectives are possible and develop plans to complete the work successfully.

Complex problems: Major programs fall solidly into the "unordered" Cynefin domains, with most being at least "complex." In these cases, the solution will neither be obvious nor attainable through simple analysis. Solving such problems starts with defining the situation as well as possible, selecting strategies that could either provide more information or represent progress. You may then initiate efforts and be guided by information that emerges as you continue. Essentially, agile management methods for project work rely on this strategy to create deliverables in the face of incomplete goals or evolving needs. Such methods assume that a solution will come into focus as the work proceeds, and the partial solutions that you create along the way will show the way to an eventual satisfactory conclusion.

Major programs tend to confront their complex environment with a combination of phased work (applying the incremental, step-by-step approach to develop course-correcting feedback as with agile methods) and decomposition of the effort aimed at converting complex problems into merely complicated ones. Although program decomposition into simpler subprograms and projects is rarely entirely successful, even the parts that are only partially successful (or fail) will provide data and experience along the way that provide the foundation for defining and planning future phases and continued progress.

Chaotic and disordered problems: The remaining two "unordered" Cynefin cases may have solutions or they may not. The approach for chaotic problems starts with taking a plausible action, hoping for beneficial results. If the outcome is adverse or carries unintended consequences, you can reverse what you did and try something else. Addressing such problems proceeds by taking additional actions that seem plausible based on prior results, and continuing either until you have solved the problem or it becomes clear that there may be no solution. Chaotic and truly disordered problems are not common for program management, because when it appears that there may be no solution or that the solution might involve prohibitive cost or effort, it is extremely unlikely that anyone will want to commit the significant investments needed to initiate a program in the first place. In fact, except in urgent situations such as natural disasters, most problems that are chaotic or disordered tend to be deferred or ignored (or, at best, monitored for signs indicating some hope of a solution).

Complex Programs

While complex programs may be approached using trial-and-error, brute-force techniques, it is nearly always much more efficient to break them down into more modest pieces that will allow a more planned, analytical approach. Breaking a lengthy undertaking into a more manageable set of shorter-duration phases deals with part of the challenge. Incremental delivery of results that will generate feedback and guidance for ongoing progress (similar to the practices of agile management) provides a useful strategy for reducing complexity.

Breaking a massive, complex program into smaller components can be even more powerful. Converting a major program into an aggregation of parallel, mostly autonomous projects begins with analysis of the complex system deliverables. Breaking complex program outputs into smaller components can yield a set of complicated, yet tractable, objectives. Deliverable breakdown starts the program planning process, and it strongly affects both the complexity of overall plans and the organization of staffing. As program plans develop, they result in multilevel hierarchies for deliverables, plans, and staffing that must be managed.

Program Deliverables

The initial complexity facing a typical program team involves the scope. Techniques for dealing with this are explored in Chapter 3 on program deliverable management. Program processes for managing scope include identifying and understanding key stakeholders, collecting requirements, resolving priority conflicts, and creating a high-level program roadmap that is consistent with overall program objectives.

Based on a roadmap, you can define details for the specific deliverables of the current phase of program work, and use system analysis to design subsystems and components that will fit together to deliver the expected functionality and value. Managing program scope also involves adopting rigorous and disciplined processes to be used for making future scoping decisions, managing scope changes, and uncovering and managing program scope risks.

Program Planning and Organization

Once the initial expected program deliverables have been defined and de-composed into smaller components, the projects needed to create them can be put in place. The structural hierarchy of the projects responsible for program efforts will generally mirror that of the system deliverables, and Chapter 4 covers techniques for managing the resulting hierarchy of projects.

Although there are structural similarities between the hierarchy de-scribing program scope and that for program projects, there are many addi-tional complexities associated with understanding workflow and developing a coordinated program plan. Dealing with this begins by defining consis-tent planning and execution methods across all program projects. The spe-cifics may be detail plan-oriented, agile, or anything that works, but the approaches used by all projects must be compatible to ensure overall pro-gram plan coherence. Project planning tools also need to be consistent to facilitate integration of the planning details from all program projects and subprograms into a cohesive overall program plan. Again, specific tool choices matter less than that the software and applications used for sched-uling and plan documentation are both suitable and consistent.

At the lowest level of program work, the project plans will focus on detailed tasks and results. At the program level, plans focus on the interfaces that define cross-project workflow and represent dependencies linking indi-vidual projects. Interfaces are a significant cause of program schedule slippage and other difficulties. Risk management is also a key part of program-level planning. Program risks include significant project risks, risks inherent to the program as a whole, and relevant risks external to the program. It is not uncommon to detect issues in schedule and risk planning that drive adjustments to scope definition and other plans.

Successful program execution depends on credible planning at all levels in the program's hierarchy of projects and a realistic baseline for each phase of the whole program.

Leadership and Staffing

Finally, each program has a third hierarchy: the organizational chart that describes the relationships of all the contributors who work on the program. This hierarchy again tends to share similarities with the structures for system deliverables and project plans, but it represents yet another source of program complexity. Program leadership and organizing the program staff are addressed in Chapter 5. Establishing structures for overall governance and alignment across the levels of program contributors is crucial to effective program management.

Near the top of your program organizational chart, you will need a competent staff (or PMO) to coordinate the work and keep things on track. You will also require skilled teams and leaders at all levels to execute the work. Program communications must effectively deal with geographic separation and other challenges. Motivating diverse teams on lengthy programs can be difficult, and there are many program risks to deal with related to managing a large staff of contributors. Program funding represents additional program challenges, because programs may be set up to have long durations, but most are only funded a year at a time. Some issues that arise when reviewing staffing-related plans may trigger additional modifications to program deliverables, timing, or other program aspects.

CHAPTER **2**

Program Initiation

Start with the end in mind.

—**Stephen R. Covey,** *The 7 Habits of Highly Effective People*

Programs require significant investments, efforts, and risks. Getting a major new program started requires assumptions about correspondingly large benefits. Although it is no guarantee, starting a new program well is essential to successfully achieving its desired results. This means digging into the initial assumptions and determining that they are realistic (or, at a minimum, plausible).

This chapter discusses processes for getting a program up and running. For a program or any other major undertaking, it is prudent to align the work with the overall objectives and purpose of the sponsoring organization. Major programs are often key to the pursuit of organizational goals, so they are usually tightly aligned with existing strategies and long-term objectives. Program initiation also requires strong sponsorship to ensure ongoing support and commitment throughout the expected duration of the work. Substantial programs consume a significant portion of an organization's resources, so the portfolio decision process plays a significant role in initiating and sustaining major new undertakings. Well-run organizations make portfolio and other program decisions using credible estimates of expected costs and benefits, in both the short and the long term. Although risks and challenges for programs may be difficult to assess comprehensively early on, effective program management works to understand and document the most significant hurdles ahead. Program initiation also must define the overall approach to be used for the work and all plans and other documents required. Finally, launching a program of almost any scale benefits from a well-planned startup event to ensure that it hits the ground running. This includes structured activities and explicit definition of initial program staffing, including the program manager and other key roles.

Throughout this chapter and later in the book, we refer to an example program of multiyear multinational information technology (IT) to illustrate the startup of a large infrastructure program. The program was conducted at Hewlett-Packard between 2002 and 2007. Some of the data have been simplified or otherwise modified to serve our purposes. In addition to showing how effective program management methods can be successfully used deliver substantial business benefits, the example also demonstrates that they can do so despite the organizational challenges in strategic direction, enterprise complexity, and management oversight of that time.

STRATEGIC ALIGNMENT AND TACTICAL OBJECTIVES

Isaac Newton's first law of motion states that a body at rest tends to remain at rest. Programs are collections, often quite large collections, of projects. Regardless of scale, programs tend to remain at rest unless and until a large-enough force comes along to start it moving. The larger the program, the more compelling the potential value of the work must be before anyone seriously contemplates taking it on.

Chapter 1 explored a number of potential sources for programs. Whatever their origin, all programs must have a credible and compelling answer to the question, What is its purpose? Many programs are initiated to serve as a direct link between stated organizational strategies and the specific project and other work necessary to carry them out. For a company that undertakes fee-for-service construction or other contract work, a new program might be a consequence of an accepted proposal. For a governmental agency, an originating program may be undertaken in support of some new agency responsibility. For an auto manufacturer, a program could involve designing a new vehicle, and for a service company a new program might entail developing and introducing an innovative new service.

Programs, however, are not always a direct consequence of stated high-level strategies. Some programs may be undertaken to meet regulatory or other external requirements, or to rework processes to make them faster, more efficient, or less costly. Still other programs might relate to expanding or developing new capabilities or facilities to support growth or to enhance the organization's viability. Whether a program directly emerges from an organization's stated strategies and objectives or is undertaken to "keep the plane in the air," each new program benefits greatly from a clear and compelling business case showing how it contributes value that supports the organization's goals.

Strategic alignment for many programs is often self-evident (the program would not exist in the first place unless some relatively high-level individual or committee saw at least a plausible business case to justify it), but even in these cases some exploration is in order. Clear program goals, embryonic as they may be, must be documented before the program starts.

If the program will be replacing an existing system or infrastructure, assess the status quo and document the "as is" situation. If the program is striving to create something new, there may be little to document, but always be skeptical in cases where the justification for a major undertaking depends upon successfully moving into a complete vacuum. Most high-tech startups are based on such programs, and statistically only about 10 percent of these are ultimately successful.

Once you have a clear notion of the current circumstances, outline what is expected from the program and when. As you flesh out the "to be" state, consider the short, medium, and long term. The short-term program goals (weeks or months) often include some project work to specify delivery goals in more detail for the program. Early objectives work to explore feasibility, or to initiate pilot or prototype efforts to refine long-term program goals. As you document early program objectives, be skeptical of assumptions that look overly optimistic—promising too much or underestimating efforts and costs. Clearly define, at least in terms of major deliverables, what the program is expected to achieve in the short run, and what is projected for the medium term—within a year or so.

Also spend some time looking at the overall long-term expectations for the program (a year or more in the future). Compare program aspirations to the organization's stated goals, and work to ensure that documented program objectives appear to be consistent. Strategies and tactics evolve over time, so major programs must evolve with them. Be wary of program goals out in the future that may be based on questionable assumptions about future needs, technical progress, market or external forces, or other factors that are likely to change. Undertaking a multiyear program to deal with a current situation can be perilous unless the objectives are sufficiently flexible to deal with future realities as they emerge.

As you work to verify that the overall direction for the program is consistent with what the organization wants to do, also consider who in the organization will be responsible for the big picture. If there is a history of frequent shifts in strategy or changes in the executive ranks seem likely in the near future, spend some time thinking about where and when probable changes may occur. Programs require long-term buy-in to be successful. A strong credible business case for the work that aligns with overall goals is necessary for establishing support early on, but things may (and likely will) change during a multiyear program. A program that seemed like a great idea to the executive committee at initiation could look very different a couple years later in the face of changing preferences and perspectives. Programs are initiated as a whole, but tend to be funded year by year. Ultimate program success requires monitoring what the organization is up to and keeping the program both visible and relevant as you progress.

A large IT effort at the Hewlett-Packard Company (HP) is a good example of a program initiated to serve a strategic need. In 2002, HP undertook to consolidate the overall management of all fee-for-service projects worldwide using a single, consistent system of processes and applications. The program to accomplish this was called COMPASS, an acronym that stood for COntrolling and Managing Projects And Services System. The program was responsible for deploying functionality to all countries and regions of the world where HP did business. The program began just after HP merged with the Compaq Computer Corporation, so one of the primary objectives was to integrate all operations into a coherent post-merger global business operation. The new systems and processes also need to be fully compliant with emerging requirements of the Sarbanes-Oxley legislation in the United States and with similar legal requirements worldwide.

The program goals were strategic; initially the program was tasked with completing its work as quickly as possible. An initial plan to deploy updated accounting and related systems in less than 2 years proved to be too expensive and to require too many contributors. Ultimately, the program was adjusted to be a phased effort with prioritized deployment waves extending over about 5 years. The program was decomposed into quarterly deployment releases, using overlapping development waves last roughly 8 to 9 months from the setting of initial requirements through system implementation. Following a pilot deployment in a single European country in mid-2003, the COMPASS program implemented roughly four to six additional countries each quarter, sequenced using business size data and other priorities. Over time, COMPASS successfully deployed systems in more than fifty countries worldwide. The program had management responsibility for an IT budget of multiple millions of dollars per year and a shifting roster of about 200 contributors, many part-time and only involved for a small portion of the overall duration.

The program was strategic, because there were substantial inefficiencies caused by material differences in methods used in the pre-merger HP and Compaq parts of the combined multi-billion-dollar global fee-for-service business. Savings were only part of the objective, though. Compliance with changing global standards was required to ensure that company managers and executives stayed out of trouble. This created a good deal of high-level interest in COMPASS, especially at its start.

PROGRAM GOVERNANCE AND SPONSORSHIP

A high level of organizational support is nearly always a given at the inception of a major new program. Someone with substantial authority starts the ball rolling, and likely thinks the new program is a superb idea. In most cases, assuming at least a modest level of initial scrutiny and analysis, there likely is a solid business case and cause for enthusiasm. As a new program begins, the expected results are thoroughly documented, including information about the people who will benefit and how they will judge its value. A clear, compelling case for the program is essential for securing, and especially for maintaining, the strong sponsor support a major program requires.

Program sponsorship may remain at the high executive level where the concepts originate, but often operational responsibility evolves through delegation, and the specifics of program sponsorship tend to change over time. Strong sponsorship of program work is essential for securing resources needed, making high-level decisions, responding to significant issues and escalations, and dealing with other needs beyond the scope of the program leader. Contending with multilevel, evolving, and often committee-based sponsorship represents a significant source of program complexity, and Chapter 5, Program Leadership, will explore ideas for contending with this in more detail.

For both projects and programs, sponsorship works best when the people involved have a substantial stake in the work. Sponsors are responsible for the ongoing health and progress of a program, so it's useful for them to directly share in both the rewards for success and the consequences of problems. Effective sponsorship also relies on a fundamental understanding of the needs and opportunities the program is expected to address and the value it is expected to deliver. Some of this will depend on communication and education initiated by the program leader, but most people involved with sponsorship activities will be well aware of the program and predisposed to be highly supportive—at least initially.

Project sponsorship is usually fairly simple, with a single individual performing the role. For programs, there are often layers of sponsorship. At lower levels there are sponsors for the projects that make up the program (many of whom may be members of the program team). Portions of the program may also benefit from independent sponsorship, originating from various functions or disciplines, different regions or geographies, or other subdivisions within the organization. Sponsorship may also phase in and out as the program proceeds through the stages of the work over time. As the program begins, effective program leaders work to identify and connect with all the individuals having sponsorship responsibilities to ensure that they understand their roles and what the program is undertaking.

For the program as a whole, it is not uncommon for sponsorship duties to be handled by a steering committee or other multiperson body with oversight responsibility. Working with numerous people who have authority over the program does contribute to program complexity, especially if there is a lack of alignment or other potential for conflict. Such difficulties rarely cause initial program problems, because at the beginning there is generally consensus (or at least apparent consensus) for program direction. (If this were not the case, the program would probably have lacked the support needed to get going.) Over time, though, as people are replaced and perspectives evolve, some conflict is probably inevitable. You will find more on dealing with this, as well as other stakeholder conflicts, in Chapters 3 and 6.

Program-level sponsors are responsible for a number of key program requirements. They will secure the initial funding and program staffing to get the program rolling. Initial funding will need to be sufficient for establishing required infrastructure and to support the core program team responsible for initial documentation, planning, and support. Programs generally have a dedicated staff, including a program manager and other roles (which may or may not be part of a dedicated program management office [PMO]). The program staff initially needs to determine the processes and methods the program will employ, often working with (or as) a PMO. The staff also interacts with sponsors at various levels to establish and confirm timing for program reviews and key decisions, and will coordinate project baselines and other program commitments. In addition, the program staff will also generally need to get one or more projects supporting program initiation started and staffed. Program startup activities and staffing will be explored in more detail at the end of this chapter.

Although for large programs the overall governance, operational processes, and infrastructure will evolve, the clearer you can make things at the start, the better off you will be in the long run. Using well-defined processes from the start of a program, even if they are imperfect, is generally a lot more effective than spending a lot of time spinning your wheels trying to select an optimal choice from among too many options. Use history and experience as guides and establish structures and processes similar to those that have worked in the past. Over the life of a major program you will be able to make needed adjustments as you progress.

Governance for the HP COMPASS program was relatively stable over the several years required for deployment. Processes were established early for the work, consistent with the operations of corporate accounting and established IT systems practices. Deployment was constrained to fall on the "middle weekend of the middle month" of each fiscal quarter to minimize impact on the company's general ledger and financial record keeping. All system changes had to be fully regression tested in advance in a development environment before deployment, with any problematic deliverable elements removed prior to production release. A steering committee of corporate executives was responsible for overall program governance, and met monthly to review status, approve high-level schedules and objectives, provide support, and to consider any major proposed changes or program modifications. The steering committee included representatives from the service businesses in each region, as well as from corporate support organizations affected by the program. Initial sequencing of the countries for deployment created a good deal of debate, but once it was set it was not controversial. Overall, governance functioned well throughout this program.

PORTFOLIO MANAGEMENT

Successful program management, particularly for large programs, depends on a coherent, rational portfolio management process. The process an organization uses to select undertakings can make the difference between programs that succeed and programs that fail.

Some portfolio processes are realistic and logical, basing decisions on analysis and resource allocations on credible estimates. Unfortunately, not all portfolio decisions are so logical. Too frequently, portfolio selections are based mostly on politics and emotion—using "gut feel" to determine what work to put into plan, and what to defer. This process, almost entirely driven top down, is depicted in Figure 2-1. Choices based on inaccurate or sparse data provide a shaky foundation for a portfolio process. Questionable decision making is a particularly common problem with large programs that need public funding (the "optimism bias" problem), but at least some subjectivity is common with even the most systematic-looking portfolio processes.

Figure 2-1 A typical top-down portfolio process.

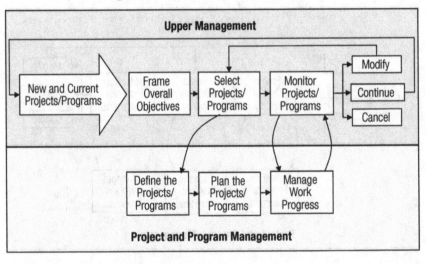

Before the staff does much analysis, most projects and programs appear to be smaller and easier than they will actually prove to be. The magnitude of this perception error tends to increase with overall scope, so early cost and duration assessments for very large programs tend to be grossly underestimated. Only with in-depth planning and analysis-based estimating will the true costs and timing come into focus. Unfortunately, such data will only be available once work commences—usually long after the decision to proceed has been made based on wishful thinking.

The low reliability data for new projects and programs also contribute to an information asymmetry problem in most portfolio decision processes. The portfolio process must allocate limited funds and staff to a mix of existing projects and programs, new projects and programs, and other organizational work. Comparing actual data for ongoing work with forecasts for new undertakings that are wildly optimistic can result in questionable decisions, frequent shifts in focus, and too few completed projects. As it is often said, the grass is always greener on the other side of the fence. In addition, systematic underestimation of program costs for new work exacerbates the frequently encountered "too many projects" problem.

Figure 2-2 A portfolio process using project and program feedback.

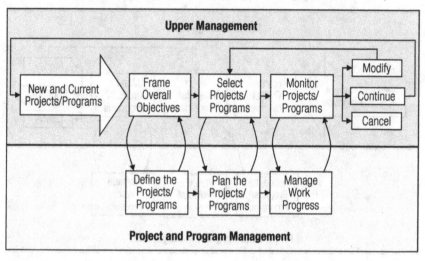

So, what does a better, more rational process look like? The process in Figure 2-2 still begins top down, but at each step there is feedback. The selection process uses data generated by the project and program managers, so it can make better informed decisions and allocate resources more appropriately.

An effective portfolio selection process also does several other things to support effective program management. It determines the ranking order for project and program alternatives based on criteria that are important to the organization, such as expected value, estimated costs, and perceived risks—all based on appropriately detailed analysis, not guesswork or hopes. (Assessing factors such as these to support return on investment [ROI] analysis at program inception is the topic of the next section.)

Effective portfolio processes also set targets for types of work, allocating a specific percentage of overall capacity for dedicated maintenance/operations effort, for evolutionary projects, and for more speculative platform/innovation-oriented efforts. Major programs tend to be in the last category, where complex, higher effort (and higher risk/reward) efforts fall. Allocating effort by category assists in managing for the future, because typical portfolio decision making tends to favor the urgent over the important, allowing short-term mundane work to crowd out, or result in inadequate funding for, program work.

For major programs there is yet another important issue for the portfolio process. The projects that make up a program are best analyzed as a coherent whole, considering the entire program as a single entity. Because there is always a limit on available resources, you may need to consider scenarios during the portfolio selection process that start with funding the largest high-priority proposals first. If you fail to put the most major undertakings in plan early, you may find that there is insufficient remaining capacity to do them at all.

As noted above, a good portfolio process must also distinguish appropriately between actual data for existing lengthy programs and the speculative forecasts for new ones. Balanced decision making requires managing the bias for the novel and counteracting any issues related to fatigue for long-duration work.

To make all of this function usefully, the portfolio process also must have realistic, up-to-date information about the organization's overall capacity (in terms of staffing hours available) and capabilities (in terms of skills and experience levels). Without accurate data for the constraints on how much work can be funded and staffed, there will be an overwhelming tendency to initiate more projects and programs than can be accommodated. Data for high-tech companies indicate that it is common to have between double and triple the amount of project work underway (at least in theory—much of what is "in plan" is actually falling further and further behind expectations) than the organization can realistically accomplish. Initiating too many projects is a typical cause of project and program problems.

Even the best portfolio process can never deliver perfect results. All projects and programs carry risk, and some will inevitably fail. At HP, founder Dave Packard was often quoted as saying, "Half of the projects here are a waste of time and money. If I knew which half I would cancel them." An effective portfolio process helps to manage this through periodic reviews. As work proceeds, the process will modify or cancel work when it becomes clear that a particular effort underway is failing to meet its stated goals. A portfolio process needs to work as "a funnel, not a tunnel," redirecting resources to productive alternatives and away from efforts that are doomed to under-deliver.

The COMPASS program at HP was initiated as a strategic, ongoing effort, but once a year it had to be listed with other ongoing and new proposed work and compete for its next increment of annual funding. As with most multiyear efforts, some annual haggling was inevitable when securing the money and staffing commitments required for future work. The strategic goals and priority for the work for the first several years made this largely a nonevent. However, toward the completion of the program an elaborate new system for overall business case analysis was introduced as part of the annual IT portfolio management process. The basis for the process was a massive spreadsheet for each project and program that focused on annual costs and annual benefits. Using it to analyze a multiyear program delivering value in phases was not entirely straightforward. Fortunately, program data was sufficiently compelling, even in "slices," that this created only minimal problems. Such analysis, though, can place lengthy programs at a decided disadvantage. (In this case, it also helped that as part of the review one of the decision makers pointed out that the program was underway, in large part, because of legal requirements.)

PROGRAM BENEFIT ANALYSIS AND RETURN ON INVESTMENT

Programs are generally large undertakings, and as such tend to be in line with strategic and other goals. They also have sufficient priority to make it through whatever portfolio selection process the organization has in place. All of this depends on a strong belief that the efforts will deliver significant results and value. At the inception of a program, document the expected benefits, and engage in sufficient analysis to build confidence that the efforts will be worthwhile.

Benefit analysis requires credible estimates of both the desired results and all anticipated costs. Program value depends on the net benefits—the measured positive effects minus the investment the program will require. While overall program value also includes any intangible or subjective benefits the program may deliver, most decision making and business case analysis depends primarily on cash flow and other numeric estimates for the work. ROI calculations are a common format for assessing value, and ROI is commonly a highly weighted criterion for portfolio decisions.

There are a number of models used to evaluate program ROI, but all the methods depend on contrasting estimated program revenue (or savings) with estimated program costs. Because programs tend to be of long duration, ROI calculations are generally made using interest rate assumptions that adjust the financial flows using the time value of money. Analysis of value begins with the reason the program is being initiated in the first place—the expected benefits.

Program Benefits

Programs are undertaken for many reasons, so their expected results vary widely. Some programs are undertaken on a fee-for-service contract basis, where the value of the program (to your organization) will be the fees called for in the negotiated contract.

For other programs, assessing value is more difficult. Some programs seek to solve a problem or address a specific organizational need. Assessing the value of this sort of work may be straightforward, using actual expense information from the status quo and estimated (presumably smaller) costs for the future. For programs that are opportunity oriented, the benefits question can be considerably more complicated, because both the value perceived by a hypothetical stakeholder and the number of such people who could benefit may both be highly speculative. Whatever the situation, begin benefit assessment by considering the stakeholders who are expected to benefit from the results of your program. Describe who they are, and document what you believe they need. Focus on what they do and how they work, and describe how the needs they have relate to what your program will produce. Dig beyond basic requests for features and specifics; document how each type of stakeholder will benefit from what you will deliver. Also describe how each of your stakeholders will evaluate what you produce.

Combine the information you have to estimate the value your organization can realistically realize from program deliverables, and when that will occur. Consider factors that could affect the value, and estimate a range that covers the minimum you expect, what appears to be the most probable, and the best case.

The larger and longer the program, the more uncertain the estimates of benefits will be. Deliverables from early, short projects may have value estimates with a relatively small range of possible financial returns. For work that is further in the future, the error bars around the estimates will be substantially larger, and in some cases a realistic minimum estimate of value may be zero (or even in some cases, negative). As the goals for your program come into focus, think about the specifics and scheduling for requested deliverables. Where feasible, consider shifts to scope and timing to deliver earlier (albeit more modest) results to enhance program value and minimize the uncertainty.

Assemble your best estimates of expected returns, laddered through the duration of program efforts and beyond. For value analysis, estimates are generally aggregated by fiscal quarter or by calendar month. Show the financial results from any efficiencies and savings, beginning when you expect to realize them, with ranges for each period reflecting estimated uncertainty. For marketable services or products, lay out the revenue streams expected through time based on contracts or sales projections, again providing range information. Be consistently conservative with timing estimates, associating inflows with dates that are credible and realistic, neither optimistic nor worst case.

At program start, most value estimates tend to be both overly rosy and highly uncertain, so as you capture the data, be skeptical of assessments that appear too optimistic or too precise—particularly for forecasts more than a year in the future. Both benefits and cost assessments should be reviewed after planning commences, and then on a periodic basis (at least semiannually) throughout the program to verify that overall objectives and assumptions remain valid.

The benefits analysis for the HP COMPASS program included both improved functionality and the opportunity to retire expensive and inefficient legacy operations processes and systems. Operationally, the program would establish new business processes and systems to eliminate redundant data entry, require less work overall, and enable faster invoicing. From a financial controls standpoint, COMPASS would make analysis easier (and possible across global regions), improve controls and accuracy, and consolidate all financial profit-and-loss data consistently into the corporate general ledger. In addition, project work undertaken on a fee-for-service basis would no longer require manual tracking because the system could provide real-time project status. The cost savings expected from higher productivity and retirement of older systems and methods were estimated to be substantial.

Program Costs

Programs begin with at least some high-level assumptions about expense. Program costs include, but are not limited to, staffing expense, program contract fees, directly charged overhead and infrastructure expenses (possibly including PMO costs), and expenses for material, services, travel, and communications. Taking on one program could mean deferring or cutting back on other efforts. If there are expenses associated with this, or other measurable opportunity costs due to selecting the program over other alternatives, capture those costs as well.

Use the same quarterly or monthly basis you chose for value estimates to distribute anticipated costs for program work along your timeline.

Costs for COMPASS at HP were also estimated and tracked throughout the program. The initial "do it as fast as possible" plan was adjusted based on a capped annual budget to spread the work over about 5 years, which moderated the rate of expense and kept the work consistent with available staffing.

When an organization commits to initiating a program, the financials ultimately always show a substantial surplus of benefits delivered over costs. At the beginning, though, there will be a period of months or even years where the costs dominate the picture. The analysis in Table 2-1 is typical for a program such as COMPASS at Hewlett-Packard, but the numbers in the table are only representative. These numbers all look precise, but it is never easy to determine the worth of any complex investment with much

Table 2-1 Costs and benefits per quarter for a multiyear program.

		Cost ($M)	Benefit ($M)	Net ($M)	Total ($M)
Year 1	Q1	($0.5)	$0.0	($0.5)	($0.5)
	Q2	($0.8)	$0.0	($0.8)	($1.3)
	Q3	($1.5)	$0.1	($1.4)	($2.7)
	Q4	($1.5)	$0.4	($1.1)	($3.8)
Year 2	Q1	($1.5)	$0.9	($0.6)	($4.4)
	Q2	($1.5)	$1.4	($0.1)	($4.5)
	Q3	($1.5)	$2.0	$0.5	($4.0)
	Q4	($1.5)	$2.6	$1.1	($2.9)
Year 3	Q1	($1.5)	$3.2	$1.7	($1.2)
	Q2	($1.5)	$3.8	$2.3	$1.1
	Q3	($1.0)	$4.3	$3.3	$4.4
	Q4	($1.0)	$4.8	$3.8	$8.2
Year 4	Q1	($1.0)	$5.3	$4.3	$12.5
	Q2	($1.0)	$5.8	$4.8	$17.3
	Q3	($1.0)	$6.1	$5.1	$22.4
	Q4	($1.0)	$6.4	$5.4	$27.8
Year 5	Q1	($0.5)	$6.6	$6.1	$33.9
	Q2	($0.5)	$6.8	$6.3	$40.2
	Q3	($0.5)	$6.9	$6.4	$46.6
	Q4	($0.5)	$7.0	$6.5	$53.1

accuracy, particularly if the investment is a long-duration program. Estimates of costs and expected value, especially early program estimates, are rarely trustworthy.

The program here invests money in excess of value delivered for about a year and a half, which is fairly common for large, complex infrastructure programs. These basic data will support examples for several ROI methods commonly used to assess program financials.

Return on Investment Assessment Methods

There are several alternatives used for assessing ROI. Each has its advantages, limitations, and challenges. The most common ROI assessments are payback period, net present value, and internal rate of return. For long-duration programs, assessing ROI must factor in an interest (or discount) rate reflecting the time value of money.

The Time Value of Money

Anyone who has a savings account or who has taken out a loan knows that money today is worth more than that same amount of money at some time in the future. Because of this, your savings grow over time at your bank, and you always have to repay more than you borrow on a loan. The size of these differences depends on an interest rate and the amount of time that has gone by. The formula for this is as follows:

$$PV = FV/(1 + i)^n$$

where:

PV is the present value
FV is the future value
i is the interest rate per period
n is the number of periods

Using an interest rate of 5 percent per year (0.05), $100 today is equivalent to $105 one year from now.

Determining an appropriate interest rate is not difficult. It is not uncommon to set an interest rate target for the organization consistent with the financial expectations of investors or other owners. ROI calculations may also use the prevailing cost for borrowing money, or the rate of interest available from external investments, such as bonds.

The data in Table 2-1 have been adjusted using an interest rate of about 4 percent per year (1 percent per quarter) in Table 2-2.

The point where the value delivered exceeds the costs remains at about 1½ years, but the estimates are discounted to lower values the further out

Table 2-2 Present values of costs and benefits for a multiyear program.

		Cost ($M)	Benefit ($M)	Net ($M)	Total ($M)
Year 1	Q1	($0.5)	$0.0	($0.5)	($0.5)
	Q2	($0.8)	$0.0	($0.8)	($1.3)
	Q3	($1.5)	$0.1	($1.4)	($2.7)
	Q4	($1.5)	$0.4	($1.1)	($3.7)
Year 2	Q1	($1.4)	$0.9	($0.6)	($4.3)
	Q2	($1.4)	$1.3	($0.1)	($4.4)
	Q3	($1.4)	$1.9	$0.5	($3.9)
	Q4	($1.4)	$2.4	$1.0	($2.9)
Year 3	Q1	($1.4)	$3.0	$1.6	($1.3)
	Q2	($1.4)	$3.5	$2.1	$0.8
	Q3	($0.9)	$3.9	$3.0	$3.8
	Q4	($0.9)	$4.3	$3.4	$7.2
Year 4	Q1	($0.9)	$4.7	$3.8	$11.0
	Q2	($0.9)	$5.1	$4.2	$15.2
	Q3	($0.9)	$5.3	$4.4	$19.6
	Q4	($0.9)	$5.5	$4.7	$24.3
Year 5	Q1	($0.4)	$5.6	$5.2	$29.5
	Q2	($0.4)	$5.7	$5.3	$34.8
	Q3	($0.4)	$5.8	$5.4	$40.2
	Q4	($0.4)	$5.8	$5.4	$45.5

they are. (And again, the accuracy of the data assembled early in a program should always be assumed to be a "rough order of magnitude," at best.)

Simple Payback Analysis

The most basic ROI model for program analysis uses simple payback. This method assumes no time value for money (or, equivalently, an interest rate of zero). This type of ROI metric has several other names, including payback period and break-even time. Payback analysis sums up all expected monetary returns minus expected project expenses, period by period, until the aggregated value of the benefits less the costs returns to zero. As programs generally have no benefits until at least some project work is completed, the cumulative financials will start negative and generally remain there for many periods, long after each period's benefits minus revenues go positive. The program in Figure 2-3 shows simple payback based on the data in Table 2-1.

The program here reaches a point early in year 3 where the cumulative returns equal the total expense up to that point. This sort of payback analysis works well when comparing similar programs, and it is easy to calculate.

Refining simple payback analysis to adjust for the time value of money is not difficult. Figure 2-4 shows discounted payback for the same program.

Figure 2-3 Simple payback graph.

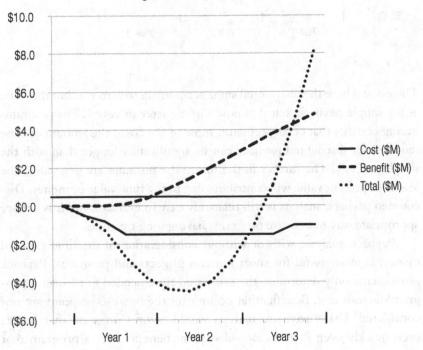

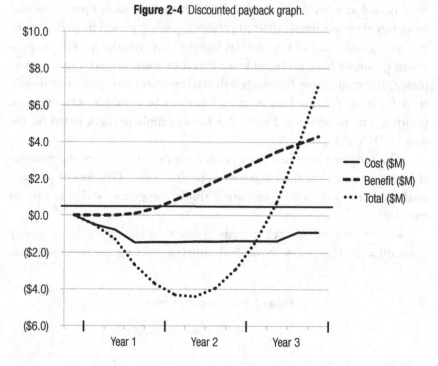

Figure 2-4 Discounted payback graph.

The point where the discounted sums accumulate to zero is about the same as for simple payback, but it is now slightly later in year 3. For programs having benefits that occur well after most of the costs, the amount of time required for discounted payback can be significantly longer than with the simple analysis. The further in the future the revenues are generated, the less their present value will contribute due to the time value of money. Discounted payback analysis is still relatively easy to evaluate, and it is a more appropriate way to evaluate programs having long timelines.

Payback analysis, with or without consideration of the time value of money, is most useful for short horizon projects and programs. Payback assessments only determine the estimated time needed to recover a program's investment. Benefits that occur after the break-even point are not considered. Using payback analysis would favor a program that breaks even quickly even if it has no subsequent benefits over a program that takes longer to recover its costs but generates a lengthy stream of ongoing revenues.

Net Present Value

Net present value (NPV) is a second method for measuring program ROI. NPV follows the same process as discounted payback analysis, but continues beyond the break-even point. NPV includes all the costs and all the anticipated benefits throughout the expected life of the program deliverables. Once all the costs and returns have been estimated and discounted to the present, the sum represents the total discounted program value for the project. NPV can be used to compare programs, even programs having very different time scales. The 5-year NPV for the program in Table 2-2 would be $45.5 million. NPV increases with scale, and in comparisons it tends to favor large programs over more modest ones, without regard to other factors such as uncertainty or revenue timing.

The profitability index (PI) is closely related to NPV, and may be more effective when assessing programs of different size. PI normalizes financial magnitudes using a ratio. PI is calculated by dividing the sum of all the discounted revenues by the sum of all the discounted costs. PI is always greater than 1 for projects that have a positive NPV, and the higher the PI is above 1, the more profitable the project is expected to be. For the program data in Table 2-2 the summed discounted costs are about $19.6 and the benefits are roughly $65.2, so the PI would be approximately 3.3 over the 5-year horizon.

These ROI assessments do require additional data and estimates of the revenues throughout the expected life of the program deliverables, but they are still relatively easy to evaluate.

Internal Rate of Return

A third category of ROI assessment for programs is the internal rate of return (IRR). IRR uses the same estimates for costs and benefits required to calculate net present value, but instead of assuming an interest rate and calculating the present value for the program, IRR assumes a net present value equal to 0 and then determines the required interest rate. Mathematically, IRR is the most complex method for ROI analysis, because it must be

43

solved by iteration and trial and error (or, equivalently, by employing a financial calculator or function in a spreadsheet to do the iterating). For programs that have exotic cash flows, there can be more than one valid interest rate for IRR. However, this can only happen when the calculated benefits less costs have multiple reversals of sign over time, so it rarely affects typical program analysis. Using the IRR function and a computer spreadsheet on the data in Table 2-2 (annualized), the IRR for the program appears to be an impressive 145%. If all the estimates are believable, this program would seem to be a very good investment.

Using Program Return on Investment Assessments

Each of these ROI methods is an attempt to analyze the expected performance of a program as a financial investment. Theoretically, any of these calculations could be an input for portfolio analysis decisions, or used to compare program opportunities with alternate investments. Selecting a method (or methods) to use, and deciding how much credibility you believe it carries, requires judgment. Comparing programs using similar ROI methods may be productive, but because risk and uncertainty increases with scale, ROI analysis for large projects and programs can be perilously unreliable.

As mentioned earlier, early estimates of cost tend to be too low. The error this contributes can be problematic, but it is often dwarfed by the magnitude of the overestimation for benefits. Not only are the expectations of value from program deliverables often based on forecasts made using guesswork (such as sales projections and other speculative forecasts far off in the future), estimates of benefits are almost always significantly larger figures. (Their anticipated magnitude compared with modest expected costs is often the reason that the program is under consideration in the first place.) In all ROI calculations, the larger estimates for the value of benefits tend to dominate the calculations.

The ROI analysis is an important input to the business case made for most programs. This sort of program analysis can be the basis for effective, rational decision making. It can also be an exercise in wishful thinking. A case using heavily biased, analytical-looking data could make a questionable undertaking appear quite plausible. Much has been written about and studied regarding before-the-fact erroneous input data for megaprojects. The optimism bias in major publicly funded programs tends to lean heavily on huge underestimates of cost, as documented in Bent Flyvbjerg's often-cited article, "Cost Underestimation in Public Works Projects: Error or Lie?" In this and other writing, Flyvbjerg points out that large public programs such as those for tunnels, bridges, or other major construction have a spectacularly poor record for initial cost estimation. He posits that the only possible explanation for this is either chronic estimation incompetence or dishonesty (and he strongly suspects the second option).

For organizations taking on major internal projects estimates of cost may be credible, but the expectations for value are often wildly inflated, such as savings from new processes or capabilities, or expected sales for new products or services.

Whether the main issues relate to underestimated costs or inflated expectations for benefits (or both), timing assumptions further complicate the problem. The business case for big programs usually rests substantially on expectations for completion. When there is delay the costs rise and the benefits tend to diminish (and sometimes they may vanish altogether).

Program cost-benefit assessments can never be any more accurate than their least precise inputs, so always be skeptical of data that look too good to be true—because they often are. When considering ROI or similar program assessment data, consider the reliability of the input sources. Review the analysis (particularly the detail data and formulas tucked away in hidden corners of spreadsheets). Examine alternative versions using historically more realistic expense and staffing data, delayed or more credible value assessments, and other "what-if" scenarios. Also ensure that both cost and value estimates are "most likely," not "best case." Spend some time considering the uncertainty of the data by reviewing or creating error-bar data, particularly for forecasts that appear to be highly speculative. (The next section explores this in more detail.)

Plan to replace initial guesses and wishful thinking with more credible estimates and actual results to adjust program ROI assessments as you progress.

PROGRAM RISKS

As discussed earlier, when a program begins, optimism tends to dominate most discussion of the work. Best-case scenarios may be employed to make the program look like an unquestionably winning proposition. Many programs are indeed excellent ideas, but all have inherent uncertainties, choices for approach, and other risks.

Uncertainty Analysis

As with all project and program estimates, cost and benefit projections are never precise. Analysis of program risk begins with probing the level of uncertainty in the initial assumptions. With cost estimates (used for staffing, sizing, ROI analysis, and other purposes), probe for worst cases. Consider historical norms for similar work, inspections, reviews of provisional project information for the program, and possible changes in the costs for program inputs over the expected duration of the work. Question assumptions about the program, especially those that relate to new methods, processes, or technologies expected to be used. Consider training needs, learning curve issues, and other factors that could impact program expense and timing. If significant work will be outsourced, review the costing assumptions for credibility, particularly for work that is unusual, novel, or otherwise requiring skills and expertise that are not widely available. Consider travel and communication costs for programs depending on widely distributed teams, and build sufficient contingency into program-level budgets to deal with periodic problems. Examine the infrastructure in place at the program start. Where there are opportunities to improve efficiency, productivity, or overall program effectiveness through better equipment, facilities, or services, contrast the costs of upgrades with potential savings. When justified, include upgrades in your program start-up costs.

Model the overall program at a high level, starting with the target cost numbers. Incorporate worst case information in your costing analysis by using weighted averages such as a PERT (program evaluation and review technique)-like formula to adjust cost estimates:

$$Cost_{(expected)} = (5 * Cost_{(target)} + Cost_{(worst\ case)})/6$$

For programs with access to Monte Carlo or other simulation tools, model your cost estimates and use them to adjust for uncertainty. Using such tools for program risk management will be explored in more depth in Chapter 4 on program planning and organizing.

As discussed earlier in this chapter, program value is also commonly overestimated. Review the assumptions about program benefits and be skeptical of both the magnitude and timing of realized value. Consider factors that could diminish the worth of program deliverables, such as technological, infrastructure, or environmental changes, shifts in target user needs and desires, new competitive alternatives, and other possibilities. Programs with long time frames will see changes, and many of these will either cause the value of your work to diminish or require fundamental changes to your program (or both). Develop scenarios for how your program will play out, and be realistic about what might change or otherwise effect how your program deliverables will be perceived.

Linear, status-quo projections are always wrong, sooner or later. For a lengthy program, you can almost guarantee disruptive change that will affect the success of your efforts. Robust program management relies on anticipating changes and setting up the work to remain viable and worthwhile even in the face of the unexpected.

Program Choices

Whereas projects of modest scale often have an obvious approach that makes sense, most large programs may be tackled in a variety of ways. The set of problems or opportunities that give rise to a program could be tackled by a series of related sequential (or overlapping) projects. They could also be addressed by developing a generalized platform deliverable and then proceeding to extend and modify it to meet a spectrum of related requirements. Component projects might be short, iterative efforts approaching desired goals step by step in an organic way, or they might be thoroughly planned lengthier undertakings that proceed through development using a sequence of preplanned phases of work. Some programs work to exploit new technologies and methods and others stick with the tried and true. Programs may also involve choices regarding major infrastructure or other changes requiring early capital purchases or other major expense.

Decisions such as these can have a major effect on program cost, productivity, risk, and even staff motivation. When there are multiple options available, the "best" choice may be far from obvious.

Decision-tree analysis is one approach used to analyze the potential consequences of alternatives. Decision trees use graphs to illustrate choices and document potential outcomes. A decision tree begins on the left with a decision, or choice node, often shown as a square. Available choices are shown as vectors fanning out to the right from this, linking to chance nodes, usually displayed as circles. Vectors fan out from the choice node, labeled with estimated probabilities and leading to described outcomes. An example decision tree for the choice of using new or existing technology is shown in Figure 2-5.

For this example, a new technology is available that could potentially reduce development costs from $300,000 to $200,000. The cost to acquire

Figure 2-5 Decision tree for technology choice.

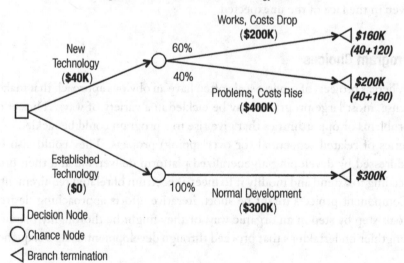

and come up to speed on the new technology will be $40,000. The technology will probably work, but there is an estimated 40% chance that there will be problems. If it fails, development will need to fall back to the existing technology ($300,000). And this development can only commence following some effort and expense associated with the new technology, for a total of $400,000. While investing $240,000 in total for the new technology and development sounds attractive and would save $60,000 if it works, the decision tree shows that this choice involves a good deal of financial risk. In addition, the diagram does not include any information about potential timing problems. Unless there are significant additional potential future savings on later work, or ideas for improving the new technology's success probability (such as a pilot or small test), the program would minimize financial risks by sticking with the known technology.

Decision trees containing this sort of financial data support analysis of expected monetary value (EMV). Comparing EMV assessments for program options can reduce the risk and improve the overall business case for the work. Effectively using EMV does require reasonably precise estimates (which may be hard to come by early in a program), and also relies on meaningful probabilities. It is fair to ask of the example in Figure 2-5, What is the 60 percent based on? Is it from a statistical analysis of lots of other cases where people attempted to adopt the technology? Is it based on an analysis of your needs and the new technology's specifications? Or is it just a guess? Often, probabilities used for project and program risk assessment are little better than educated guesses, so be wary when interpreting analyses based on decision trees.

Overall Program Risks

Programs are collections of projects, and managing program risk does share a good deal with the overall processes for project risk management. Programs are more complex than projects, though, so managing risks within the component projects is only the beginning of program risk management.

Programs must indeed manage some of the specific risks that arise from within projects. Programs also have risks that are related to work at the program level. Programs are large, often strategic efforts, so still more risk will be due to organizational or other factors outside the program. The need to manage risks from above (the organization and strategy), from within (intrinsic to the program), and from below (component projects) makes program risk management a significant challenge. Each of the following three chapters (Chapter 3 on deliverables, Chapter 4 on plans, and Chapter 5 on leadership) will explore aspects of program risk management in some detail as it relates to each topic. At the start of a program, however, you need to assess overall program risk and determine your approach for managing it.

Risks in the Projects

The most straightforward part of program risk management is ensuring that good project risk management practices are employed within all the component projects. If there are dozens of projects, hundreds or even thousands of project-level risks may be identified. This is far more than could, or should, be managed at the program level. However, even though most project risks are best managed by individual project teams, some project risks will also be program risks.

The most obvious example of such a project risk is the "showstopper" risk—a risk that will bring its project to a screeching halt and have major impact on the program as a whole. Such project risks are clearly also program risks. Even at the start of a major program, some of these will be evident. Identify the parts of projects that require innovation, novelty, untried technologies, new development methods or equipment, changing processes, or other sources of potential trouble for the program as a whole. As program deliverable analysis evolves (discussed in Chapter 3), identify project risks contributing to deliverable complexity that may interfere with integration at the program level.

Some additional project risks warranting program-level attention are the interconnections and cross-dependencies between the projects that make up the program. As planning proceeds, particularly workflow-related planning as described in Chapter 4, note all project interfaces and plan to track them as program risks.

Also, identify any situations involving risk within projects that could persist after the project is completed. Projects are time-bounded and have defined closure dates. Programs have longer durations and some are open-ended, so any risks that outlive the project in which they originate (for example, a scope risk related to a project deliverable that will serve as an input for a succession of future projects) will need to be tracked and "adopted" by the overall program.

Finally, projects always carry some level of overall risk. Identify any component projects that are inherently risky as a whole. Projects managed by other companies or using a substantial amount of contract labor will be risky, as are those depending on widely distributed teams. Projects longer than about 6 months tend to carry substantial risk. Programs decompose the work into component projects to simplify the work and manage risk, but this is only effective when you do a good job of creating a balanced mix of projects having modest size, substantial independence, and reasonable levels of inherent risk. As the initial structure for a program begins to take shape, keep an eye on the big picture to detect pockets of risky projects.

NASA projects have long used computer applications to develop program schedules. In the late 1960s on the Apollo program, computerized PERT analysis was employed to track work by all of the various parts of the program as it proceeded. An overall massive database was populated with dependency and estimate information for all these interlocking pieces. Critical path analysis showed the minimum time required to reach program milestones. Any delays on the critical path would result in slips to scheduled launch dates. *Angle of Attack* by Mike Gray is a fascinating book summarizing the history of the Apollo program. He reports on the computer analysis for the initial launch: "The second stage (S-2) was on the critical path from the very first computer run. Among all the other contractors—who were having plenty of problems on their own—the S-2 became known as the 'umbrella' for the way it shielded them from NASA's wrath."

At any given time on a large program, one or two projects will tend to dominate the risk discussion.

Intrinsic Program Risks
Some program-level risks are related to scale. Staffing, funding, duration, and technical complexity are all significant sources of risk, especially if they significantly exceed that of previous programs. If past efforts of comparable

size have encountered substantial unanticipated problems, chances are that this program will too. Document program risks that relate to large staffing levels, big budgets, lengthy timelines, or other scale factors.

Programs are made up of projects, but may also require non-project effort. Consider potential risk sources related to support, administration, infrastructure, and other "white space" contributions to the program.

Project risks that seem relatively trivial can aggregate to levels warranting program attention if they recur in multiple projects. Risk management for portfolios depends on the risks associated with items in the portfolio being independent. This works well for insurance companies writing policies, banks making loans, casinos hosting gamblers, and other aggregations where there is little expected correlation. Programs are large collections of items, but the risk factors affecting the component projects are anything but independent. Correlation effects are substantial within a program, so overall program risk may far exceed expectations based just on detailed project analysis. This happens due to shared work methods, common staff and resources, workflow dependencies, and other project interconnections.

Projects in a program will often describe the same or similar risks on many of their risk registers. Some risks that seem relatively minor for a single project may aggregate to substantial consequences at the program level. Plan to review the risks identified in projects on a regular basis, and note any potential chronic problems that could result in program-level headaches.

Also consider risks related to staffing expectations (or access to other resources such as testing equipment, systems, work areas, or other specialized facilities) that are noted as risks by multiple projects. Loss of specialized staff or even serious queuing delays can create program-level traffic jams if they affect several projects simultaneously.

Cascade effects also can cause major program-level problems. Failure to assess risk correlation effects can result in significant misperception of program-level exposure. A minor-looking risk in one project could ripple through a program with devastating effect if there are unintended consequences overlooked in workflow analysis. With an assumption of independence, the listed risks for projects and programs may look benign. In fact, however, should one risk occur, there may be others for which the probability will jump to 100 percent, resulting in a flurry of problems all at once that can snarl up an entire program. Identifying workflow interfaces between projects is a good method to catch many such program-level risks, but without diligent correlation analysis some exposures may remain out of sight.

Also at the program level, risks can be identified by the program staff (or PMO). These risks tend to be most visible when considering the program as a whole, rather than inspecting the detailed pieces.

Risks from Outside the Program

Finally, programs must consider risks inherited from their sponsoring organizations. This can begin with the sort of unrealistic assumptions used to initiate a program discussed earlier in the chapter. Excessive expectations for results and unrealistic constraints on resources and time contribute much to program risk. Inappropriate initial assumptions that are not adjusted early contribute to chaos and failure.

Programs are also bound up with organizational goals and strategies. In many cases a program's primary purpose may be aimed at managing an enterprise-level risk situation. Such risks that are delegated to programs are never solely the responsibility of the program team, because they also must be closely monitored and managed where they originate. Nonetheless, there are inevitably aspects of managing a typical program related to managing organization-level exposures. Some specific areas where program managers may need to deal with inherited risk include the following:

- Organizational reputation and brand protection
- Fraud and financial liability
- Safety and security
- Compliance with legal and other regulatory requirements
- Casualty loss and disaster preparedness
- Protection of confidential information and intellectual property

There are many other potential sources of organization-level risk, and for sufficiently large (relative to the enterprise) programs, even the ongoing existence of the organization may be at risk.

One of the primary objectives of the COMPASS program at HP was related to an important company-wide exposure: compliance with changing legal requirements for tracking and reporting of financial information. On major programs there may be multiple exposures with consequences that reach far beyond the program itself.

Program Risk Management Process

Due to size, complexity, and other factors, program risks are numerous and arise from many sources. Program risk management warrants a formal process, established during program initiation.

The basic process for program risk management is similar to the process for project risk management: plan, identify, assess, respond, monitor, and control. Program risk management is often a responsibility of someone on the program staff (or in a PMO), but for very large programs there may be a dedicated separate risk management staff with its own budget. Begin the risk management process by determining the following:

- The risk tolerance for the program (thresholds for cost, timing, and other risk consequences set by your sponsor and key stakeholders)
- The owner for the program risk management process
- Other contributors to the program risk management process, and their roles
- The processes for program risk management and the format for the program risk register
- The location for archiving program risk information and plans for access and security
- The frequency and structure of program risk reviews
- Defined tracking metrics for monitoring program risk

Document the process and verify support for it at program inception by key stakeholders, and commitments by contributors who will participate.

Using the process and keeping up with risks as a program proceeds is covered in Chapter 6.

Program "Pre-Mortems"

Another useful risk management exercise for new programs involves the concept of prospective hindsight. Post-project retrospective reviews and other after-the-fact analysis are powerful tools for identifying root causes and data for process improvement. However, you do not have to wait for problems to occur to conduct such an analysis. You can challenge people to envision failure scenarios at the start of a major program, and then analyze them to develop strategies that would avoid or at least mitigate those outcomes.

The starting point for prospective hindsight involves imagining that a possible event in the future has already happened. Such a mindset not only increases the understanding of the situation described, it improves people's ability to uncover possible root causes and helps them make a more realistic estimate of its probability.

A program "pre-mortem" is based on the process used for medical postmortems. As with project "lessons learned" analyses, medical postmortems work to uncover the cause of problems to understand them and deal with similar situations better in the future. A program pre-mortem is conducted at the start of a program instead of at the end, and used to avoid problems and improve the chances of success for the upcoming work.

A program pre-mortem begins with the assumption that the program has failed, and probes for plausible scenarios that may lead to this result. A pre-mortem can begin once the overall program objectives are established and the program team understands the initial high-level plans. The program manager starts the process by gathering the program team members and asking them to put themselves into a future where the program has just failed spectacularly. Each participant is then independently challenged to capture as many plausible causes as they can think of for the failure. People should be encouraged to include even scenarios that might imply criticism or that could be considered impolite. One such session at a large company uncovered a failure scenario for a billion-dollar environmental sustainability program due to diminished support following the retirement of the current chief executive officer (CEO).

Capture all the scenarios and reasons for failure by sequentially having each participant select and read one idea, different from any already mentioned. Working quickly and without debate, continue to list reasons, one by one, until all have been recorded. Review the list, and clarify any that seem too vague or imprecise. Also, work to consolidate any items that seem essentially similar.

Use the list to seek program alternatives that would be more robust and to adjust the objectives to be more realistic. A pre-mortem can be an effective way to temper initial excessive enthusiasms and to help the team identify and deal with early indicators that may be signals of later problems. Forewarned is forearmed.

PROGRAM CHALLENGES

Programs are difficult for a wide range of reasons, many summarized in Chapter 1. Program startup poses a number of specific challenges, some arising from causes outlined in the earlier sections of this chapter. Program challenges include the following:

- Scale and complexity
- Misalignment of funding and program results
- Stability of the external environment
- Retaining long-term support and managing stakeholder expectations
- Effective communications
- Delegation of authority and control
- Staff motivation

The list for any particular program might not include all of these challenges, but it would doubtless also list additional challenges particular to the specific program.

Scale and Complexity

The scale of the work is a universal program challenge, and is perhaps the most daunting of the items listed. Initially, most programs are far too large and complex to really understand. Techniques for dealing with technical and functionality-based complexity are explored in Chapter 3. Chapter 4 addresses managing workflow and interface hand-offs between projects. Leading a complex hierarchy of teams responsible for projects, subprojects, program staff, and other contributors adds another layer of complexity, and methods for effective program leadership are outlined in Chapter 5.

At the start of a major program, one of the first tasks is to establish how you plan to manage the complexity, defining the methods to be used, documenting what is known, and initiating project activity to explore options, address feasibility questions, and fill in the most critical knowledge gaps. Techniques for contending with system complexity rely heavily on decomposition, but there are always trade-offs. While the smaller pieces (of things, work, or staffing) make managing the parts more straightforward, the program still depends on the interconnected whole for success. If you break things up well and handle the resulting interactions successfully, you will enhance program control. If you fail to do this carefully, it can make things worse. As you proceed, however well your decomposition choices may appear to be working at the start, monitor the program for issues that arise from misunderstood or poorly managed complexity, and be prepared to make adjustments promptly.

Misalignment of Funding and Program Results

As discussed earlier in this chapter, one challenge that nearly all long-duration programs face sooner or later is a threat to the required budget. Program results are generally delivered only well after significant investment and effort. As periodic (generally annual) staffing, budget, and portfolio decisions approach, develop a presentation that summarizes past program accomplishments and emphasizes the value and expected benefits of future work.

Later phases of lengthy programs will need to compete with new, shiny, exciting alternatives within the organization, so the more compelling you can make the business case for ongoing funding, the more successful you are likely to be in securing it.

Even initially, program funding or staffing may be insufficient to support an effective launch—especially if the expectations for cost are set with insufficient understanding of what the program actually requires. Identify the business case for the program at the start, and use it to justify funding of initial phases of work. Also, whether it seems entirely necessary or not, consider ways to deliver value early and frequently throughout the overall arc of the program. Programs increasingly are adopting agile, or at least agile-like, methods to accelerate producing demonstrable results. Even results that do not achieve all of what might be ultimately expected provide unambiguous evidence of the program's overall value. Prototypes, pilots, and other "proof of concept" work can provide solid validation of the business case for ongoing, perhaps even increased, funding.

It is dangerous to take program funding for granted based on the apparent priority of the work, even at the start. There are always too many good ideas in any organization than can be funded, and the temptation to pull resources from current work to start up "just one more project" can be overwhelming. Always be prepared to defend your turf and be ready to describe the consequences of any changes to funding or staffing in terms of cost, results delayed, or other program impact.

Stability of the External Environment

Programs have long timelines, and the world never stands still while they progress. Long-duration programs need to be ready to deal with changes related to technology, competition and alternatives, regulations and standards, and other factors.

Some programs depend heavily on key technologies. At program initiation, explore the possibilities for technological changes that could disrupt creation of deliverables, tools, methods, or other aspects of the program. For technologies that are intrinsic to your deliverables, plan to keep abreast of new developments and work to develop designs that incorporate flexibility that could allow you to swiftly and smoothly integrate new capabilities. Technical changes affecting tools and methods may not be essential to adopt, at least right away, but they could represent ways to raise efficiency or productivity. For changes that appear imminent or at least soon enough to benefit your program, build some contingency funding into your budget to cover acquisition or upgrades, and also plan for any training or other effort needed for implementation.

Regulations and standards also evolve over time. Legal and regulatory changes are rarely big surprises, because significant changes to rules generally go through periods of public debate and scrutiny, which takes time. However, they can be problematic for large global programs if no one is monitoring what is being proposed in distant countries or regions that could affect the program. If changing legal requirements could represent a potential threat to your program, plan periodic reviews of any areas that could be relevant, at least semiannually (perhaps as part of an overall planned program review).

Standards also tend to evolve somewhat slowly. For programs subject to standards from organizations such as the International Standards Organization (ISO) or the American National Standards Institute (ANSI), or industry standards [from the American Society of Mechanical Engineers (ASME), the Institute of Electrical and Electronics Engineers (IEEE), the Telecommunications Industry Association (TIA), the World Health Organization (WHO), or many other organizations from a lengthy alphabet-soup list] for equipment or product categories, plan to regularly monitor what has been proposed that might be inching toward adoption. The best way to avoid problems related to changing standards is to be part of the group setting them (or to encourage someone in your organization do so). Influencing the standards that emerge can enhance your program's potential value and ultimate success.

As computing equipment was becoming more ubiquitous (and much less costly) in the 1970s, HP engineers developed a standard connector, cable, and protocol to streamline development of system components (including automated instruments). This HP interface bus (HP-IB) made development and integration of systems employing HP products a lot easier, and the design was soon made available to other companies. A standards committee for the IEEE, which not coincidentally included several HP engineers, soon adopted this as the IEEE-488 standard. The standard was widely adopted throughout the computer industry (outside of HP usually referred to as the general purpose interface bus [GP-IB]). Global acceptance of this standard increased the sales and utility of HP computer peripherals and other products for many years.

Retaining Long-term Support and Managing Stakeholder Expectations

Funding over the long term is only one of the challenges faced by lengthy programs. Stakeholders over time have a tendency to change their minds, so work to develop a deep understanding of their connection to the program. Stakeholders who can affect the program have the greatest potential for harm, so meet with them to discuss their goals for the program. As the program begins, communicate regularly with the key decision makers, supporters, and those who have a sponsorship role to keep all of them informed of what you are doing. Use your knowledge of their interests to focus your communications on aspects of the program they care about. Throughout the program, work to keep track of any changes in stakeholder priorities, and regularly inform your key stakeholders of program progress, particularly in areas that support their interests.

Also pay attention to stakeholders who will be affected by the program, or at least people who can represent their viewpoints. Programs are initiated to solve complicated problems, and the complex deliverables will have no value if they do not adequately meet the need (or worse, are never used). The business case and ROI for a program depends on benefits with measurable and credible benefits. Know how the program results will be evaluated and used by customers and users, and focus your analysis of system deliverables on how they will be used to address specific needs. While you are listening to the "voice of the customer," you may also need to do some persuading or selling. Complex program deliverables may require new methods, education, or other investments on the part of users and adopters. Whenever business process changes will affect users, or if your deliverables will not be precisely what users expect to receive, develop a communications and implementation strategy to facilitate necessary changes and to adjust expectations where required. Plan to monitor user preferences and feedback as the program proceeds to ensure adoption of what you produce and realization of desired value.

The needs and expectations of any stakeholder for the program may shift during the program, as a result of external changes, other factors, or even whim. As the program proceeds, the roster of stakeholders your program works with may evolve significantly, due to job changes, health issues, retirement, or other personnel shifts. In addition to connecting with key stakeholders at the program start, develop plans to engage with them on a regular basis throughout the program to keep them aware of your progress, verify their connection to the program, and to confirm their continuing involvement.

Losing a stakeholder may be a nonevent, with a new individual quickly named and engaged with the program with little or no disruption. Losing key stakeholders who have a sponsor role or authority over the program (or even just a reduction in their engagement), however, can be disastrous. If you find a gap in needed support, work to fill it as quickly as you can. As mentioned earlier, the most effective sponsors have something at stake with the program. If your program lacks the high-level support that you need to get started (or later, to keep running), consider who at an appropriate level in the organization would have the most to gain from your success—or the most to lose with your program's failure—and use your best persuasion skills to secure their support and ongoing interest in your program.

If you find any skeptics or critics of your program among high-level executives or other leaders who could interfere with your progress, work to win them over, too. Programs need as many friends in high places as they can get, so plan to be friendly with everyone and avoid making enemies. Should there be high-level people in your organization who do not support your program, find out why. Use your business case data, your connections with other high-level supporters, your expertise in program management, your sunny personality, and any other tactics you can think of to secure their backing. Connect your program and its objectives to their imperatives and interests, and work to secure a commitment to support, or at least tolerate, the program. If you do find that the program has adversaries in high places, at least be aware of them and work to retain the support of others with at least as much authority and power who will defend your program in case of conflict.

Communications, Delegation, and Long-term Motivation

Programs face many other challenges. Program information management and communications are difficult, both because of the amount of information and the distributed (and diverse) teams that staff most programs. Managing information for a large program so that people can find what they need without assistance and with minimal delay is crucial to a healthy program. Provide a good start toward ease of use and ready access by organizing a coherent online program information system that mirrors the hierarchy of the program's teams. Similarly, structure and tailor communications to provide the status and other data contributors need without unnecessary clutter relating to parts of the program with which contributors have little interaction. Organizing information and communications to serve your needs—all of everything, all the time—is a formula for overwhelming everyone. Too much information can be worse than too little; no one will have the patience to tease out the parts they really need. Communicating well on large programs is a lot of work, and requires planning. Effective program information methods will be explored in more detail in Chapter 5 on program leadership.

Programs also depend on successful delegation of authority and control. The purpose of decomposing the work is to make it more tractable and straightforward. This only helps if the projects that make up the program are largely autonomous and able to operate independently most of the time. If the project leaders are not able to run their own projects without constant interaction with the program manager, you have accomplished little. Delegation presents a challenge because there is a fine line between too much independence among projects and too little, and your goal is to remain near that fine line. As the workflow connecting projects comes into focus, use a formal process to identify and track all cross-project interfaces. At the program level, resolve each interface and gain agreement from the project leaders involved, and establish plans to track the status of each interface as the program progresses. Leaving full responsibility for other project efforts in the hands of the project leaders and their teams generally works well for programs, with the exception of any current project-level issues that have been escalated to the program level for tracking. Using interface management to track overall program progress is discussed in Chapter 4.

Successfully securing meaningful commitments for delegated work is yet another big challenge. Delegation is not a challenge unique to programs, but it tends to be particularly problematic because of program scale. The number of distributed locations involved, especially on programs having multiple layers of hierarchy, provides much potential for trouble. Although initially there may be only a manageable number of teams, as a program expands the web of delegated responsibility expands dramatically. The number of people you need to secure reliable commitments from can be very difficult to keep track of, to say nothing of keeping them under control. Managing delegation for programs is covered in more detail in Chapter 5.

Staff motivation, both initially and (especially) over the long haul, is yet another program management challenge. Program size can both help and hurt with staff motivation. On the one hand, programs are big and important, so many of the people involved will be impressed and enthusiastic about participating. On the other hand, programs are complicated and may produce few tangible results right away. Getting people excited about a program early on can be difficult, especially on programs that will require effort for months, or perhaps even years, before there is much to show for it. Ideas for engaging people early and keeping them motivated over the long haul are also explored in Chapter 5.

PROCESS MATURITY FOR PROGRAM MANAGEMENT

As a program begins, it is useful to reflect on similar recent work and identify any aspects that were especially problematic. Much of what goes wrong in programs is a result of poor, or even nonexistent, processes, so it is worthwhile to conduct a review aimed at improving work methods and management practices that have not served you well. If you need to do something only once, it makes little sense to spend a lot of time perfecting the process—in most cases applying brute force and figuring it out as you go will be more efficient. For small to medium-sized projects it makes sense to invest time, at least periodically, in refining methods for work and management tasks that recur, to improve productivity and provide higher confidence that you will achieve your expected objectives. For large programs, formal, well-defined processes become essential, because without them there will be no basis for organizing and tracking the many aspects of the work in a coherent, understandable way. Inadequate program management processes result in a chaotic aggregation of project teams marching in random directions with little chance of success. Big undertakings warrant at least some investment in developing and reinforcing processes for coordination and use of consistent techniques.

What this means for a particular program, however, varies a great deal. Good process for a program building a bridge may little resemble the details of effective processes for developing a new computer operating system. What does matter is that the processes for a specific type of program be aligned with the work well enough to improve productivity and facilitate coordination of ongoing effort. In reviewing processes to be used for a new program, analyze specific new challenges, technologies, work methods, and other expected differences compared with past work and consider their impact on existing methods. Think about recent problems that could have been avoided or reduced through the use of better, or different, management techniques. Overall, review the approach you plan to use for program setup, requirements management and testing, planning, monitoring and communication, measurement and control, and for other essential program responsibilities. Work to reduce overhead, eliminate unnecessary effort, streamline processes, and address gaps and shortcomings.

A common approach for process assessment involves the use of a maturity model. There are many models and frameworks that can be used to analyze process maturity. Most owe a debt to the first maturity model to be widely applied, the capability maturity model (CMM). Watts Humphrey of Carnegie Mellon University led the effort to develop the CMM for the Software Engineering Institute (SEI) in the late 1980s, funded by the U.S.

Department of Defense. The CMM effort was initiated because at that time computers and software were becoming a larger and more dominant aspect of military programs, and were causing a disproportionate share of timing and cost problems. At the core of CMM were definitions for five levels of maturity: initial (using ad hoc processes or no processes), repeatable (using known but undocumented processes), defined (using documented processes), managed (using measured processes), and optimized (using processes that were continually improved).

Based on this basic framework for software, many other models have been developed, including the current capability maturity model integration (CMMI), which evolved from CMM and remains at Carnegie Mellon. For almost 30 years, CMM concepts have been used to assess the process maturity of organizations developing software. The basic belief behind this is that an organization having greater process maturity would be more productive and write better software. When post-project analysis shows that poor or inappropriate processes are among the root causes for chronic problems, this belief has obvious merit.

The CMM initially placed most processes associated with project and program management at levels 2 or 3, and the current CMMI structure still has most project management processes at level 2, with risk management and "integrated project management" (program management) at level 3. Neither the CMM nor the CMMI defines the specifics for individual processes, only their purpose and guidance for assessing them. It remains up to organizations to choose the details of the processes they use for requirements management, planning, monitoring and control, and other responsibilities.

The CMM, and now the CMMI, focuses on software development and related work. Over the past several decades many similar models of process maturity have emerged for other undertakings, most with about five levels of maturity and borrowing heavily from the work done by SEI at Carnegie Mellon.

A few years ago, the Project Management Institute (PMI) introduced the organizational project management maturity model (OPM3), which defines levels of maturity for processes for managing projects, programs, project portfolios, and for the organization overall. The OPM3 defines graduated

Table 2-3 Process maturity models.

Level	CMM	CMMI	OPM3
1	Initial	Initial	(None)
2	Repeatable	Managed	Standardize
3	Defined	Defined	Measure
4	Managed	Quantitatively Managed	Control
5	Optimized	Optimizing	Improve

levels of maturity and, like most other models, resembles the CMM. A comparison of the CMM, CMMI, and OPM3 is shown in Table 2-3.

The assumption of a maturity model is that lower levels are "bad" and higher levels are progressively better. This may or may not be the case in specific situations, however, for several reasons. Higher levels do require effort and overhead, so it is always prudent to assess where you are, what the benefits of the next level might be, and the costs to achieve and to remain at the next level. For a significant program, moving from level 1, with no defined processes, to level 2, where known methods are routinely applied would seem to be easily justified, and in fact the PMI's OPM3 begins with the assumption that there are standard methods. The CMMI explicitly includes a process for managing integrated projects, which implies that programs should have little or no difficulty justifying well-documented processes at level 3. Analysis regarding climbing to the next levels is more complicated, however.

In the 1990s HP put a good deal of effort into assessing the maturity levels for software development labs across the company. The initial set of assessments, using methods outlined by the SEI, found that most of the development organizations were somewhere between levels 2 and 3 in the CMM hierarchy. A second set of audits of the same labs about a year later showed some improvement, but not a great deal. Most of the organizations were at about level 3. Subsequent assessments found that most software development organizations appeared to be "stuck" at about level 3. While this was initially considered to be a problem, after some reflection the concern diminished.

An organization at level 1 or 2 is easily improved. Lists of recommendations that will help are easy to assemble, and changes can be made confidently with high expectations that they will be helpful. At level 3, beneficial advice becomes harder to come by. When a group of people is already working well, developing proposals for beneficial change is difficult. A proposed change might improve things, but for performance already above the norm there is at least some chance that unintended consequences of a particular change might make operations *less* productive. In addition, business process changes are never free. The costs of making a change (including training, implementation, equipment or other capital expenses, and persuasion) may be significant, so the value expected from the change would need to be compelling and sufficiently large to justify the effort and expense. For level 4 organizations, improvement efforts aimed at the next level become even more difficult to justify. The philosophy of "If some is good, more must be better" does not always apply to processes.

Tom DeMarco and Tim Lister comment on this in *Peopleware*, a book focused on building high-performing software development teams. Having a well-defined, optimized process is great, if it's the right process. In an environment where changes are frequent, focus on process management can divert attention from where it most matters—achieving good results. They state, "If you are already a CMM level 2 or higher organization, remember this: The projects most worth doing are the ones that move you DOWN one full level on your process scale."

There are many methods and techniques that can be useful for program work. Determining which ones will work well for your particular program requires judgment and experience. As a new program begins, review the processes that have been used in the past, and consider changes where you think they will be worthwhile. (You will find many ideas for program processes throughout this book.) Thoroughly document the processes you intend to use, communicate how they are to be applied, obtain buy-in from relevant stakeholders, and be watchful as your program progresses for further revisions.

PLANNING FOR THE PLAN

Initiating a major program is a significant undertaking, best approached by managing it as project. There are a number of tasks necessary for getting a new program off to a running start that can be organized into a plan and tracked to completion. The magnitude of the effort will depend on the specifics of the program, but a typical program would benefit from a plan something like this (some activities will run in parallel):

- Investigate the program
  - Draft program charter — 1 day
  - Assess stakeholder priorities — 1 day
  - Document early deliverables — 2 days
  - Establish information system — 2 days
  - Review feasibility — 1 day
- Develop a preliminary plan
  - Assemble core program team — 5 days
  - Plan startup workshop — 2 days
  - Do initial project breakdown — 3 days
  - Conduct startup workshop — 2 days
- Develop detailed plans
  - Validate program breakdown — 1 day
  - Commit core project teams — 5 days
  - Plan initial projects — 5 days
  - Integrate project schedules — 1 day
  - Identify and resolve interfaces — 4 days
  - Analyze program resources — 2 days
  - Assess program risk — 1 day
  - Validate program plans — 2 days
- Set initial program baseline
  - Review plans with stakeholders — 2 days
  - Negotiate required changes — 2 days
  - Finalize program charter — 2 days
  - Set program baseline — 1 day

- Transition to execution
  - ○ Commit program staff   5 days
  - ○ Notify stakeholders   5 days
  - ○ Initiate program monitoring   5 days

This plan-for-the-plan template runs roughly 2 months. Planning for a small program will take less time, but for a major program initial planning might take considerably longer. The intent of laying out the work for initial program planning and managing it as a project is to organize it well, and to ensure that it is done efficiently and effectively. A "plan for the plan" would look similar to the one in Figure 2-6.

The inputs to this "meta-plan" include program definitions, records from earlier programs, and information about formats and requirements for various planning and other program documents. You need to determine who in addition to the program manager should be involved with developing the plans, and who should review and approve the program-level plan (such as sponsors and other key stakeholders). As you work to get the program up and running, use your plan for the plan to monitor and control the initiation process.

Begin planning for the program by drafting an initial program charter. Program charters vary in content based on scale, specifics of the work, and other factors, but most include the following:

- Business case for the program
- Vision and strategic alignment
- Overall program objectives and priorities
- Expected benefits and value to be delivered
- A roadmap for deliverables including target timing goals
- High-level definitions for the expected deliverables and results
- Known user and customer data
- Descriptions of key stakeholders
- Initial cost and resource estimates
- External dependencies
- Key constraints and assumptions
- Known issues and high-level risks

Figure 2-6 The plan for the plan.

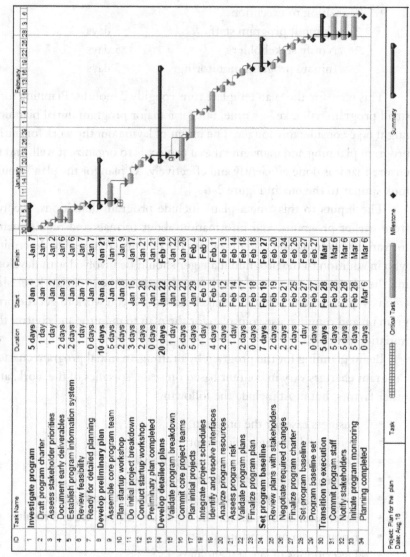

ID	Task Name	Duration	Start	Finish
1	**Investigate program**	**5 days**	**Jan 1**	**Jan 7**
2	Draft program charter	1 day	Jan 1	Jan 1
3	Assess stakeholder priorities	1 day	Jan 2	Jan 2
4	Document early deliverables	2 days	Jan 3	Jan 6
5	Establish program information system	2 days	Jan 3	Jan 6
6	Review feasibility	1 day	Jan 7	Jan 7
7	Ready for detailed planning	0 days	Jan 7	Jan 7
8	**Develop preliminary plan**	**10 days**	**Jan 8**	**Jan 21**
9	Assemble core program team	5 days	Jan 8	Jan 14
10	Plan startup workshop	2 days	Jan 8	Jan 9
11	Do initial project breakdown	3 days	Jan 15	Jan 17
12	Conduct startup workshop	2 days	Jan 20	Jan 21
13	Preliminary plan completed	0 days	Jan 21	Jan 21
14	**Develop detailed plans**	**20 days**	**Jan 22**	**Feb 18**
15	Validate program breakdown	1 day	Jan 22	Jan 22
16	Commit core project teams	5 days	Jan 22	Jan 28
17	Plan initial projects	5 days	Jan 29	Feb 4
18	Integrate project schedules	1 day	Feb 5	Feb 5
19	Identify and resolve interfaces	4 days	Feb 6	Feb 11
20	Analyze program resources	2 days	Feb 12	Feb 13
21	Assess program risk	1 day	Feb 14	Feb 14
22	Validate program plans	2 days	Feb 17	Feb 18
23	Finalize program plan	0 days	Feb 18	Feb 18
24	**Set program baseline**	**7 days**	**Feb 19**	**Feb 27**
25	Review plans with stakeholders	2 days	Feb 19	Feb 20
26	Negotiate required changes	2 days	Feb 21	Feb 24
27	Finalize program charter	2 days	Feb 25	Feb 26
28	Set program baseline	1 day	Feb 27	Feb 27
29	Program baseline set	0 days	Feb 27	Feb 27
30	**Transition to execution**	**5 days**	**Feb 28**	**Mar 6**
31	Commit program staff	5 days	Feb 28	Mar 6
32	Notify stakeholders	5 days	Feb 28	Mar 6
33	Initiate program monitoring	5 days	Feb 28	Mar 6
34	Planning completed	0 days	Mar 6	Mar 6

Project: Plan for the plan
Date: Aug 18

Task ▬▬▬ Critical Task ▦▦▦ Milestone ◆ Summary ▬▬

- Methodology or life-cycle requirements
- Program governance structure
- Program manager and defined program staff roles

Capture the charter data you know at the start of planning, and include activities in your plan for the plan to flesh out and define what you do not.

PROGRAM STARTUP

Program startup is a primary component of your plan for the plan, and many of its scheduled activities will depend heavily on the outputs from a startup meeting. There are many terms used to describe program startup events, including *kick-offs*, *initiation workshops*, *planning summits*, and *launches*. Whatever name you prefer, getting a program off to a healthy start requires that you conduct one.

This chapter has emphasized the need to examine program assumptions carefully, and to be skeptical of things that seem excessively optimistic or unrealistic. Successful program startup relies on all of this scrutiny and analysis, but it also needs to focus on all the overall positives the program represents. Most programs, especially very large, ambitious ones, have a great story to tell, and represent substantial benefit to the organization. A compelling program vision is a major part of this, so make understanding how the future will be better following successful completion of your program central to your startup activities.

Craft a clear and motivating program vision that describes why the program matters. Work with your program sponsor and key stakeholders to develop a vivid description of the future created by your successful program. Outline the benefits expected and why they are important to the organization and to your core team. Use clear, engaging, and emotional words to convey a strong image. Effective visions are inspirational. Create a compelling vision that will motivate your teams and get the program off to a great start.

As with a project startup workshop, there are several objectives for a successful program startup event. The main purpose is to establish a clear and consistent understanding of the overall program and its objectives. You also will be working to get a rapid start on program efforts and begin to build enthusiasm for the program and strong relationships across your core program team.

The people who should participate in the program startup activities include all the members of the program core team. This begins with the program leader, and includes other core program staff who have defined roles on the program team, such as planners, functional managers with responsibilities on the program, leaders of any projects already defined, and other program contributors as appropriate. If there are people involved with an organizational PMO who will be involved with your program, get their commitment to participate as well.

Plan the Program Startup Meeting

Meeting preparation begins with building a strong case for holding a face-to-face meeting. For global, virtual, or other distributed program teams, bringing the program team together in one place can mean the difference between program success and disaster. Meeting in person will help you build the solid foundation of trust that the program team will rely on during the complex work and inevitable problems and stress ahead.

There will be costs and expenses that come with these benefits, for travel, logistics, and other needs. Build the strongest business case you can for holding a face-to-face program startup meeting, and secure the funding and approval necessary. If despite your best efforts you are unable to justify an in-person meeting, plan to hold a series of teleconference or videoconference meetings. You will not motivate the program staff or build teamwork as effectively, but a sequence of short meetings can foster a good common understanding of the program's objectives and facilitate initial planning.

Before the startup meeting, assemble the program documents you will need, including a thorough program description, the charter, your program vision, what is known about requirements, information on key customers and stakeholders, and other available program information.

Develop an agenda for the meeting that will get your program off to a strong start. The length and content of the agenda will vary depending on the type and size of your program, but program startup meetings generally will need a minimum of a day, and most will require more than that. Major programs may profit from a succession of multiday workshops. Begin the agenda with introductions. Include time on the agenda for team-building activities to allow program contributors to get to know one another, especially if they have not met previously.

Include a review of the overall justification for the program and the overall vision for the work. Emphasize why the program matters. Present and discuss the high-level program objectives. Consider including the program sponsor and other key stakeholders at the start of the meeting to reinforce the program vision and importance of the work, and to assist in describing the overall goals.

Add agenda items for program imperatives such as planning, process definition, role refinement, program breakdown and roadmap analysis, communications plans, and other needs. Clearly specify expectations for each item. Allow sufficient time on the agenda to at least establish a solid foundation for key planning deliverables having owners and committed dates for resolution.

Finally, plan your meeting logistics. Off-site locations are best for program startup meetings because they minimize distractions and allow people to focus exclusively on program issues. Secure a meeting room with sufficient space to hold all who will attend. Plan to set up the room to stimulate discussion and interaction, with all seated in a circle or other arrangement where people can see each other (and supply identifying name tags, especially if some participants are initially strangers). Consider enlisting the help of a facilitator from outside the program team to enhance participation by the program leaders during discussions of complex matters. If some participants will be remote, arrange for telecommunications access, and test the capabilities you plan to use prior to the meeting.

Distribute the agenda and any documents you want people to be familiar with before the meeting.

Conduct the Program Startup Meeting

Use initial introductions to help break the ice and start people interacting. As meeting participants are introducing themselves, have them describe their role and contribution to the program. Start the business portion of the meeting with an agenda review, and clarify the overall objectives for the meeting. Initiate discussion of the program by emphasizing the positive—lay out the business case and vision to share the program's importance and benefits. Present the overall program objectives (involving a sponsor when possible), and facilitate a discussion of the overall program to confirm that all understand its priority and goals.

As the meeting proceeds, use flip-charts (or a computer and projector) to capture information and findings: decisions, plans, issues, key comments, significant side issues, and action items. After each agenda item is completed, summarize what was accomplished or decided. Involve all participants in discussions and analysis, calling on individuals in turn for their thoughts and comments, and employing techniques that encourage broad participation such as using yellow sticky notes to analyze situations, initiate planning, and collect inputs.

Include activities during the meeting where people work together in small groups to facilitate team building, and employ collaborative processes such as brainstorming, Delphi estimating, affinity analysis, and team problem solving. Schedule short social interactions during the meeting where people can have some fun and eat together.

Programs are complex, so spend some time discussing the overall approach the program will use. Focus on the assumptions and expected roadmap for deliverables, major milestones, and the initial breakdown of the program into projects. Develop a graphical depiction of the anticipated timing for the program roadmap, and inspect it to understand high-level dependencies, potential resource or other conflicts, and overall credibility. If adjustments are needed, determine what they are and document justifications to support them.

Conclude the meeting by summarizing what you have accomplished, and identify activities for follow-up. For all action items and identified tasks, assign a responsible owner and a deadline. End the meeting by thanking all who participated.

Follow-Up After the Program Startup Meeting

Write up minutes for the meeting and send them to all participants and other relevant stakeholders. Discuss the meeting outcomes with the program sponsors. Start to track any action items or unfinished meeting business. Archive the startup meeting results and other updated program documents in your program information system.

KEY IDEAS FOR PROGRAM INITIATION

- Align program goals with organizational objectives and priorities.
- Confirm strong sponsorship and establish effective program governance.
- Get involved with the overall process for managing the portfolio of projects and programs, and ensure that the selection process is based on realistic information.
- Verify that program expectations of benefits and value appear credible.
- Understand stakeholder risk tolerance, and establish an effective risk management process for the program.
- Review recent program experiences to uncover past problems, and update program processes to address issues that could affect your work.
- Treat initial program planning as a project, and develop a thorough plan for creating the documents, plans, and infrastructure the program requires.
- Schedule and hold a program startup event (or events) to ensure you will hit the ground running.

CHAPTER 3

Program
Deliverable
Management

Dividing an elephant in half does not make two small elephants.
   —**Peter Senge**, *The Fifth Discipline*

Programs are complex. The first type of complexity faced by most program managers involves the expected deliverables. The size, scale, and often fuzzy nature of the problems confronted by programs often present an impenetrable barrier to understanding, especially initially. Little progress will be possible until program deliverables are broken up into simpler, more tractable pieces. The decomposition process is not benign, however. Much can be lost when attempting to convert a complicated system into pieces. Inadequate analysis of the interconnections between components may result in serious integration problems. Doing system decomposition carefully and well is central to successful program management. The strategies adopted for system design also provide the starting point for dealing with the complexity of workflow analysis (discussed in Chapter 4), staffing of the work (discussed in Chapter 5), and for tracking and managing program progress (discussed in Chapter 6).

   Programs are expected to deliver benefits, but there may be many possible ways do this. Developing a program roadmap provides a context for considering various alternatives and documenting the overall program scoping over time, showing what you plan to produce. Some programs have a roadmap that begins with research and development of extensive tools, infrastructure, and a platform to provide a foundation for delivering a succession of project results quickly and efficiently. Other program roadmaps might rank order expected results and then initiate projects in sequence, one by one, based on capacity. Some roadmaps begin with prototypes or pilots—based on simple subsets of the larger program objective—and work to create the information needed to move on to deliver more comprehensive results in successive projects. Still other programs might choose to tackle the most complicated (and highest value) problem first and then move on to treat simpler variants as derivative cases of the work already done.

Choosing the "best" roadmap for a given program can be far from obvious. Fortunately, programs do not need a perfect roadmap that never changes to be successful. This is a good thing because a perfect roadmap for most programs is rarely possible. A good roadmap based on solid analysis, that sets out a credible, realistic scope for the work and requires only modest changes as you proceed, will give you the best chance for successfully delivering the value expected from your program.

Decomposing large, complex system deliverables into understandable components requires two steps: understanding the problem (or opportunity) and converting this information into program specifications. When confronting complicated situations, it is best to keep these parts separate. Developing solutions primarily using analysis of all the needs and requirements (or at least all you are able to gather) yields better results than defining deliverables based on user whims, management fads, or other emotion-based demands.

Understanding the problem (or problems) you are trying to solve begins with developing a deep understanding of the needs and desires of key stakeholders. It also relies on extensive knowledge of relevant technologies and capabilities, to provide the foundation for defining what will be produced. Developing program scope uses system analysis techniques to guide design decisions, manage complexity, and understand program scope risks. Once the specifications are set for deliverables, effective program scope management relies on a disciplined formal process for managing changes and scoping decisions for later projects as the efforts progress.

MANAGING PROGRAM SCOPE

In many organizations, project and product management are handled separately and by different staff. Program management relies on both project

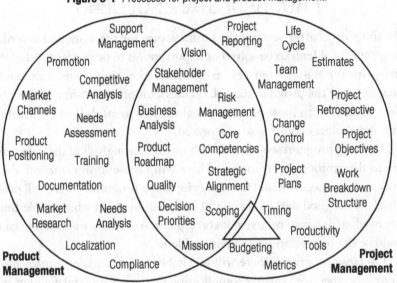

Figure 3-1 Processes for project and product management.

and product management (and more) to be successful, so an effective program manager needs to ensure that the processes for both project and product management are handled competently. Many of these processes are depicted in Figure 3-1.

Effective program scope management focuses particularly on the processes that are in the overlap area of the Venn diagram in Figure 3-1. It is always dangerous for any task to have two (or more) owners, because this may result in everyone thinking someone else will take responsibility. Multiple owners can also result in turf battles, conflicts, and other unpleasantness. The functions that are part of both project and product management are particularly important, especially for initial program scoping, so work to ensure that each receives proper attention and monitor progress to identify and resolve any issues promptly. As a friend at Hewlett-Packard often observed, "Around here, marketing is just too important to be left to the marketing department."

PROGRAM STAKEHOLDERS

The program charter sets out the business case for the work and describes the specific problems to be solved or opportunities to be pursued. All of this starts with the inputs from key stakeholders, the people who successfully agitated to get the program started. It takes a lot of momentum to get a big effort underway, so most programs begin with a great deal of information from stakeholders about what is expected.

Defining program scope starts with sorting through all of the data available to determine what it means. There will be useful information about needs and the specific issues that gave rise to the program. There will probably also be a good deal of less useful information about what people think they need, which may or may not correspond to what they actually need or would be the best solutions to their problems.

On large programs, there will inevitably be information representing multiple perspectives, further complicating matters. Some stakeholders will be powerful and influential, others less so. What is expected by some stakeholders may be inconsistent with what other stakeholders want, resulting in conflict (or, at a minimum, timing issues).

All project and program work must be aware of and attend to the "voice of the customer." On big programs there will be many voices, so the first order of business is to collect the information available and to then prioritize and make sense of it. In all of your discussions, focus on why people want what they are requesting and the value they expect from it. Especially in initial discussions, work to steer the conversation away from specific technologies or solutions. Focus on problems and opportunities, not concrete end results. The most useful program deliverable roadmaps are based on priorities and plausible plans, not on imposed constraints and political pressures. While exploring needs, avoid making delivery commitments for specific outputs and timing.

Stakeholder analysis begins with the most influential individuals in the mix, those with sponsorship responsibility for program work. The sponsors and key stakeholders who got the effort underway and are on the hook for paying the bills generally have the most clout in determining the shape of initial program scope. Meet with the people who make decisions and control your program funding and approvals. Document their goals for program results, focusing on what they most care about and timing assumptions. Probe for how they plan to evaluate program deliverables, and what they would like to see the program accomplish. Seek to understand their priorities. Get a sense of what is urgent, what is important, and what is desired but not essential. Using the technique of "asking why five times" can help develop a deep understanding of the fundamental source of the articulated needs.

Stakeholders who will be affected by program deliverables must also be part of your analysis. Especially for program deliverables that will be marketed as products or services, work to gain a thorough understanding of the people who will purchase, use, and interact with what you produce. For program deliverables that will change the way people do their work, invest the time to understand the status quo by interviewing, watching, and interacting with the people who will experience the most impact from the program results. Gain an understanding of what will be accepted and useful, documenting user needs that are credible and realistic. Delivering what managers want but then having it be ignored by users will result in a failed program.

What can be at least as important as defining program requirements during this process is listing specific items that could be requirements that you plan to explicitly exclude. Program scope will evolve over time, but for each phase of program work it is prudent to isolate potential requirements that are not currently part of your scope. The concept of "Is/Is not" lists is a powerful tool for projects. It sets a boundary around the project scope that makes it clear what you *do not* plan to include. While this works well for projects, the "Is not" concept may be too extreme for programs. At the program level the dichotomy might be better characterized as "Now/Not yet."

As you assemble what you do know, also keep track of what you still need to learn. There will be inevitable gaps in the data from stakeholders on major programs, particularly at the start. Some gaps will occur when the current situation is not acceptable but no one can articulate exactly what to change or fix. Other cases will be easier to understand, but have fuzzy or uncertain objectives because of novelty or uncertain upcoming changes. Whenever stakeholders have difficulty articulating what they need, take note and plan to initiate efforts to fill in the gaps (through analysis of proposed deliverables, testing using models or prototypes, iterative development and feedback, or other techniques discussed later in the chapter).

Development of the Boeing 777 provides a specific example of complex scoping that was managed quite well. The basic need for the 777 development program in the mid-1990s was fairly obvious. There were many modest-capacity, short-range, mostly domestic passenger jets in service at the time from Boeing and from its competitors. There were also very large, long-haul jets in service, including Boeing's 747. There was a large gap between these two types of aircraft. There were no medium-sized, long-distance jets available, and Boeing saw a significant opportunity to introduce a modern jet that would be attractive to commercial airlines and enable them to open new routes and expand markets for the flying public.

A program to develop such a jet would be a multiyear, very expensive (and risky) undertaking, however. The first step Boeing took toward initiating the program was to set up exploratory meetings with its biggest airline customers, the "gang of eight," a year before the decision to go forward with designing the new plane. In *Twenty-First-Century Jet*, Karl Sabbagh notes that this was unprecedented for a major aircraft maker at the time, and it surprised the people at United Airlines, Boeing's largest customer. Gordon McKinzie, responsible for new product engineering at United, participated in those early discussions, and he noted, "They made a point inside the meetings of repeating back to us what we told them, and then followed up after each meeting with a little document. . . . We had three sessions, and each was about three days long and there were a lot of airlines in attendance." Even after Boeing made the decision to design and build the 777, it continued to keep the airline representatives in the loop. Subsequent discussions ultimately led to the realization that the 777 would not be a single design but a family of five configurations tailored to the specific needs of Boeing's various airline customers.

GATHERING PROGRAM REQUIREMENTS

Assembling program requirements begins with stakeholder analysis, but it does not end there. You also need to consider external requirements, organizational and other standards, technological capabilities, and other factors.

External factors place significant constraints on many programs. There are legal requirements for many programs that restrict what can be done or mandate specifications that must be part of the program. Regulations for protecting privacy, handling financial information, ensuring safety, and many other concerns may affect program deliverables. There may also be constraints that control where and when work can be done, such as zoning laws, permitting regulations, timing restrictions, and other limitations. Review the overall environment for your program to identify any situations where what stakeholders are requesting diverges from what is possible.

Also consider organizational processes you will need to follow and any standards that your program will be subject to. Some requested scope may either be in conflict with existing standards or require extra effort to ensure compliance.

Based on the work of Noriaki Kano in Japan in the 1980s, requirements can be thought of as falling into three broad categories: basic, performance, and excitement. His model of how users respond to these three types of needs is summarized in Figure 3-2. Most of the needs articulated by stakeholders tend to fall into the *performance* category. These needs and requirements are the ones people ask for and mention when they are interviewed. When performance needs are met, users are satisfied, and when they are left out, users are dissatisfied. Overall satisfaction is generally proportionate with how fully these needs are delivered.

Some deliverable requirements are so *basic* that they are rarely mentioned or discussed. Such expected needs matter to users and customers mostly if they are missing; when they are present, they are unnoticed, but if they are not delivered or perceived as deficient, users are unhappy. Over time, performance needs tend to evolve into basic ones—no longer valued very much but still essential to ensuring acceptance of what your program produces.

Maximizing the value derived from program deliverables depends on discovering and incorporating *excitement* needs. These needs are often unknown to users or may be considered to be unaffordable or otherwise impractical. Delivering what users will be excited and delighted by requires

Figure 3-2 The Kano model.

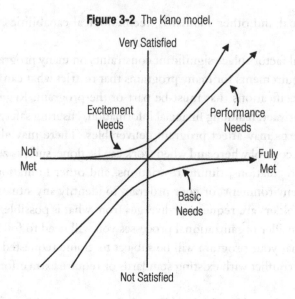

understanding both what will be appreciated and what is possible. As you collect the stated and other needs of stakeholders, users, and others, consider emerging technologies and other innovations. New capabilities or methods might better serve user needs than what has been requested, so use your knowledge of available options when analyzing requirements. Your responsibility as a program leader is to align the needs with the best available solutions, and you may find better solutions incorporating excitement needs during discussions within your program team far earlier than from your other stakeholders and user community. The overall process for managing program requirements is summarized in Figure 3-3.

One of the primary requirements for the Boeing 777 required a significant change to the engine configuration. Many jets with two engines were in service, but all were restricted to flying short routes and over land. The 777 would have only two engines, but was to be rated for long-distance transoceanic flights. The design would save weight and fuel, but there was no precedent for "extended twin-engine operations" (ETOPS). Technology and engineering enabling single engine, long-distance flying, if one engine

Figure 3-3 Program requirements process.

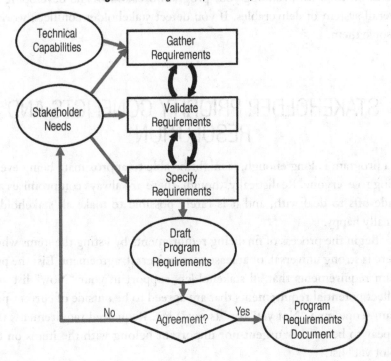

failed, appeared possible, but at the time there was considerable uncertainty. It was not clear that the airline companies would buy it, nor was it a given that the authorities who would need to approve it would do so. The business case for the plane restricted to flying only short-distance domestic routes was questionable, as was the option of adding two more engines. After a good deal of discussion with customers and regulators, Boeing decided to proceed with the novel configuration. The 777 program team planned to do what was necessary to gain approval to fly international overwater routes with initial commercial delivery. This move, while risky, was managed well and paid off handsomely for Boeing and the 777.

As program requirements begin to take shape, document them and review your results with your key stakeholders. If you find overall agreement, proceed with refining your program breakdown and developing the overall system of deliverables. If you detect stakeholder conflicts, work to resolve them.

STAKEHOLDER PRIORITY CONFLICTS AND RESOLUTION

If a program is long enough, it might be able to approximate being everything to everyone. Realistically, though, there are always compromises and trade-offs to deal with, and it is rarely possible to make all stakeholders equally happy.

Begin the process of finalizing requirements by listing the items where there is strong universal, or at least near-universal, agreement. List the program requirements that all stakeholders support in your "Now" list, and collect potential requirements that are agreed to be outside of current program scope on a "Not yet" (or "Is not") list. Requested requirements that appear to be neither urgent nor important belong with the items on the "Not yet" list.

Some requirement requests will not fall unambiguously on either list because of conflicts caused by differing stakeholder perspectives or other factors. Some proposed requirements may be of significant interest only to part of your stakeholder community. For some of these cases further discussion might yield consensus.

Other items may represent genuine conflicts, however, with some stakeholders demanding a requirement and others feeling it should be excluded. Some proposed requirements may be in conflict with regulatory or other external constraints, organizational directives, mandatory standards, or other imperatives for the program. There may even be some situations where two parties propose requirements that are inconsistent with each other—cases where you could meet one requirement but not both. Collect the information you have on requirements where there is controversy, including the source, justifications for the proposed requirements, and any other relevant data. Discuss the disputed requirements with your primary program sponsor and press for opinions on them. Where your sponsor is strongly favorable to a requirement that is on the fence, provisionally add it to the "Now" list. If a requirement lacks sponsor support, demote it to the "not yet" list.

Circulate your "Now/Not yet" list to the key stakeholders from whom you need agreement and request feedback. There will probably be little disagreement on the "Now" list if you have done a thorough job in capturing the requests and priorities of your stakeholders. You will almost always collect a good deal of spirited response to the "Not yet" list, however.

For some controversial items, there may be enough support to promote a requirement from the "Not yet" list to the "Now" list. If there are only pockets of enthusiastic support for some proposals, solicit a statement from the most vocal supporters describing why a particular requirement must be part of the program scope. Circulate the information to other key stakeholders to see if it changes anyone's mind.

If you have any issues where there are strong opinions on both sides, bring the stakeholders who are most engaged together to hash things out. Sometimes pulling disparate viewpoints together into one place will cause opinions to shift, especially if one faction has significantly more organizational power. For some disagreements, there may be options beyond those already being considered, and a "third way" compromise might emerge that would be acceptable to all.

As a last resort for issues where discussion and principled negotiation fails to bring consensus, it may help to escalate to higher authority. Even when sponsors and high-level managers initially appear to be indifferent, you will usually be able to engage them when dealing with program ambiguity.

Update your "Now" and "Not yet" requirements lists based on the final dispositions, and use the resulting prioritized list to refine your program roadmap and begin developing detailed scoping. Work to soothe the feelings of any stakeholders who believe that they have been slighted, and when appropriate reassure them that future phases of program work will reconsider their inputs. Verify overall acceptance of the current program requirements on your "Now" list with your stakeholders. The sorts of items that will end up in your two-column list are summarized in Table 3-1.

Table 3-1 Documenting "Now" and "Not yet" requirements.

Now	Not Yet
• Urgent needs included in current work • Functional requirements for current work • Physical and other parameters for current program deliverables • All "musts" • All "wants" where there is sufficient stakeholder consensus	• All requested requirements that are excluded from current work • "Wants" that lack stakeholder consensus • Requested requirements that are omitted despite expectations of some stakeholders • Reasonable and important stated program needs excluded from current work

CHARACTERIZING PROGRAMS

Like projects, all programs are unique. The differences between programs can be enormous, with the most significant variances involving program deliverables. Generalizing the process of defining program scope is difficult for many reasons, but many of the challenges stem from the type of program. Two useful distinctions that can help with this are the timing of the deliverables (integrated "big-bang" delivery versus incremental "step-by-step" delivery) and the type of deliverables (tangible versus intangible). These dichotomies influence the processes used for defining what a program will produce. Some examples of program deliverables that fall into the four resulting categories are listed in Table 3-2.

Programs requiring integrated delivery generally have carefully planned scoping based on significant up-front investment in design activities. Risk management for these programs focuses on risk prevention. Programs that are set up to deliver a succession of results on a periodic basis rely on feedback-based iterative scoping and a more evolutionary, emergent approach to scoping. Risk management for these programs tends to be more reactive, either dealing with problems as they arise using a "break–fix" model or by making adjustments in the next cycle.

Table 3-2 Program deliverable categories and examples.

		Timing	
		Integrated Delivery	**Incremental Delivery**
Deliverables	Tangible	Phase oriented (new products and platforms, bridges, buildings, tunnels, spacecraft, artwork, transit systems, airports, sports complexes. . .)	Product-line or segment oriented (consumer products, tract housing, customized items, highway systems, automobile models. . .)
	Intangible	Architecture oriented (financial and high-reliability systems, motion pictures, complex applications, integrated processes. . .)	Agile oriented (software applications, television series, standalone processes, education curricula, websites, online services. . .)

The most traditional category on the grid (and what comes to mind for most as a "program") is the phase-oriented program. These programs are generally large efforts that derive all of their value at completion. Errors and problems are painful, and delays and scoping shortfalls are expensive and potentially disastrous. In some cases, programs of this sort are complex in ways that have been studied extensively and are fairly well understood, so planning may be more tedious than difficult. Other programs rely on novelty and innovation, however. Platform development and other single deadline programs involving new technologies or methods are very difficult to define and plan.

The use of agile methods for software development has grown substantially in the recent years, including on large programs. Agile-oriented programs producing a succession of intangible deliverables have become increasingly common. (Actually, all work involving agile methods represents a succession of related project iterations, so each is, by definition, a program.) The coordination of scoping and synchronization of frequent deliveries can be daunting, but methods for applying agile methods at scale have emerged that can be quite effective. Such methods are not overhead free, though. The successful use of agile methods on a large scale tends to afford less freedom at the project level than for typical agile (independent, self-managed) teams.

Using iterative concepts for programs of all types is not particularly new, and good program managers have always worked to deliver results as soon as practical by prioritizing the work and scheduling completion of the highest priority results in early phases. Product-line–oriented programs that produce a sequence of tangible outputs apply many of the same techniques as the programs using agile methods, although generally with "time boxes" measured in months rather than weeks. Whether or not a project delivering on fiscal quarter deadlines or two or three times per year is "agile" is not a very interesting debate. Applying methods that work effectively is more important than getting too hung up on what they are called.

The remaining category involves architecture-oriented programs that deliver complex intangible systems. These programs, like other phase-oriented efforts, often involve undertakings that are fairly well understood. For work that mirrors past program efforts, definition and planning can be straightforward (although not necessarily easy). Not all such programs involve routine types of deliverables, however. Platform development for new products and other work employing novel methods and technologies involves challenges and uncertainties that make scope definition difficult.

ESTABLISHING THE PROGRAM ROADMAP

Because all programs are unique, roadmaps differ. The density of the map depends on the overall scale of the work, with larger programs having more complicated maps. Roadmaps are time-scaled summaries of deliverable expectations, showing the work involved at an appropriate (generally project or subprogram) level of detail. Regardless of program type, the initial portion of the roadmap focuses on program initiation deliverables, and, except for programs with no planned closure dates, the final portion includes termination deliverables. Roadmaps reflect the breakdown of program deliverables. Like a work breakdown structure for a project, program roadmaps may involve a multilevel hierarchy.

Integrated delivery programs have roadmaps with milestones signifying interim deliverables with reviews or checkpoints scheduled across the program timeline. The phase-oriented construction roadmap in Figure 3-4 shows a typical example. Synchronized program and project milestones indicated are plan review (PR), design review (DR), site review (SR), build review (BR), customer review (CR), and sign-off (SO).

A software development program roadmap for an architecture-oriented IT solution is shown in Figure 3-5. This roadmap is in fact based on the release plans used for each wave deployment for the COMPASS program at Hewlett-Packard, introduced in Chapter 2.

One program management approach that is gaining traction for large-scale system development for agile-oriented programs is the "Scaled Agile Framework" ("SAFe") developed by Dean Leffingwell and others. Project teams in the roadmap in Figure 3-6 use agile methods (Scrum in this case). System releases are scheduled every fourth iteration here, and a program team manages the integration and overall mechanics for each release. The program team is also responsible for centrally controlling the system backlog and scoping for the effort (with guidance from the organization). As is generally true with large-scale programs, central coordination based on timing and other constraints is key to success. Within these constraints, the teams responsible for development employ agile methods to deliver their portions of the overall system.

Still other types of programs use product-line–oriented roadmaps to summarize plans. Derivatives and extensions are common in roadmaps like the example in Figure 3-7, populated with new products that offer either comparable performance for a lower price or additional capabilities for a similar price. Programs responsible for deliverables that will be sold as retail products generally manage the roadmap so that there are new (or new-looking) offerings several times per year—often aligned with "Dads

Figure 3-4 Construction program roadmap with milestones.

Month:	1	2	3	4	5	6	7	8	9	10	11	12	13	14	15	16	17	18	19	20	21	22	23	24
Program Team	Program Startup			Plan		Design			Prepare			Build					Inspect		Fix				Program Close
Project Team 1					PR			DR			SR						BR		CR			SO		
Project Team 2					PR			DR			SR						BR		CR			SO		
Project Team 3					PR			DR			SR						BR		CR			SO		
Project Team 4					PR			DR			SR						BR		CR			SO		
Project Team 5					PR			DR			SR						BR		CR			SO		
Project Team 6					PR			DR			SR						BR		CR			SO		
Project Team 7					PR			DR			SR						BR		CR			SO		
Project Team 8					PR			DR			SR						BR		CR			SO		

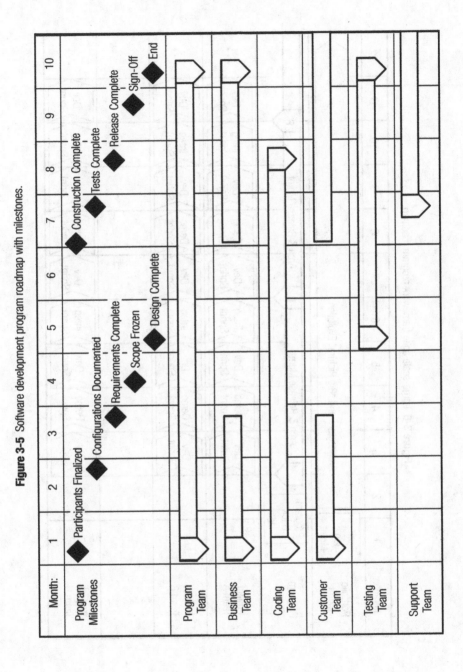

Figure 3-5 Software development program roadmap with milestones.

Figure 3-6 Large-scale agile framework program roadmap.

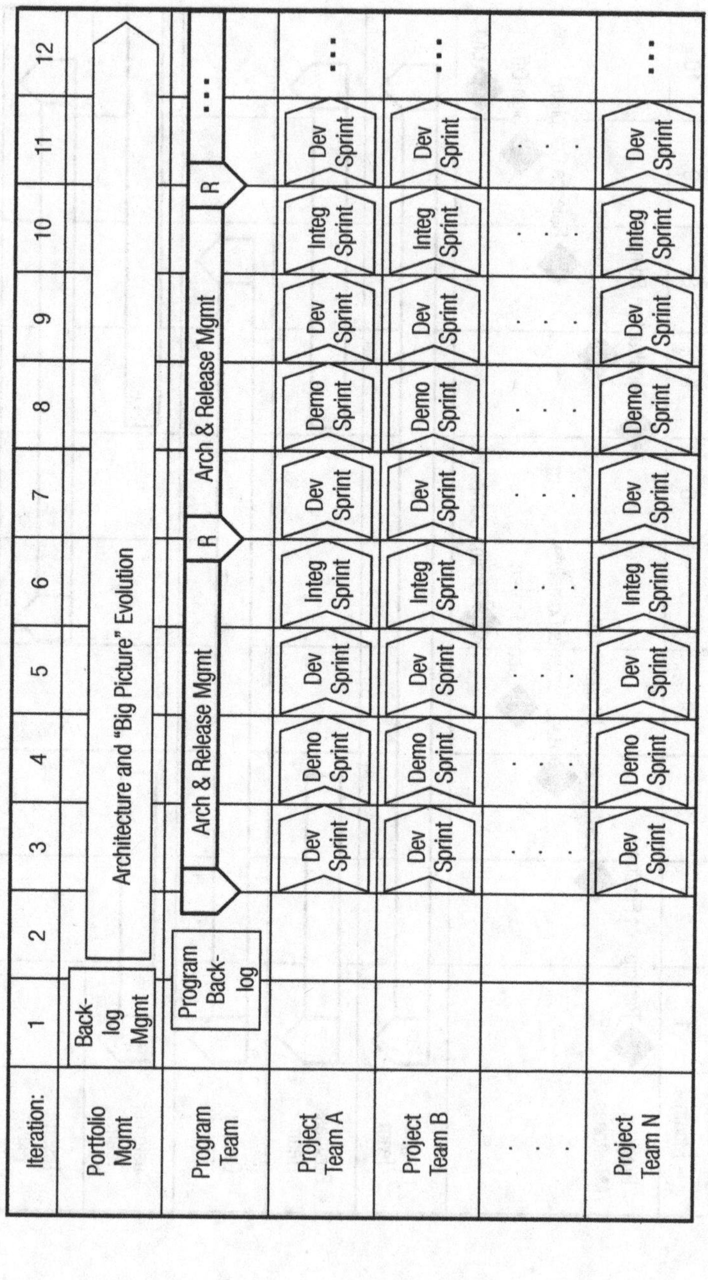

Iteration:	1	2	3	4	5	6	7	8	9	10	11	12
Portfolio Mgmt	Backlog Mgmt		Architecture and "Big Picture" Evolution									
Program Team		Program Backlog	Arch & Release Mgmt			R	Arch & Release Mgmt			R	⋯	
Project Team A			Dev Sprint	Demo Sprint	Dev Sprint	Integ Sprint	Dev Sprint	Demo Sprint	Dev Sprint	Integ Sprint	Dev Sprint	⋮
Project Team B			Dev Sprint	Demo Sprint	Dev Sprint	Integ Sprint	Dev Sprint	Demo Sprint	Dev Sprint	Integ Sprint	Dev Sprint	⋮
⋯			⋯	⋯	⋯	⋯	⋯	⋯	⋯	⋯	⋯	
Project Team N			Dev Sprint	Demo Sprint	Dev Sprint	Integ Sprint	Dev Sprint	Demo Sprint	Dev Sprint	Integ Sprint	Dev Sprint	⋮

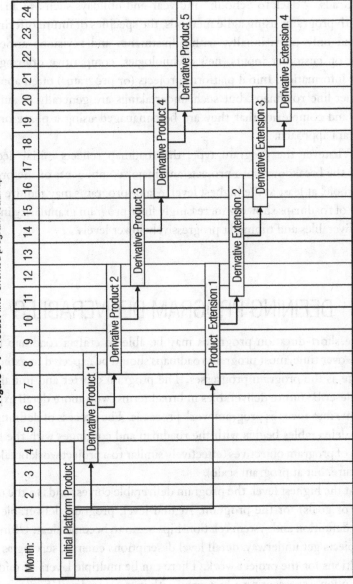

Figure 3-7 Product-line–oriented program roadmap.

and Grads," "Back to School," and year-end holidays such as Christmas. As with programs using agile methods, the specifics of future offerings are defined only provisionally, with adjustments and revisions anticipated based on customer inputs, new technologies, competitive offerings, and other information. Initial platform projects (or programs) often appear on product-line roadmaps, but such undertakings are generally of sufficient scale and complexity that they are best managed using a phase-oriented program approach.

Whatever the program type, the roadmap reflects initial decisions about the breakdown into projects and major components of the program as a whole, at least at the highest level. Major programs may require a hierarchy of roadmaps showing increasingly finer program granularity in terms of deliverables and timing at progressively lower levels.

DEFINING PROGRAM DELIVERABLES

While short-duration programs may be able to craft a roadmap that is stable over time, most program roadmaps should be expected to extend and change as the program progresses. The program charter and initial roadmap describe future deliverables in broad terms, with more detail expected to come into focus as program work proceeds. The process of defining program deliverables begins with the roadmap and continues with the breakdown of program objectives (effectively similar to a project work breakdown structure, but at program scale).

At the highest level, the program deliverable corresponds to the overall goal (or goals) for the program. At mid-level, program deliverables gain more definition and system relationships begin to become clear. Ultimately, as projects get underway, detail level descriptions emerge, serving as scope definitions for the project work. There can be multiple layers of mid-level description, representing a hierarchy with increasing detail. Such a scoping hierarchy documents the intermediate deliverables that fall between the overall program objective at the top and detailed scoping of each lowest-level component.

High-Level Program Deliverable(s)

As the information gathered from stakeholders takes shape, develop narratives for the items documented in your roadmap. Describe each element in a paragraph or two, using a format similar to a catalog description that might promote its sale to a prospective customer. Include diagrams where appropriate to illustrate what functions or components the element contains, and explain how each deliverable will be used. Emphasize the benefits expected, and make the value proposition clear. If a succession of program deliverables will be created, describe only the current deliverables in detail. Define later deliverables broadly, including any provisional information you may have on them.

The overall program deliverable serves as the first level of program scoping, so describe how it addresses program objectives. Review your description and diagrams to detect any missing information or issues. If you find gaps or any aspects that seem fuzzy or less than credible, revise the narrative to fix it.

In addition, focus on how the highest-level results for your program will be evaluated and approved. Work to define all acceptance tests or other decision criteria. Creating deliverables without knowing how their value and usefulness will be assessed can be a waste of time and money; for major programs, the waste of time and money can be enormous.

High-level deliverables are central to your "elevator speech" for the program, so refine your descriptions to make them concise and compelling.

Mid-Level Program Deliverable(s)

Describing mid-level deliverables fleshes out the program and aligns your work with the program roadmap. Programs involving complex systems can have several intermediate levels of decomposition before reaching the point where the level of complexity is appropriate to start initiating projects. At the mid-level(s), descriptions elaborate on the major components for the program as a whole. The process of creating specifications based on collected requirements begins with defining mid-level deliverables.

One common model used for many types of system deliverables employs a V shape to show the process of progressive elaboration for program scope. The V-model version in Figure 3-8 is typical of those used for medium-scale software development projects. There has been a good deal of debate in recent years about how useful this concept is, mirroring the debates about life cycles and phase-oriented planning versus agile methods for software development.

Regardless of how you come down on that particular debate, the need to define and decompose systems for scoping a large program is unavoidable. If you find that you are unable to break up program scope into manageable components, you are highly unlikely to be able to even get a program started, let alone successfully complete it. The value of the V-model for program scoping is twofold: it emphasizes the need to logically decompose complex systems into simpler components, and it shows the relationship between the definitions at each level and their corresponding assessment processes.

The first step for the V-model is to derive system specifications from business requirements. While this is rarely easy, the process for all but the most "bleeding-edge" program need not be insurmountable. Developing

Figure 3-8 "V-model" (verification and validation) for software development.

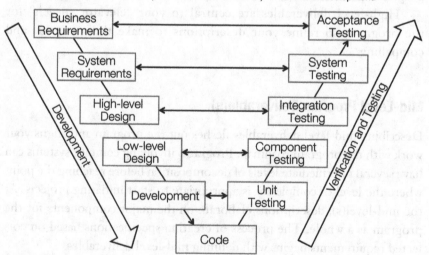

the system specifications begins with a survey of requirements, constraints, and other information collected from stakeholders. The highest priorities will be reflected in the roadmap, and experience from earlier programs will guide the definition of system specifications.

Begin with the business requirements associated with the earliest deliverables on your program roadmap. As you start to lay out the high-level specifications for each deliverable, consider the main drivers for the overall design of your program outputs. Developing an appropriate structure for your program begins with a clear idea of what matters most to your sponsor and key stakeholders. Deliverable design can be optimized for a number of criteria, such as the following:

- Project (sunk) costs
- Unit (variable) costs, for programs creating service-oriented or manufactured deliverables
- Deliverable performance
- Project duration

This list is based on the work of Don Reinertsen in *Managing the Design Factory*. His book focuses on designing physical products, but much of his advice relates to system design for almost any sort of complex program deliverable.

When overall program cost is the dominant priority, concentrate your efforts in system specification on reusing components and capabilities from earlier work. Favor the use of existing, "tried-and-true" technologies and methods over speculative new ones. Plan to maximize the use of "off-the-shelf" parts and components in creating your deliverable. You may be able to simplify your efforts by revising the boundary defining your system. If there are functional requirements that can be met using existing capabilities, consider incorporating them instead of developing new functionality.

Cray supercomputers did this in an interesting way for many years. At Cray Research, all efforts were focused on developing very fast central processing units (CPUs) and system memory. That was essentially all that the company did. Cray systems had no storage, no peripherals, not even any devices for entering or retrieving data. When you purchased a machine from Cray, you also had to purchase (or have) a general-purpose system on which you could run "Cray Station" software. All interaction and use of the super-computer was actually done through the attached computer. By eliminating the need to design anything except the CPU, memory, and a fast system-to-system connection, Cray simplified its overall design work. Because of this system prices (while still very high) were considerably lower than they would have been otherwise.

For programs developing deliverables that will be produced or delivered in quantity, unit costs are a major concern. One way to minimize the cost of each product or service delivered is to design it to be easily manufactured or provided. Developing high-efficiency infrastructure (manufacturing capabilities or support systems) are often part of the strategy for this—trading off high up-front costs for much lower ongoing operational expense. For tangible products, "design for manufacturing" principles will be a key factor. Developing ways to assemble things more easily (for example, to snap together instead of using fasteners or screws) and to use custom connectors that prevent assembly errors can improve efficiency. As with overall project cost, use of standard parts can save money, both through avoiding specially developed custom components and being able to take advantage of economies of scale and quantity discounts. In some cases, there may also be opportunities to reduce cost through designs based on fewer, but more complex components. While this may prove effective, it could result in adverse trade-offs involving design complexity and troubleshooting difficulty.

If deliverable performance is the highest priority, limiting modularity may be useful. Highly modular systems are easier to design and simpler to build, but the number of interfaces involved can limit performance, reliability, and overall system integrity. High performance also requires a fundamental understanding of which design elements contribute most to system bottlenecks and queuing. For novel systems, the slowest interfaces and components may be difficult to find through analysis. Experiments, simulation models, and trial and error may be more successful in detecting the system elements that are most likely to impede performance. Finally, high-performance systems require optimization at the system level. Component-level optimization is easier, but improving individual components could result in unintended consequences and slow down the system as a whole.

Some programs are urgent, and for these the highest priority will be execution speed. Finalizing the design and delivering results as fast as possible starts with adequate funding and staff to avoid workflow bottlenecks and maximize parallel development efforts. Simultaneous development (or concurrent engineering or "fast tracking") can significantly shorten programs, but this only works well if the specifications are stable and frozen early. Doing a lot of work that later must be redone due to sloppy analysis or specification changes may even cost time. As with minimizing overall cost, reusing components and parts from earlier work can facilitate rapid progress with little incremental effort. Similarly, employing standards that contributors are familiar with will speed the work. You can also enhance your rate of progress by avoiding requirements for innovation by sticking with known methods and technology. Co-location of staff and visible and enthusiastic support from sponsors and managers can also boost program progress. It always helps to staff the work with the best, most experienced people available, and high-priority, urgent programs can often make a good case for top-notch staff. Finally, setting a rapid pace and sustaining it starts with defining frequent, visible milestones for the program and consistently meeting them. Plan to schedule checkpoints often on urgent programs and publicly recognize teams and individuals who achieve them.

SYSTEM DECOMPOSITION AND ANALYSIS

Scoping for a program begins with roadmaps and the setting of general objectives and requirements assembled from key stakeholders. Before work can commence, though, you need to define the actual detailed specifications for deliverables that can be delegated to project teams. Large complex program deliverables involve aggregations of components, parts, and subsystems, which in turn may be made up of still smaller pieces. Developing a hierarchy of components for program deliverables depends on systems engineering, architecture definition, or other similar analysis techniques.

For complex systems the initial decomposition could represent an acceptable approach, but more often some additional work, "what-if" exploration, and detailed examination provide insight into designs that better suit the program's objectives. For some program deliverables, graphical representations or analysis techniques can help to identify weaknesses, provide insights, and reveal options for improved designs. Before committing to a design, it is always useful to examine the assumptions and build confidence that the scoping you are committing to can in fact plausibly support your program objectives.

Graphical and Modeling Techniques

System diagrams are common for a wide spectrum of complex design jobs. Construction and mechanical systems rely on scale drawings, blueprints, exploded parts diagrams, and three-dimensional computer representations (Figure 3-9) depicting the deliverables and results expected. Physical models, sometimes full scale, are also used by many programs to gather feedback about what is to be built. Review and inspection of such drawings and

Figure 3-9 Three-dimensional computer representation for a construction plan.

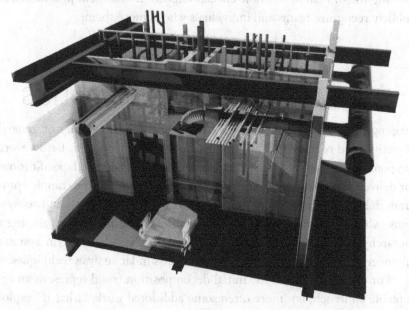

Figure 3-10 Example of a system block diagram.

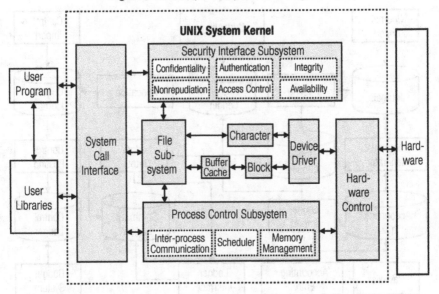

models may provide early opportunities to detect operational, functional, or aesthetic issues at very early stages of the work.

For complex engineering systems, functional block diagrams are useful for examining the component-level pieces of a system, including the connections and interactions. Figure 3-10 shows an example block diagram for a typical UNIX operating system kernel. Multilevel block diagram hierarchies can be used to identify potential failure or performance issues, by looking for excessive inter-component interactions, queuing bottlenecks, or other weaknesses.

Similarly, software applications use flowcharts or data-flow diagrams to illustrate how a system is expected to function that also provide insight into possible problems. Business processes may also be summarized using flow charts. As with functional block diagrams, you can use inputs, outputs, and branches to analyze of decision points, loops, and other complex flows and behaviors. An example of a system flowchart is in Figure 3-11.

Graphical or physical representations for complicated systems are useful for several reasons. It is always simpler and cheaper to create a picture or

Figure 3-11 Example of a system (general ledger) flowchart.

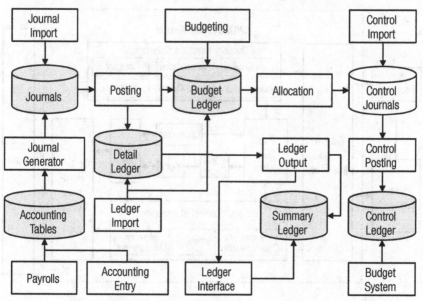

model of something than to actually build the final version. Each problem you can detect and correct at the concept stage will be one less you will need to deal with at the end—when changes are costly and there is little patience. When there are several alternative possibilities for the end result, models and drawings are a useful way to select an alternative that will suit the largest number of your stakeholders. Graphical or physical representations are also a good way to find and begin addressing functional defects and other potential problems.

System Analysis

System analysis generally starts with detailed narrative descriptions to provide powerful insight into systems. Describing how the components of a system will interact and function helps you determine if such a system will do what it is expected to do. Detailed use cases, scenarios, and other text-based descriptions can be an effective way to summarize the flows of data, inputs, outputs, and the other interfaces that make up a system. Role-play exercises involving individuals on the program team who assume the functions of components to model the workings of the overall system can also provide deep insight into potential bottlenecks, weak points, and overlooked connections. Any analysis that illuminates the interactions of system subcomponents can be useful in detecting potential flaws or inefficiencies in the design of a complicated system.

Other analysis techniques rely on formal inspections. Inspections use teams of people, often people who have relevant expertise from outside the program team, to review the proposed designs, system specifications, prioritized backlog databases, or other proposed scoping. Detailed reviews at defined stages of program design are a common method for identifying issues, defects, and omissions before committing to development work. Formal, disciplined walk-throughs of major software systems can be used to verify completeness and system coherence. Inspections by governmental agencies and officials are often part of the approval process for large construction or other publically funded programs. Whether it is legally required or not, a thorough inspection to review proposed specifications, ideally using a fresh set of eyes, is a prudent step in system analysis.

Many methods for analyzing complex systems involve matrices or tables to keep track of what is going on. A two-dimensional grid provides a useful way to monitor how system requirements are to be implemented. The simplest type of relationship matrix contains requirements ("Whats," or the voice of the customer) along the side and project specifications ("Hows," or the chosen approaches for addressing the stated requirements) across the top. A two-dimensional grid such as the diagram in Figure 3-12 provides a useful way to track the correspondence between what is desired and what will be produced. You can use such a matrix to document which project specifications contribute to fulfillment of documented requirements, and detect any situations where a requirement is not fully addressed.

To construct a relationship matrix, first populate the row headings on the left using your collected program requirements. They will include all the assembled and agreed upon information you have pieced together from your stakeholder analysis, roadmap discussions, and other initial scoping work. The number of rows with defined requirements may be large, and

Figure 3-12 A relationship matrix mapping requirements to projects.

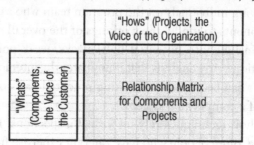

include listings related to functionality, performance, usability, safety, reliability, maintenance and supportability, cost, manufacturability, environmental factors, regional specifics, or other aspects.

The next step populates the column heads above the relationship matrix using your initial program breakdown and defined deliverable components and parts. You then can use the cells in the matrix to capture the interactions between the requirements and projects, showing the cases where projects support ("+") or strongly support ("++") the requirements listed. If there are cases where a project interaction is adverse to a requirement (such as a project striving to implement new high-performance capabilities and a requirement for minimizing cost) indicate a negative ("–") or a strong negative ("– –") correlation. (Use blank or "0" to indicate no or negligible interactions.)

When completed, examine each row to ensure overall coverage for all high-priority requirements. If you find inadequate support for any essential requirements, consider adjustments to the projects in your program breakdown to better address them. The matrix is also used to demonstrate why the projects as specified are necessary, and to identify situations where project specifications may appear superfluous.

Quality function deployment (QFD) is a useful system analysis technique that expands on the basic relationship matrix. QFD was developed by Yoji Akao in Japan in the mid-twentieth century, and it was initially used successfully at the Kobe Shipyard run by Mitsubishi Heavy Industries to track the construction and maintenance of large, complex ocean-going vessels. Akao has said that QFD "is a method for developing a design quality aimed at satisfying the consumer . . . [and] to assure the design quality while the product is still in the design stage." QFD methods not only represent an effective way to ensure that the specifications you are adopting will meet the requirements you have assembled, but also provide insight into the complexity of your designs.

The overall QFD process begins by constructing a relationship matrix:

- Identifying key requirements based on customer/stakeholder inputs (rows)
- Defining projects and design specifications to address the requirements (columns)
- Populating the two-dimensional relationship matrix to indicate the relationship between the "Whats" and the "Hows"

Quality function deployment then builds on this foundation, as shown in Figure 3-13. It uses the box at the right in the figure to assess how well the proposed aggregation of "Hows" meets the documented expectations. For each requirement, document a minimal acceptable standard in quantitative terms that can be used in testing and evaluation of ultimate deliverables. Particularly for requirements that have high priority and significant effect on the value of final deliverables, you should also estimate the incremental worth of delivering results that exceed the minimum standards. QFD additionally uses the rows below the matrix to determine the estimated difficulty, relative priority, and quantitative goals for the defined projects in each column.

In addition to all of this, QFD provides an effective method for assessing program complexity. To do this, it uses a triangular matrix to analyze potential conflicts or issues between the "Hows" of the relationship matrix grid. (The triangular matrix at the top of Figure 3-13 inspires the phrase "house of quality" associated with QFD.)

Populating the diagonal grids at the top of the diagram in Figure 3-13 again uses "+" and "−" indicators to show where the defined projects can be expected to support or conflict with each other. Ideally, the projects that

Figure 3-13 The quality function deployment "house of quality."

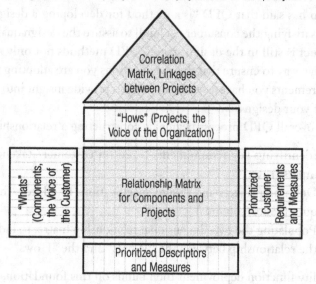

represent the program breakdown are consistent with one another, and the interactions among them are harmonious and support the program as a whole. It rarely works out this way, however. For example, goals within a project responsible for minimizing the cost and size of a power supply (or any other component that provides inputs to other project deliverables) are often in conflict with the design goals of projects that strive to deliver maximum speed or other high-performance capabilities.

Based on this analysis, you can reexamine your program breakdown and consider alternatives that could result in fewer negative correlations or provide better alignment with requirements.

Quality function deployment methods can be extended well beyond this sort of initial high-level analysis of "Whats" and "Hows." You can use QFD matrix analysis techniques to further examine the lower levels of a design hierarchy to test concept selection options and detect issues in detailed system design work. While QFD techniques by themselves can never solve system design or other problems, they can provide a disciplined, structured way to find potential issues and system problems so you can confront and deal with design trade-offs early. It is always best to resolve unnecessary complexity and other problems during design, before you have invested a lot of effort. If you fail to do so, you risk developing things that will not perform to expectations or that will require extensive rework.

If you have interest in QFD, you can find a good deal of useful guidance in reference books on the topic, on the Internet, and in materials related to "Six Sigma" quality management processes.

System Tools

Diagrams and analysis techniques provide considerable insight into complex systems. Tools can also be an effective method for developing insight into complex systems during scoping and design work. System analysis tools fall into two major categories: simulation tools and computer-aided design tools.

Simulation tools are a useful way to probe the operation of any system where there will be high volumes of inputs and outputs flowing through and extensive interaction among the system components. Large multiuser software applications, complex business processes, web-based transaction systems, large manufacturing installations, and many other types of systems can be modeled using software that can simulate various levels of activity, random timing, and other system parameters. Simulations can reveal bottlenecks and other queuing problems, cases that are not properly handled, and situations where volume could present problems. Simulations for some kinds of systems can be devised to provide user interaction that is functionally identical to the expected workings of a final system, although such prototypes will operate generally much more slowly. Providing a platform where the look and overall functionality can be seen by users can be a powerful proofing tool, even though the performance may be sluggish.

One area where simulations can fall short is in cases where system demands will be very high and the simulation capability has no effective way to model the stresses expected on the final system. A very visible example of this was the introduction in the United States of the Affordable Care Act's Healthcare.gov website in the fall of 2013. The portal and all of the connected web-based services were designed and tested in advance, and functionally it seemed to work reasonably well. All of the possible paths and options were exercised, and all the scenarios that were checked worked as they had been designed.

But the testing only went so far, and the design depended on a main contractor and over fifty subcontractors. It was complicated, and network connections were never tested using the expected level of transactions (50,000 simultaneous users), let alone the roughly 250,000 who attempted to access the system in the days following the web portal's opening. There was much finger-pointing and lots of blame to spread around concerning this very public failure of program management. There is some evidence that testing just prior to the opening of the system showed that it would have substantial performance issues even with only 1,000 simultaneous users.

Problems at startup were epic, with massive delays, users being dropped, and almost no successfully completed transactions. Following these well-publicized failures, a huge response effort was mounted to make the system work. The initial problems were tackled using a large number of fixes and changes aimed at transaction bottlenecks and related problems. In fact, much of what ultimately resolved the performance problems was a fairly common remedy used with modern computing problems—throwing more and faster hardware at the problem. Many program deliverable performance problems (and risks and program issues in general) arise from scale, and many of these problems only reveal themselves after the system is in production and under the operational stress that emerges. Simulation has its limits in revealing what can be expected when the floodgates open.

A similar scale-related problem that was narrowly averted occurred at the Golden Gate Bridge in San Francisco when it opened in 1937. It was designed to carry loads based on vehicular traffic, and tested to ensure that it could bear those loads. The design engineers were taken by surprise when on opening day people were invited to walk out on the bridge prior to its official opening. There were at one point so many people packed on the bridge that the weight far exceeded the bridge design specifications. The flexing began to worry those who built the bridge—imagining that it would disastrously collapse into the bay before it even officially opened. Ultimately all the pedestrians were cleared from the bridge and the invitation for many thousands of people to amble across the bridge has never been repeated.

A second type of tool for modeling complex systems is based on computer-aided software. The utility and power of three-dimensional software has increased to the point where a good deal of design work can be completed almost entirely on computer screens. The Boeing 777 program described earlier in this chapter was the first at Boeing to employ computer-aided design (CAD) software systems. Boeing used it to significantly lower costs and improve quality compared with earlier design efforts. Philip Condit, the initial program manager for the 777 and later CEO of Boeing, strongly supported adoption of CAD systems because the existing methods were so cumbersome and expensive. Designing a complicated multifunction mechanical system component such as a wing involved building it and then discovering all the issues with placement of fuel lines, support struts, hydraulic controls, wiring bundles, and other parts by trial and error—lots of error. Condit observed that, on average, each and every drawing in the Boeing system was changed almost five times before final release; thus, Condit said, "We design four and a half planes for every plane we build." For the 777, all designs were done using Boeing's Computer-graphics Aided Three-dimensional Interactive Application (CATIA) and Electronic Preassembly In Computer (EPIC) systems. No mock-ups were needed, and all space-related or other design issues could be resolved entirely in the computer.

PROGRAM SCOPE RISKS AND OPTIMIZATION

Chapter 2 explored overall planning for program risk management, including decisions about program risk management. Assessing risks requires their thorough identification, including the risks associated with planning and workflow (which will be examined in Chapter 4) and those arising from staffing and organizational structure (which is a major topic in Chapter 5). Identifying risks related to scope management focuses on potential failure modes and performance shortcomings. It begins with systems analysis, particularly looking for the various ways that a particular system might misbehave. As the overall structure of a complex system comes into focus, scope risks emerge. Some risk is due to novelty or excessive complexity associated with specific components or subsystems. Other scope risks arise from the interactions among subsystems. Still more risks relate to choices made concerning how much scope is delivered, and how frequently.

Novelty and Uncertainty

Programs, like projects, are unique. At least some aspects of program scope involve novelty. The more ground-breaking and "bleeding edge" the objectives are, the more uncertainty there will be. As your program breakdown process proceeds, review the major components and project objectives to understand how the program differs from work where you have background and experience.

Some program scope risks are intrinsic to the components you are defining; at least a few aspects of any program will be fundamentally dissimilar from deliverables created for past projects and programs. Most programs have some subsystem requirements that are new and uncertain. Whenever you uncover a portion of the program where your only alternatives involve unknowns, note them as risks.

Scope risks also can come from the methods and processes you plan to use. If your program requires changes to equipment, systems, the work environment, or any other aspect of your infrastructure, assess the potential impact on your program and note any significant changes as risks.

Your program may also face changing regulations, organizational mandates, or other constraints affecting the work. If so, assess the possible consequences on your processes or procedures, and note anything that might cause problems as a program risk.

Successfully dealing with complexity starts with understanding where your background and experience is shallow. Dealing with the related risks involves seeking ways to substitute alternatives where your understanding is better or gaining the needed experience and dealing with learning curve issues. Identify as program scope risks all novelty and uniqueness that you are unable to plan around.

Subsystem and Component Interactions

System analysis also documents linkages and interactions following the decomposition of complicated deliverables into smaller, interrelated parts. Analyzing functional block diagrams, flowcharts, and other graphical system representations provides a good start for locating potential bottlenecks, queuing problems, or other performance issues. Simulations and scenario analysis can also provide insight into aspects of an overall system that are likely to be problematic. Look for system components that have excessive numbers of inputs, outputs, or control linkages to other parts of the system. In designs having a multilevel hierarchy, trace out the connections at each level, seeking to identify subsystems where the levels of interaction appear too high.

Interaction between modules and components of a design can also create problems if the volume or scale of the interaction is extreme. Estimate the amount of interaction expected for documented inputs and outputs, and analyze the performance that will result using your design assumptions. Both excessive quantities and types of subsystem interactions can result in system performance problems or failures, so note any examples you find in your system design as risks.

Phasing of Deliverables

Programs having integrated delivery responsibility (construction, major systems, and other types of single-delivery programs) must accept the risks inherent with efforts where the entirety of the defined scope has to be delivered all at once.

However, most programs have at least some latitude in delivering results incrementally. Some scope risk arises from choices made about deliverable timing. For programs that will deliver a stream of deliverables, it can be problematic to deliver results either too often or too seldom. Minimizing risk associated with deliverable frequency depends on finding the Goldilocks zone where the rate of delivery is "just right."

Some programs adopt a philosophy of delivering large results infrequently. This would appear to free up more effort for development by reducing the amount of overhead for testing and replanning. In theory, you would conserve resources by not having to mount activities associated with delivery very often. This philosophy works well only in cases where the scoping for each of the infrequent deliveries remains stable and well understood. The longer you go without feedback and adjustments, the more risk you assume, particularly if the needs could shift or program stakeholders change their minds.

Other programs choose to deliver smaller results more often—monthly or even weekly. "Time boxing" releases to occur frequently can be very effective when dealing with small programs, stakeholders who are integrated into the program team, and modest levels of complexity. For larger programs, delivering results too often may result in excessive overhead and frustration on the part of users and customers. ("I haven't even figured out how to use the last version yet, and here is the next one.")

For complex system deliverables, selecting the right release schedule can be tricky. In general, you want to ensure that the increment of change and value delivered will more than justify the cost of delivering, documenting, training, and supporting what you produce. For some programs with closely aligned users and stakeholders the time box chosen could be monthly. Advocates of the agile methodology Scrum argue that a 30-day sprint cycle for software development releases works well in most cases, including for multi-team system undertakings. For programs delivering systems to a larger, more diverse population of users and customers, "time boxes" of 6 to 8 weeks (or even longer cycles) can substantially reduce the overhead and be easier to manage. Programs responsible for tangible deliverables tend to adopt even longer cycles of multiple months, based on feasibility, realistic development time frames, and the effort required for each release.

There is always some risk associated with adopting a release or delivery cycle having an inappropriate length. A cycle that is too long involves risks of misalignment between evolving needs and what is delivered. A cycle that is too short may consume excessive resources for testing, feedback, and support, and may even involve some risk of annoying key stakeholders. Choosing a release cycle that is not optimum is undesirable, but for longer programs this can be managed by making adjustments that experiment with different timeframes to determine what works best.

System Adjustments

Managing program scope risk starts with system analysis to identify potential issues related to design choices, and adjusting them where possible to better deal with obvious risks.

When the design of a system deliverable depends on invention or a creative breakthrough, investigate alternatives for solutions that could use existing methods or technologies. System design based on components that have worked before and are well understood, if they will be sufficient, will yield the most predictable results. A bias for known methods and components can significantly reduce overall deliverable risk and complexity.

Reuse of known methods and components is a technique that can be effective in nearly any environment, including (perhaps especially) in those where there is a bias for the novel and innovative. One example of this comes from a program manager who is far better known for other accomplishments, the master sculptor Auguste Rodin. By the 1890s, at the height of his career, Rodin was managing a staff of more than fifty people in his gallery and salesroom in Paris (now the location of the Musée Rodin). This large team supported his booming business of producing bronze sculptures in whatever volumes, sizes, and configurations customers requested. Most of the works he produced were done on commission and could be made any size desired by the purchaser. Because he worked in bronze, his team could produce large numbers of original sculptures. It is estimated that in the last 20 years of his life at least 319 versions of *The Kiss* were produced, in four different sizes.

Rodin's staff was able to make his works both larger and smaller using a machine invented in 1836 by French engineer Achille Collas. The device could be used to create duplications of any sculpture in any size desired, and it enabled his assistants to make multiple original sculptures at whatever scale a purchaser requested. Rodin's most famous piece, *The Thinker*, was originally less than 1 meter (only about 28 inches) high. Before long it was also being reproduced and sold at half that height as well as in a version enlarged to roughly 2 meters.

Rodin also created art by recycling his own works. The process for making bronze figurines produced many leftover arms, heads, legs, hands, and other body parts. Rodin created many entirely new sculptures by combining these available pieces. Rodin also made new works using multiple castings of the same figure, combining them to create a completed sculpture. His *Three Faunesses* comprises a single female figurine that he cast three times and then joined together by braising. Reuse is a tried-and-true technique for efficiently creating project and program deliverables of many types.

Program scoping analysis will also reveal aspects of your program breakdown where there are potential issues with subsystem interconnections—another significant source of scoping risk. Whenever there are excessive numbers of inputs, outputs, or control connections linking system components, or potential volumes or scale that could result in performance or queuing problems, investigate alternative subsystem definitions and configurations that might improve the design. Realign flows, combine or adjust components, and in general seek changes that would result in a more robust, lower risk system design.

Analysis reveals many sources of scope risk, and at least some of these can be avoided by adjustments in scoping and through reuse of components, processes, and methods. Regardless of how successful you are in this, however, at least some scoping uncertainties will remain. Dealing with residual scope risks starts with recognizing the uncertainty and consequences of potential problems. For particularly risky aspects of program scope, establish a high priority for the related activities and projects. Ensure that the work is adequately funded and staffed, and start working on any education and skill development that will be helpful to the program team members involved. Work to build the skills and knowledge you will need to deal with new or otherwise unknown undertakings early, before you need it. Tap into any expertise within your organization relevant to risky scope items, and secure commitments from those with experience to at least mentor people on your program staff. Whenever possible, build the case for acquiring contributors who have needed experience for your program team, using outside consultants where appropriate. Solicit help from people who have successfully worked with the aspects of your program scope that you are concerned about, through benchmarking exercises with similar organizations, networking with peers in professional societies, consultations with academics who have applicable expertise, and others who have appropriate backgrounds.

For risky portions of program scope that you cannot avoid or mitigate, schedule all related activities and projects as early in the program timeline as possible. Focus on tests, prototypes, pilots, and feasibility explorations first, to verify whether the concepts you plan to use are viable. Scheduling the work related to significant scope risks early will provide you with the largest possible buffer for resolving any problems you may encounter and exploring workarounds and alternatives. If you ultimately find that you will be unable to deliver an essential part of program scope, it is much better to be aware of it early, before you have consumed a great deal of effort, time, and money. Whenever the scope for a major program requires something that is in reality not possible, canceling the program early is always in everyone's best interest.

Finally, being too aggressive with the amount of scope committed to a given phase, release, or iteration is a major source of risk. Accepting excessive lower-priority items into scope not only makes it less likely that those aspects can be delivered, but also diverts efforts and threatens the program's ability to successfully complete the highest value work.

Make all the necessary adjustments to program scope and overall system design needed to minimize program risks for the current phase of work, and clearly document all significant scope risks that remain in your program risk register.

DOCUMENTING PROGRAM SCOPE

Documenting program scope relies on many of the ideas explored earlier in this chapter: roadmaps, narratives, graphical and other program deliverable depictions, models, and other descriptive artifacts. For programs in general, more scope documentation is better than less, as long as the content is clear and the descriptions at each level of the scoping hierarchy aid in understanding what is to be developed.

Scoping Roadmaps and Function Hierarchies

The highest-level scope documents for most programs tend to be overall roadmaps that outline major deliverables and timing. Roadmap documents may be documented using a variety of methods, but because they are used for general communications and will be distributed to a wide audience of program stakeholders, it is best to adopt a format that is accessible to all and can be easily understood, attached to communications, and printed. Some program teams use output formats such as a graphics format (.jpg or .gif, for example) or a generalized document format (such as .pdf) to capture and distribute outputs from specialized planning or scheduling tools to document program roadmaps, but interpreting the output from such tools (and controlling the contents) can be a challenge.

It is most common to use a general-purpose graphics tool to clearly show the planned flow of program deliverables; Figures 3-4 through 3-7 earlier in this chapter were created with MS PowerPoint. Even a spreadsheet program can be useful in documenting an overall roadmap. General "office-type" tools provide a good mix of clear documentation and relatively easy update, and make creating presentations and reports fairly easy.

The next layers of scoping rely on a range of documents, starting with clear definition of the scoping at all applicable levels for the current phases of work. This begins with a well-defined dichotomy showing what is presently in scope and what is not, generally in the form of a "Now/Not yet" (or "Is/Is not") table, usually backed up with a database containing scoping, backlog, change proposals, or other requirements information. All items in scope require clear specifications to define them and explicit owners responsible for their delivery. The same level of documentation is needed at lower levels for any system requirements currently in scope that have been decomposed into smaller subsystems. This is true at each level all the way down to the specifications delegated to specific project teams responsible for implementing them.

All identified program requirements must be documented, including those that will be considered for inclusion later in the program. The definition for future requirements may be broad and general, but it must provide at least the minimum data needed for the scoping decisions pending for upcoming program phases or iterations.

Scoping Status Repository

Establish a location in your program information system (discussed in Chapter 2) for tracking the status of all program requirements. Ensure that it is visible to all contributors and stakeholders who need to understand what the current program phase is committed to deliver. Whether you choose to use a simple spreadsheet, table, database, or other format, include the information that people will need to identify, describe, and display the status for each item. Establish a process that will be easy to use for access for program contributors. Specific structures for program scoping systems vary a good deal, but most include the following fields:

- Identification number or code for each requested requirement
- A short description
- Status (at least "In" or "Out")
- Link to a detailed request document
- Source and requestor name
- Priority
- Stakeholder sponsor
- Project(s) affected
- Implementation owner
- Timing or release requested (or committed)
- Estimated effort
- Link to any other related documents

Other information may be relevant, such as additional contacts, progress data for items in scope, and additional items extracted from the original request documents or results from analysis activities. It is best to keep program scoping documentation simple, to make interpreting the current status straightforward. Links to more detailed information are a good way to keep online program-level scoping lists simple and reduce the need for replicating excessive amounts of detailed information and analysis.

Program scoping information is useful to all, so read access should be freely available to every program contributor. It is a good idea to restrict update access to program staff responsible for managing the scope, however, to reduce the possibility of inappropriate change.

As the program proceeds, retain all scoping document versions, requests, proposals, and change decision information. More information on managing program scope and scope changes is provided in the Program Scope and Change Management section, below.

Scoping Documents, Reports, and Diagrams

In addition to the roadmaps and status of program requirements or backlog items, you will need other documents. The program charter is one such document, along with all the tests, acceptance criteria, and approval requirements applicable to your program. You should also collect any flowcharts, functional block diagrams, or other drawings or figures that relate to your program scope.

If you have developed narratives or scenarios describing your program deliverables, include them in your program information archive. All programs are subject to constraints, so include documents summarizing their effect on deliverables in your scoping documentation. Document the reasons for all program timing constraints (such as fiscal periods, market cycles, or trade shows) that impact your deliverables. If there are organizational standards, legal or other regulations, regional requirements or other external constraints, document them. Also document the results of any market research, competitor analysis, or user needs surveys that will affect your program scope.

Models and Feasibility Studies

Program scope documentation also includes all the prototypes, physical models, pilot studies, and simulation results you have produced or have plans for. Include all summary documents, pictures, mock-ups, and other representations you have for your program deliverables. Be thorough in documenting the results of all research, prototyping, models, pilot programs, and other work done to validate the credibility of your scoping assumptions and decisions.

PROGRAM SCOPE AND CHANGE MANAGEMENT

Managing program scope requires a formal process. An effective process has two parts: *scope management*, to establish the content of each phase, release, or iteration, and *change management*, to adjust the scope of each individual program phase.

Program Scoping

For large, complex programs, decisions concerning what to include (and what to exclude) can be difficult, and should not be made casually. In general, scoping decisions are best made on a periodic but infrequent basis and with careful analysis of stakeholder inputs, realistic development capacity limits, value and effort assessments, and other relevant considerations. The main purpose of program scope management is to accept requirements that deliver value to stakeholders. Adding to scope is primarily a function of the infrequent scope management part of the process.

Program Change Review Process

Programs also need a disciplined process for managing scope changes between the overall scoping decisions. The main purpose of the more frequent change management portion of the process is to assess proposed changes as requests are received and to defer most of them to a queue to be considered for inclusion in future program efforts. An effective change process ensures that only the most urgent changes submitted will be accepted and only after sufficient analysis to minimize unintended adverse consequences. The program change management process also generally operates as a zero-sum game; for any change that adds to scope, some aspect of the current scope will be dropped to make room for it.

Program Scope Control

Managing scope on a multiphase program using such a two-level change regime employs a process similar to that of projects employing agile management methods, such as Scrum. With Scrum, the team defines a series of sprints, with detailed scoping defining the initial iteration and general descriptions of the requirements to be addressed during some number of future development cycles. At the end of each sprint, the scoping for the next will be locked down after making adjustments to the broad descriptions drafted earlier based on feedback and results. Scoping for each cycle is fluid and evolving until each sprint begins, and then it is tightly controlled for the duration of the cycle (generally 30 days) until the next scheduled release.

Programs tend to have "time boxes" that are longer, perhaps several months. Nonetheless, they are well served by a scoping philosophy where the overall roadmap is defined in general terms, the individual phases are defined as they begin, and changes are restricted during development for each release to enable predictable delivery the next increment of value. Using this sort of scoping process to manage program scope is explored in more detail and with an example in Chapter 6.

Managing scope for a major program is complicated and difficult. Anything you can do to simplify it and make it more predictable and straightforward will make your job easier and your programs more successful.

KEY IDEAS FOR PROGRAM DELIVERABLE MANAGEMENT

- Establish unambiguous responsibilities for managing program project and product decisions.
- Determine stakeholder needs and desires for program scope, focusing on problems and opportunities not on solutions.
- Assemble and prioritize program requirements, working to resolve or at least minimize conflicts and inconsistencies.
- Develop a high-level roadmap for program deliverables, defining phases, releases, or iterations that are as frequent as feasible.
- Use systems analysis and related techniques to develop a coherent multi-level design for program phase deliverables.
- Thoroughly assess the quality and effectiveness of your solutions, and adjust them to minimize complexity.
- Capture scope risks, and revise scoping plans where possible to better manage them.
- Clearly document current program scope, and explicitly define what is and what is not included in your current program phase, release, or iteration.
- Define and use a process for managing program scope that is flexible for setting phase scoping but disciplined in limiting changes for committed program work.

CHAPTER 4

Program Planning and Organizing

Essentially, all models are wrong, but some are useful.
  —**George Edward Pelham Box** (statistician and scientist)

One approach to dealing with the inherent complexity of programs is to develop a model of the work based on planning. Such models can be very useful in determining whether or not to proceed and how to do so. Program plans comprise multiple project plans, and modeling the overall program using these lower-level plans provides a powerful tool for understanding and organizing the work. For many reasons, however, it is never possible for a program plan based on such a model to be precisely accurate or predictive. Effective program management recognizes this and works to develop plans that will be useful—despite being incomplete and lacking certainty—for at least the short term.

As discussed in Chapter 3, program complexity begins with the expected deliverables. Interactions between subsystems and components can be difficult to analyze and understand, and some systems are inherently chaotic and unpredictable. Program failure modes related to scoping are significant, but program complexity does not stop with the deliverables. Workflow interrelationships, which are the main topic of this chapter, also create program problems. Much of the complexity arising from the project interactions within a program is linked to how deliverables are decomposed into components. Addressing program workflow issues often requires adjustments to the initial design decisions.

Dealing with program plan complexity begins with adopting processes and tools with capabilities that are adequate to the task of organizing and understanding the effort required. Managing workflow complexity also demands a thorough and detailed focus on planning for all included projects and subprograms. This is true even (perhaps especially) in cases where most of the work will be delegated to teams adopting agile, iterative development methods, because in a dynamic environment cross-team linkages can break down and quickly lead to chaos.

Program planning efforts depend on appropriate tools. Informal methods and low-end tools may be sufficient for undertaking small projects, but the complexity and magnitude of information that you need to manage on a large program requires tools with sufficient functionality. Big programs rely on establishing and managing complex program plans. Tools for effective program planning include specialized project and program management applications, communications and networking systems, and facilities for archiving and organizing program information.

Where the focus of project management planning is on activities (or tasks, stories, or other terms describing units of work), the main focus for program planning is on interfaces—the connections that bind the related projects together to make up the program. Failing to identify and manage cross-project dependencies leads to potentially disastrous timing and other program problems. Program-level planning also requires effective risk management, which includes, but goes well beyond, project risk management. Developing effective program plans relies on bottom-up, credible plans for each included project that can be used to validate program plans, guide revisions to program roadmaps and scoping, and establish realistic baselines and commitments for program objectives.

PROGRAM PLANNING PROCESSES

Some of the processes central to program planning and organizing relate to life-cycle management and change control, both of which have been explored to some degree earlier in this book. Other necessary processes include planning standards, issue and problem management, and program reviews.

Program Life Cycles

Most life cycles for project work have a straightforward high-level structure that boils down to "thinking, doing, and checking." The exact terms vary, and there are often specific subcategories defined within these broad categories for specific types of project work. As an example, projects employing iterative techniques go through these stages within each iteration, using a "design–build–test" structure.

As outlined in Chapter 1, a program life cycle employs the same three fundamental phases. The Project Management Institute documents the program life cycle as having a definition phase to initiate the work (discussed in Chapter 2), an execution phase in which projects are undertaken to deliver benefits and value (generally by far the most significant in terms of cost, effort, and time), and finally, for most programs, a closure phase to verify satisfactory completion and conclude the program efforts.

Life cycles are generally more about upper management's need to standardize and synchronize work than they are about project management. Programs in particular use life-cycle definitions to establish the project standards that will make planning, monitoring, and controlling within the program more straightforward. By imposing specific methods, checkpoints, and other life-cycle requirements across an aggregation of projects, program leaders can more effectively coordinate and understand what is going on. At the highest level within the "doing" part of a program, this takes the form of the program roadmap. Different types of program employ various forms of roadmaps, and their structure usually resembles one of the examples in Chapter 3 (see Figures 3-4, 3-5, 3-6, and 3-7). The program roadmap sets out general timing and scoping objectives for the work that define what concurrent projects are expected to deliver.

To ensure coherence, it is best to define a consistent life cycle that will be followed by each project in the program. Having a common life cycle provides for effective synchronization of work undertaken by separate project teams and a foundation for aggregating project plans into useful program-level schedules for analysis and tracking. Whether the project life cycles are plan based (plan, analyze, design, develop, test, release) or composed of a sequence of agile iterations, common structures and definitions provide the program leader with a foundation for coordinating program efforts. Specific details for life-cycle phases and required deliverables are less important (as long as the choices are appropriate to the work) than establishing a consistent basis for coherent planning and tracking.

Program Planning Standards and Templates

Consistency in project planning is also essential. Providing clear, thorough documents describing the process is a necessary staring point. Guidance from program staff or a program management office (PMO), including training, mentoring, and coaching, can be useful in ensuring consistent planning methods. Especially early in the program, facilitating planning sessions and project startup workshops is a great way to encourage development of appropriate project plans and schedules. However you choose to go about this, work to ensure that project plans will be compatible and sufficiently detailed across the program.

For project work using agile methods, mandate the use of a standard method for all teams, for example Scrum. Establish an overall common cadence for the work to synchronize the time boxes used by all development teams and establish which iterations will be focused on internal, potentially releasable results and which will focus on integration and external release.

Templates are a useful tactic for ensuring plan consistency across project teams. Establish templates for all software applications you expect to use for project planning (ideally based on a single project scheduling tool, as will be discussed in the next section). Define milestones and common terms for life-cycle transition points in the program. Include tasks (or activities, stories, or whatever is appropriate) and milestones (with specific, measurable criteria) in the templates to support program reporting, communications, testing, integration, reviews, and other coordination requirements. Incorporate relevant holidays (for all regions and countries involved in the program) and key organization dates and events into the templates to ensure that everyone can plan around them appropriately. By providing the project teams with detailed templates, you will encourage robust and compatible project planning. The easier you can make developing consistent, thorough project plans, the more straightforward your program planning efforts will be.

Program Plan Change Management

Managing program scope and deliverable changes as you proceed is central to program control and ultimate success. Chapter 3 discussed the value of a formal process, and Chapter 6 will explore the process in some detail. Programs benefit from an open process for planning phases (or releases, iterations, stages of work, or whatever term is applicable) and a more disciplined process applied during those phases to limit changes to current work. Plan changes are best managed in line with this overall process—with flexible overall plan development for the next phase of program work based on the project-level input and feedback, and a disciplined change process that tightly controls plan changes within each phase of work. Plan changes, like scope changes, may appear benign when first considered but represent significant unintended consequences for the program as a whole. Once a baseline for the next stage of program work is set, establish a formal process for detailed assessment of any plan changes that are proposed, with a default disposition of "reject" or at least "defer" that ensures that only essential plan changes representing significant, credible value to the program will be accepted.

Program Issue and Problem Management

Good project management depends on prompt resolution of issues and problems as they arise. In general, projects will identify issues and use a table, web-based list, database, or spreadsheet to describe each issue and track it using information, such as when it was opened, the responsible owner, a due date for resolution, the priority, current status, and any comments.

Program issue management does not materially differ from this, but you will need to decide whether to track all issues associated with project and other work or to track only the most important issues at the program level. Managers of programs of modest size often elect to track all issues for the program as a whole, because even situations that appear to affect only a small part of the program may have unintended consequences or quickly escalate into major program consequences. This can be unwieldy for very large programs, though, so it is common to establish criteria for bringing project-level issues to the attention of program management.

Whether you track all issues for the program or the most critical subset, establish a central location for all problem and issue tracking, preferably within your program management information system. Establish processes for monitoring of issues at the project level at least weekly to ensure that listed issues are receiving prompt attention. Plan to track issues at the program level at the same frequency, reviewing (at least briefly) all project-level issues to detect any that are new, overdue, or rising in significance. At a minimum, track issues at the program level that represent significant program impact, such as the following:

- Overall schedule slippage
- Program budget consequences
- Significant staffing problems
- Program deliverable quality, performance, or other scoping concerns
- Contract problems
- Program-level risks or potential changes
- Stakeholder expectations

Monitor program issues weekly, and more frequently when warranted. Provide status in your program reporting using "red–yellow–green" stoplight indicators or other clear indicators to provide public visibility and ensure that each open issue receives the attention it requires.

Strive to resolve issues within the program as promptly as possible, to avoid additional problems, unexpected consequences, and cascade effects. If resolving an issue requires more authority than you have within your program or you encounter significant conflicts concerning how to proceed, promptly bring the issue to the attention of your sponsor (or another key stakeholder) who has sufficient power to close the issue. It is good practice to do this sparingly and only as a last resort, however, because escalating issues to a higher authority too frequently will erode management's confidence in you and your program team. When it is clear you have no feasible alternative, always escalate promptly. Establishing an effective process for dealing with problem escalations to the program level (or even higher) when it is necessary will be explored in more detail in Chapters 5 and 6.

Program Reviews

Programs that run a year or longer exceed the horizon for accurate planning, so they benefit from periodic review. A program review focuses on much of the same information developed at program startup, including program roadmaps, assumptions, constraints, and stakeholder expectations. Reviews are also used to update plans, budgets, risks, and other program documents using current information, recent history, and any changes the program faces.

The planning horizon for some programs may be very short because of uncertainties and frequent changes. Such programs will adopt more agile, iterative methods and may conduct overall reviews approximately monthly. For programs where there is greater stability, reviews might be conducted quarterly or even semiannually, but no program should go longer than about 6 months without revisiting the overall plans. Program reviews often coincide with major releases, major program milestones, the end of a fiscal period, or other significant organizational dates.

Program reviews, like program startup workshops, work best when you can meet face to face for sufficient time to thoroughly assess the program. Calling a meeting of all the parties whose contributions are important to planning will ensure both better results and more effective ongoing teamwork. The length of a review will vary with the type of program, but even agile programs holding monthly reviews will probably require most of a day, and larger programs often benefit from reviews lasting several days.

When planning for a program review, set an agenda covering topics such as the following:

- Current program objectives, stakeholder needs, roadmaps, and priorities
- Changes to program constraints and assumptions
- Updating program schedules, budgets, and risks

Focus a program review on future plans, to clearly define the next phase of work. Make adjustments to benefit from past successes and to modify your approach to future work to avoid earlier problems. Reviews are also a good opportunity to reinforce goals and relationships, and to recognize significant program accomplishments.

Program reviews will be further discussed in Chapter 6, which focuses on program execution and control.

PROGRAM PLANNING TOOLS

Processes for planning are only one part of the foundation for a healthy program. Implementing program processes depends on planning tools, communications and networking capabilities, risk and decision modeling tools, and information management systems.

Planning Tools

For large programs there may be several decisions to make regarding planning software. At the highest level, summary plans may be best managed using generalized office-type applications such as spreadsheets, tables in documents, or standard presentation applications. For summary plans having minimal detail, these methods can be very effective in providing clear information to stakeholders who do not have access to (or do not want to deal with) specialized project management software. At the highest level, it is important to establish standard formats based on widely available software, and to ensure that there will be no problems with either access or interpretation.

Similarly, you want to minimize any potential for confusion or information access for your lowest-level project planning information. In general, at the project level it is best to select (and develop planning templates consistent with) a single software tool that all projects will use for defining, planning, and tracking program work. For overall program coherence and control, consistency is generally much more important than the specific project planning tool you select. For conventional planning, a midrange tool such as Microsoft Project or any of a wide range of similar applications will likely be sufficient. For programs using agile methods, tools for defining and tracking work increments from suppliers such as Rally, VersionOne, Atlassian (Jira), and others represent good options. Mandating the use of the same approach for planning all projects in the program will make program-level plan analysis and status management much more straightforward than if each project team in the program is using a different format and tool. Cloud-based planning tools or web-based applications can also work well, but choose a standard planning tool that at least meets all the needs of the most complicated projects in the program.

Some tools that work well at the project level may prove to be inadequate for program management. Midrange tools may have limited features or capacity that make them unsuitable for program-level planning and tracking. You may need more expensive software with additional capabilities to adequately document, monitor, and control large, complex undertakings. With more functionality, however, comes a steeper learning curve and greater challenges in establishing program plan baselines. Many organizations select and standardize specific high-end applications for major programs based on the recommendations of the PMO or other centralized support group. If you do plan to use a high-end planning tool, identify a competent program-level planner who will be able to dedicate the time required to become sufficiently knowledgeable about the tool, as well as the effort needed to keep the program plan consistent with the underlying project plans. Program management requires consistency and plan coherence to manage inter-project scheduling conflicts as the program proceeds.

If you are in a position to select a tool for program planning, there are several high-end options from which to choose. However, because of industry consolidation, there are currently fewer full-featured program planning tools than there once were. Most offerings are now aligned with a small number of major suppliers, such as Oracle, Hewlett-Packard, and Computer Associates (CA). In determining your best option for program-level planning, assess both the history and likely future of the software packages you are considering. Some high-end packages continue to operate as they did when they were mainframe based, and have limited capabilities for offline use. Consider also that many high-end, enterprise-level tools provide additional functionality for risk assessment and simulation, contributor time tracking, portfolio management, and a wide variety of other features that might be of interest (or, conversely, might get in the way).

For all the tools you plan to use to support planning and scheduling, spend some time exploring the capabilities for importing and exporting data (especially if project teams will be using a different project management application for planning and tracking). Also check that the tools you plan to use support all the languages and computing platforms that will be needed across the program.

Before committing to using a new program-level scheduling tool, consult with others who are using it to determine how it is working for them. Locate peers who are doing similar program work and discuss what they like about each package you are considering, and what, if anything, they find frustrating, challenging, or otherwise undesirable about the software. In general, it is best to adopt software that others in your own organization also use, so favor packages where you have a substantial community of local users over ones where you will be on your own when you have questions and encounter problems.

Acquisition and support costs can also be a significant consideration. For tools that will be used by many program contributors, estimate the costs "per seat" for users and how much you will need to expend in training and learning curve investments over the life of the program. Some high-end applications can be expensive, so ensure that you have the funding, other resources, and approvals needed to make them work.

Finally, for all levels of planning, select tools that will make managing a hierarchy of plans at different levels of granularity as straightforward as possible. While keeping executive-level summaries, program-level plans, and detailed (possibly at multiple levels) project-level plans synchronized is never easy, selecting an inappropriate tool can make it practically impossible.

Communications and Networking Capabilities

Programs have extensive communications needs, so you should consider using any and all reasonable options for communications. Establish easy-to-use communications for working with geographically remote parts of your program team, and select technological options that will be available to all who will need to use them. Conduct tests of any communications methods you plan to employ to ensure compatibility at program initiation and recheck their utility when any new global teams or contributors join the program.

For program planning and other meetings that include geographically remote participants, teleconferencing is the most universal tool. Telephones, videoconferencing, and computer networking methods can all be effective. For meetings where you need to share images, graphics, software applications, live video, or other complex visual program information, specialized media rooms set up for videoconferencing and web-based meetings are helpful. Whenever you plan to hold technology-assisted meetings, ensure that everyone involved will have consistent access and will be able to participate fully.

Program teams rely heavily on email and other computer messaging technologies for formal and informal communications. Most messaging capabilities these days are universally available, but it is always prudent on a new program to check with your entire program team to ensure that you will not encounter later difficulties. Verify that there will be no potential issues with access, technical compatibility, types of attachments, bandwidth, data volumes, or security with any the messaging technologies you intend to use. Program communication planning will be further discussed in Chapter 5.

Information Management Systems

Carefully plan the structure for your program management information system. Determine how best to establish a central repository for file and information sharing across the program. Ensure that the access methods you select support collaboration and have universal compatibility, an adequate performance level, and appropriate security. Consider your program requirements when planning the use of web-based tools, e-rooms, file servers, distributed project and program management software applications, and other tools for remote collaboration.

As you establish your program management information system, work with the program staff and contributors to understand their needs, and organizing the information you need to store. Include all the program information that contributors will need for their efforts, and set up the data to make their access simple and logical. A program's information archive is an essential tool for execution and control, as will be discussed further in Chapter 6.

Simulation, Risk, and Decision Modeling Tools

Tools for modeling deliverables, discussed in Chapter 3, can be very useful in managing the complexity of program scope. Similarly, software for analyzing plans, schedules, and decisions may be used to better understand the complexities in program workflow and organization.

Project and program risk management software (including both stand-alone applications that can use data from midrange project scheduling tools and functions built into high-end project management applications) can provide a useful perspective on potential worst-case program schedules, analyze correlation problems affecting project timing, and assess overall plan credibility. Such tools use computer simulation to vary program parameters (in most cases including schedule duration estimates) using randomly selected values within defined ranges to analyze program timing assumptions. One of the most important uses of the output created by tools using this sort of Monte Carlo analysis is to challenge the illusion of precision fostered by the deterministic-looking schedules created using typical project management tools. Instead of the firm ending dates generated by single-point estimates, Monte Carlo analysis displays a range of possible timing outcomes, along with probabilities estimated for delivering results by various dates.

The most common technique for schedule uncertainty analysis uses three-point duration estimates in place of the "most likely" single-point estimates that serve as the foundation for basic critical path and other program schedule analysis. Some midrange software scheduling tools provide for entry of three-point estimates (optimistic, most likely, and pessimistic) in their databases, but these software packages only use the data to calculate weighted-average program evaluation and review technique (PERT)-type estimates of expected duration. In midrange project management scheduling applications such as Microsoft Project, the use of these data can be somewhat mysterious, and it is peripheral to the application's main function.

True Monte Carlo schedule analysis requires either additional specialized software or adoption of a high-end scheduling package that provides it (or at least supports simulation analysis as an add-on feature). When considering either one of these options, be aware that simulating complicated program schedules is difficult. Even an experienced program planner who has access to a fancy tool and possesses a solid understanding of the process may still fall prey to the "garbage in, garbage out" scenario.

There are a number of applications designed to provide simulation-based program schedule analysis based on data stored in the database of midrange scheduling tools without having to reenter or convert your program plan data. Simulation capabilities built into high-end program and enterprise planning applications offer similar opportunities for analysis based on plan estimates stored within the tool. Either of these alternatives generally requires less work for schedule risk analysis than methods that depend on extracting program data before inputting it into stand-alone Monte Carlo simulation software.

There are obvious benefits to using full-function Monte Carlo methods, but there are also costs. In addition to the up-front investment in software, you will also need to generate at least the two range-defining duration estimates for key program work, and in some cases, you may find it necessary to use more elaborate definitions or distributions for duration estimates. You will also need to consider correlations between projects and related activities, and specify these interactions as well. At least one person on the program staff will also need to build expertise with the application selected, and allocate the time to carry out the analysis, produce reports, and communicate the results. Carefully consider the costs and added complexity, particularly in cases where there is little or no previous experience with program-level Monte Carlo simulation analysis.

As noted, a major benefit of Monte Carlo risk analysis is the graphic and visible contrast between the apparently precise schedules generated using basic critical path methods and the range of possible outcomes (and probabilities) generated by computer simulation. Demonstrating the potential variation for program completion dates can be an effective antidote for excessive initial program optimism.

Use of Monte Carlo computer applications to analyze programs is not limited to schedules. Many programs also use simulation techniques for decision support and scenario analysis. The same overall considerations of effort, expense, and value are relevant, but when making complex decisions involving multiple alternatives—"make vs. buy," "replace or repair," and similar situations—statistical simulation software can be an effective tool for exploring financial considerations and other consequences. Such analysis can reveal worst cases and extreme outcomes that would otherwise be difficult to see. Specialized decision analysis software (often available from the same vendors who provide "bolt-on" applications for schedule analysis) can provide insight for making better decisions and for considering alternatives.

For relatively simple cases, it is even possible to do Monte Carlo–type assessments using only a basic spreadsheet. There are functions built into Microsoft Excel, for example, that can be used to generate random outputs from common statistical distributions, and analysis functions you can use to assess the data generated.

In implementing computer simulation to support program planning and decision making, be aware that the outputs generated may be replacing one illusion of precision with another. The output of a simulation model can never exceed the precision of its inputs. For example, work duration estimates are rarely very accurate, and are often rounded. Monte Carlo simulation software can deliver results reporting many more decimal places in schedule analysis than are justified. Plan to use the results of simulation analysis only generally, for guidance rather than for precise guarantees.

PROGRAM DECOMPOSITION AND PROJECT PLANNING

As we have noted earlier, the Project Management Institute defines a program as "a group of related projects . . . managed in a coordinated way." Decomposing a program into a set of projects is one of the sources of complexity that makes program management challenging. Managing this complexity requires reviewing the initial program breakdown structure to explore adjustments that might result in a set of projects that could be more easily managed. This analysis involves developing detailed project plans for each of the projects relevant to the program, and then using these data to review and refine the program plans, set a baseline, and document the basis for program monitoring and control.

Creating the Program Breakdown Structure

As discussed in Chapter 1, breakdown of program work into projects results in project collections that execute in parallel, in series, or both.

Programs with large staffs are made up of projects running in parallel, as in Figure 4-1.

Programs also may comprise projects that run in sequence, delivering a series of releases or products, as with undertakings employing agile methods. An example of such a program is shown in Figure 4-2. Programs of this type generally have a single team that takes on the project objectives one after another. Planning for this sort of program differs only a little from basic project planning, unless for some reason the project team is quite

Figure 4-1 A program having a large staff and multiple project teams.

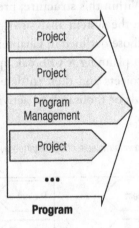

Program

Figure 4-2 A program made up of a sequence of projects.

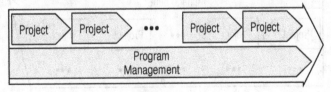

Program

large. (When there are a large number of contributors, breaking each of the successive projects into smaller, parallel efforts, similar to Figure 4-1, would likely result in a more easily managed program.)

Big programs contain both projects running in parallel and projects running in sequence (Figure 4-3). Such programs generally involve phases (or iterations) defined by the columns, and are staffed by teams associated with the rows—including the program staff (or PMO). Programs may contain a few projects, hundreds of projects, or any number in between.

Program management planning focuses on understanding and managing workflow complexity. This begins with decomposition of the overwhelming program detail; efforts that require thousands of activities and large numbers of contributors are unwieldy to plan. There is also too much going on at any given time to monitor as a single effort. Decomposing a program into projects generally begins at a high level using guidance from the program roadmap. Within this structure, projects tend to be defined, at least initially, based on the system analysis of the program deliverables (using processes such as those outlined in Chapter 3).

The goal of program planning is to break up large undertakings into (mostly) independent projects and then to delegate to qualified project leaders the many hundreds or thousands of activities the program will re-

Figure 4-3 A program with multiple phases staffed by several project teams.

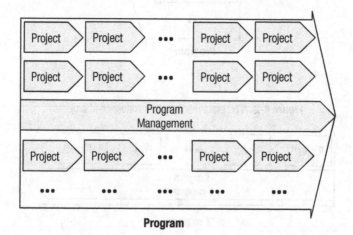

quire. The objective of decomposing a program into projects is essentially the same as that for the work breakdown structure at the project level—to reduce the complexity that must be managed by creating smaller undertakings that will be easier to understand and deal with.

A program breakdown structure made up of independently staffed projects does reduce complexity on one front, but it introduces new complications. It would be nice if programs could be broken up into a set of completely autonomous parts, but this is never possible. The projects that make up a program always have interdependencies because of the overall business justification, system connections, integration requirements, and other interactions. When scheduling project work, linkages between projects emerge due to these and other cross-connections. Because these dependencies cross project boundaries, each linkage represents an interface that will need to be tracked and managed at the program level.

Reviewing the Program Breakdown Structure

If done well, improvements in manageability gained from decomposing the program into projects will more than compensate for the effort required to manage the interconnections. As with the breakdown of system deliverables, maximizing the benefits requires analysis. Some breakdowns may make things worse by creating excessive numbers of cross-project dependencies. Other choices may create excessive new risks and failure modes that will threaten the program as a whole. A thorough review of your program breakdown structure will help you identify beneficial adjustments to improve your overall program plans. The first step in the review starts with examining the initial program breakdown and looking for alternatives that reduce the amount of interdependency, risk, and complexity.

List the projects that constitute the current phase of program work, and identify the interconnections between them based on system analysis techniques such as quality function deployment (using the correlation matrix in an analysis similar to the one depicted in Figure 3-13). Assess the functions and disciplines required for the staffing of each project, looking for projects that will require many types of contributors for successful completion. Also evaluate the need for geographically remote or contract staff on each project. In general, the more self-contained each project is, the less dependent it is likely to be on other teams, inputs, and projects. Project teams that can work independently most of the time will be less likely to be blocked in their work by external delays or other program problems.

Excessive duration is another source of potential complexity. If the projects envisioned will be responsible for complicated deliverables requiring lengthy timelines, consider alternative approaches for incrementally delivering the functionality needed. Providing less functionality sooner not only delivers value earlier, it can make the program phase planning easier and can lower risk through the use of frequent feedback. Iterative approaches using agile management techniques do entail some overhead, but shorter projects are more straightforward to run and the overall program will face fewer and less complicated interactions. Although adopting a rolling wave approach such as this delivers less functionality, it can more than compensate by delivering value sooner and more frequently. Reducing planning durations can also significantly decrease workflow complexity and risk, and it can reduce overall program effort.

As you explore alternatives, some potentially useful program decomposition changes may have consequences affecting the program roadmap, architecture, or system design. In cases where the shifts are minor or do not involve priorities for key stakeholders, adjust your plans. If changes you are considering would result in material scoping changes, retain the ideas as "what-if" scenarios and proceed with more detailed planning. You may uncover additional issues as you proceed into detailed project planning and risk analysis, and it is always better to deal with all necessary changes in a single negotiation than to request a series of smaller changes.

PROJECT PLAN INTEGRATION AND INTERFACE MANAGEMENT

The heart of program planning involves applying a coherent process to plan the projects and using "progressive elaboration" to analyze and make adjustments needed for a workable program baseline plan. This is a multistep process that starts with the initial program breakdown structure documenting the initially defined projects. Very large programs may have a hierarchy with several layers of subprograms, but the overall process for planning mostly involves the program plan at the top of the hierarchy and the basic projects at the bottom of the hierarchy.

Developing Project and Program Plans

The project plans that make up most programs tend to be deeply intertwined. Because all of the work is in service of an integrated goal, there will inevitably be a good deal of interdependence among all the plans. A key goal of iterative program planning is to identify and document the interfaces that connect each project to other projects, so they can be understood, discussed, adjusted as appropriate, and ultimately used for program tracking and control. The process begins with defining the foundation projects, identifying the core team for each, and initiating the project planning process. As the project plans come together, timing and other details emerge. For the relatively simple program with the handful of parallel projects depicted in Figure 4-4, the project timing appears to support a program starting (S) in January and finishing (F) in August.

In reality, however, the program is unlikely to meet such a deadline, because the plans at this point are based only on the individual projects,

Figure 4-4 A program made up of five parallel projects.

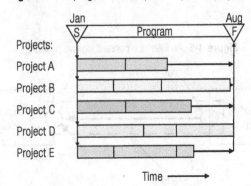

Time ⟶

with no consideration of inter-project connections. Planning at the project level will inevitably reveal dependencies that link each project to other projects in the program. Figure 4-4 shows places in the project plans where cross-connections are anticipated, segmenting the project timelines.

Interface identification typically begins when project planning detects an external dependency outside of the project. Resolving external linkages in project plans requires coordination with other project teams. Managing these connections is one of the fundamental responsibilities of program management. Identification of cross-project interfaces is intrinsic to project planning, but documenting and managing them is a program planning responsibility.

Project linkages are inevitable in any program involving parallel project activity. Each cross-project dependency involves a minimum of two project teams. Effective management of these interface connections between projects is essential to program success. The relationship between two projects sharing an interface is depicted in Figure 4-5. The project on the receiving end of the linkage is shown as the "customer," because that project will need to receive the input in order to proceed. The project team providing the output that fulfills this need is shown as the "supplier" project. Interfaces always have a single supplier, but they will have more than one customer in any situation where an output from one project is required by multiple other project teams.

Interface identification can initiate on either end of the connection, but most are first identified as a predecessor dependency during customer project planning.

Figure 4-5 An interface connecting two projects.

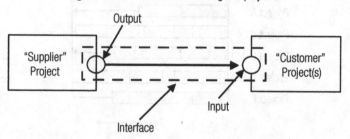

Figure 4-6 A program with five parallel projects showing interfaces.

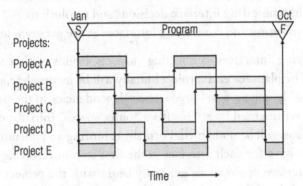

Identifying interfaces starts within project planning, but managing interfaces is ultimately a program management responsibility. A portion of an interface lies inside a project, but most of it is in a no-man's-land. None of the involved projects has sufficient control to manage the entire interface. Because of this, poorly managed interfaces are a major cause of many common program management problems. For the program made up of the projects in Figure 4-4, a very different picture emerges once the plans account for the interface connections. Figure 4-6 shows that the overall program duration will be substantially longer because of the timing effects of the interfaces, ending not in August but in October. In addition, large gaps have opened up in the project schedules where the integrated plan shows each of the project teams sitting idle. Program planning must deal with these timing problems, as well as any other potential difficulties that may arise in the interface handoffs.

Identifying and Managing Program Interfaces

A process for managing the interfaces that link the projects that comprise a program involves the following:

- Identifying all program interfaces
- Documenting each inter-project connection using a single consistent format

- Gaining agreement and reconciling schedules and deliverables
- Communicating interface decisions and resolutions
- Monitoring and controlling interfaces at the program level

Identifying interfaces connecting projects begins with project-level planning. The plans for each project initially will be incomplete, containing a few—possibly quite a few—predecessor dependencies in the project network chart represented by arrows from "outer space." Initially, one side of most interfaces will be undefined. Formally capturing and documenting the data you do have for each interface is the first step in resolving these unknowns. Interface descriptions generally begin with the project where the input side of the linkage resides, because work in the project needing an input cannot begin until a satisfactory input has been received.

There are several types of cross-project interfaces. Some examples include the following:

- **Handoff of responsibility between projects** for a specific component or deliverable. (Example: A quality assurance team cannot begin assessment tests until the development team completes module programming.)
- **Required completion of actions** by another project. (Example: The programming team cannot begin development work until the support team completes updates of database software.)
- **Information developed by one project** needed by other project(s). (Example: The development team must complete all user documentation before the testing team can begin final user acceptance testing.)
- **Materials, facilities, or other physical project outputs** required for other project work. (Example: The drywall team cannot begin mounting finished walls until the electrical and plumbing teams have finished their installations.)
- **Management decisions, reviews, or approvals** required for work to proceed. (Example: Project teams cannot proceed to the next phase of work until the management team finalizes signoff approval.)

- **Customer decisions, reviews, or approvals** required for on-going work. (Example: The market research team must review and approve final specifications before the development teams can commence.)

Examples of any or all of these types of dependencies can occur on large programs. One useful format for documenting interfaces is in Figure 4-7. The fields on this form collect the information needed to document and track each interface at the program level.

Using a form such as this formally documents interfaces and provides a basis for written agreement. When interfaces are defined by legally separate parts of a program team, some form of actual contract will capture these details. However, even when the two or more parties involved across an

Figure 4-7 Interface definition form.

Interface Definition Form				
Program: _____				
Interface Name: _____				
Interface Code ID: _____				
	Project Name	Agreed by	Organization	Date
Supplier				
Customer(s)				
Interface Definition and Completion Criteria:				
Completion Date:				
Prepared by: _____		Revision _____		Date _____

interface are part of the same organization, it is still wise to treat each finalized interface definition form as though it were a contract. Writing down the specifics and getting formal agreement encourages the responsible contributors to pay attention to the details, and a formal signature provides a much firmer foundation for the commitment than conversations or other verbal agreements.

As project planning proceeds, interfaces start to come into focus. As noted, the team needing input will generally begin the documentation process, noting the specifics of what the team members require and, based on their initial planning, when they would like to have it. Program interface management strives to match each of the inputs identified in the project plans with an appropriate output. Completing and signing off the interface definition form initiated by the leader of the customer project requires review and agreement by the leader of a supplier project. In an ideal case, a documented external input will be quickly paired with an existing output planned by another project in the program, and there will be a quick and easy closure on all the details.

On most programs, such ideal cases are rare. For some required project inputs, there may be no planned matching outputs. Sometimes, even when there are outputs, there may be differences in expected timing, completion criteria, or other issues. There also may be planned outputs in some projects for which there is no defined need by any projects in the program. Resolving interfaces and developing a coherent program plan requires iterative planning, using a process that shifts its focus back and forth between the project and program levels.

Iterative Program and Project Planning

Developing a useful program plan often involves more than one planning cycle, using feedback and adjustments along the way to develop a program plan that minimizes disruptions and streamlines the overall work. The process can vary, but a three-step process is generally sufficient for creating a workable, realistic program plan.

Using three iterations for program planning can be compared with the process a woodworker uses in building furniture. The first step involves cutting all the required pieces to size, so they can be checked in that rough state for general fit. The second step requires making adjustments and adding slots, miters, joints, and other details to each piece. After again checking the parts for fit, the furniture craftsman makes further adjustments and proceeds with sanding, finishing, polishing, and final assembly.

A process map for three-step program planning is shown in Figure 4-8, which depicts the program and project level activities involved.

The program planning steps are identified here as "Straw," "Tin," and "Gold." These names are based on an effective process for program planning and interface management used by the Hewlett-Packard Medical Group for major product development programs some years ago. What you call the steps and exactly how many planning iterations you need are less important than the overall goals for the process. The main objective is to gather useful planning information based on bottom-up planning to develop the best program-level view at each stage. Program analysis can then be used to provide feedback and make adjustments as you proceed to create workable, credible program and project baseline plans.

The initial step of the process is usually neither very realistic nor pretty. The "Straw-man" program plan will be based only on project-level planning data, so at this stage it will be rife with problems and gaps, and there will be both incomplete interfaces and interfaces with timing problems,

Figure 4-8 A three-step program planning process.

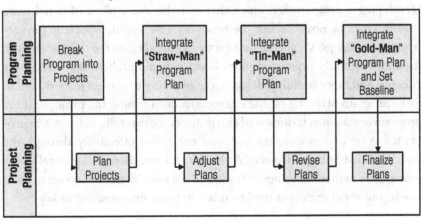

specification problems, or both. At the program level, document the interface definition problems and program schedule issues that emerge from integrating the project plans. Based on the Straw-man program plan and a review of all the interface forms, summarize the information needed by each project leader to initiate project plan adjustments.

Providing these data to the project teams kicks off the next step of planning, where project leaders work with their teams and the leaders of other projects to close the open interfaces and adjust the plans into more coherent alignment.

Integrating the resulting revised project plans at the program level results in a much-improved "Tin-man" program schedule. At this stage the overall program plan will work better, but there are always a few unresolved interfaces that require attention, remaining schedule problems, and inevitably some resource and budget issues.

The feedback from this second plan integration triggers further project plan revisions. The plans resulting from these efforts will usually come together successfully, with interfaces well defined and a "Gold-man" program plan that can serve as a credible baseline both for the program as a whole and for the individual projects.

Specifics for such a three-step process are explored in more detail below.

Developing a "Straw-Man" Program Plan

Developing a program-level plan that includes every piece of detail work required may be possible, but the result is rarely useful, especially for very large undertakings. When the list of activities numbers in the thousands, even the most carefully organized plans become incomprehensible. It is more effective and more useful to delegate the planning to project leaders, and to focus program planning on the interconnections among the projects. If the program breakdown is done well and projects are carefully defined, the program can be understood, tracked, and controlled effectively through the interfaces that link the projects. At any given time, there will generally be a manageable number of things to track, and the most significant program risks, issues, and other concerns tend to relate to these inter-project linkages.

When a project is part of a program, it is useful to establish clear planning standards, tools, and formats that will ensure that the documents and other planning outputs can be compared, reviewed, and integrated with minimal effort. Enforce the use of common processes and tools to make project-level planning outputs consistent. This applies to such outputs as work breakdown structures, schedules, prioritized backlogs, burn-down lists, responsibility matrices, and other documentation. Projects that are part of a larger program always have linkages to other program work, and such external linkages are often noted in project schedules using milestones.

Each cross-project interdependency is also a program interface, so as project planning proceeds, ensure that all project teams develop interface definitions using a common format for their external inputs and outputs. Disciplined documentation created as project planning proceeds will make managing program interfaces as straightforward as possible. Initiate a process for your program that will make identifying interfaces thorough and efficient. Remember, there are two ways to discover a program interface: in advance as part of planning or as a rude (and potentially disastrous) surprise during execution.

Identifying interfaces as planning moves ahead involves paying attention and asking the right questions. For inputs, ask about what materials, components, or parts will be needed before activity work can begin. Focus on defining the specifications, data, approvals, and decisions that projects will require to get started on the tasks the project leaders have defined. Initiate a customer interface for anything needed originating outside the individual projects. Leaders of customer projects with external requirements must document what they need, and specify when they would like to have it based on their plans and draft schedules.

Similarly, for deliverables that projects intend to create, the project leaders should specify who will be using the deliverable. For deliverables that will be delivered to others or integrated with outputs from other projects, verify that the specifications and acceptance criteria are reliable and credible. Leaders of projects that plan to deliver external outputs must define the supplier interfaces, specify what they will produce, and indicate on their preliminary schedules when they anticipate delivering them.

The Straw-man program-level plan involves aggregating and matching up interface definition forms emerging from all the project-level plans. Integrating all of this at the program level starts with analyzing the forms, aligning any matching interface definitions, and identifying any remaining issues or problems. Begin the process by creating a master interface definition table to track and manage all of the program interfaces (Table 4-1). For modest programs, a table created using a spreadsheet or on a website could be sufficient, but for large programs a database may be necessary.

One way to simplify the procedure for matching interfaces is to make the exercise part of a program startup workshop or other planning meeting where key project leaders are present. You can speed up the matching process by using sticky notes summarizing the interfaces (and using one color for inputs and a different color for outputs). You can further expedite the overall process by drawing a timeline on a whiteboard or large piece of paper that shows all the program milestones associated with the schedule templates and project planning guidelines you are using. Many interfaces tend to fall on or near milestones, and multiphase programs tend to define milestones as they progress to reflect the main handoff and interface transi-

Table 4-1 Interface tracking table.

Master Program Interface Table					
Interface Code	Interface Name	Owner	Supplier Project	Customer Project(s)	Status

tion events. Matching up clusters of sticky notes along a program milestone timeline is not difficult even if there are many dozens of interfaces to deal with. Building the master program interface table as you proceed with interface matching is an excellent way to develop an understanding of the overall program as a whole.

For matched interfaces where everything the supplier and customers have defined is in alignment, create a single consolidated interface definition form and add the interfaces to the master program interface list.

During Straw-man planning, unfortunately, most interfaces are not so tidy. There are always many unresolved linkages, and adding these with a status of "open" to the program interface table is an effective way to highlight and track them.

One common type of open interface you will encounter involves dependencies that do not explicitly connect to defined projects in the program. For interfaces involving management decisions or customer interactions, the supplier may be an individual who is an integral part of the program staff. If so, identify the program staff (or PMO) as the project team for the purposes of the interface resolution. Similarly, whenever the program staff is either the customer or the supplier for an interface, identify the program staff as the responsible project team. Also use the program team as the interface owner for any external linkages where the true owner is not actually part of the program team. In each such case, name the individual on the program staff who has agreed to represent the viewpoint and perspective of the actual owner, as a liaison, agent, surrogate, or in some other appropriate capacity.

At this initial stage of program planning, there may be many customer-generated interface definitions documenting inputs that have no corresponding supplier at all. In some cases, there may be an obvious project that should be the supplier. If so, either the leader of the customer project or someone on the program staff can approach the project leader to begin documenting the supplier end of the interface. Changes to the supplier project's plans are often necessary to incorporate activities for creation of the requested output.

In other situations there may be no obvious source to fulfill a legitimate project requirement. In such cases, the leaders of the customer projects may need to revise their plans to meet the need themselves, modify their needs to enable them to use an input that is available from an existing source, or involve the program team in resolving it.

Initially, many interfaces identified by customer projects that do match up with suppliers will reveal disagreements on specifications or timing (or both). Whenever there are differences in the way an interface is defined by the supplier project and the needs of one or more customer projects, note the issues on your program interface list and summarize them for all the project leaders involved. Ultimately, the owner of each interface definition will be the supplier project, so encourage the leaders of the customer projects to work with the project leaders they will depend on to settle on specifications and timing that are realistic for the supplier. It is best when the interface differences can be resolved between project team leaders, so provide feedback to the project leaders to facilitate project-level discussions aimed at aligning interface specifications and timing.

Some supplier-based interface definitions may have no customer claiming them. In cases where the outputs are really required, unclaimed interfaces uncover planning shortfalls in one or more of the program's projects. For these, the program manager will need to identify the projects with missing inputs and provide guidance to the project leaders for integrating the linkages into their project plans. If a planned output proves not to be needed (for example, a piece of documentation that will no longer be required), advise any project leaders planning to produce it to drop it and any associated effort from their plans.

Rarely, you may find multiple supplier projects that are planning to create outputs aimed at fulfilling the same customer needs. In most of these cases, the program staff will need to get involved to determine which of the possible sources will be the most appropriate to produce the output, and then to let the leaders of the other projects know that their outputs will not be needed.

As the master interface table takes shape, use the timing information supplied by the supplier (owner) projects to create a milestone chart for the program as a whole. Create a draft program timeline based on the interface definitions and bottom-up project plans. Analyze it to produce a list of issues concerning the specification differences or other issues identified in the interface analysis.

As the interface map of cross-project connections for the program as a whole comes into focus, reexamine how the program was broken down into projects. Large programs often get into difficulty because they have been dissected into projects hastily, with minimal consideration of project interactions. If any projects have what appear to be an excessive number of interfaces, reexamine the program decomposition to see if there is a different structure having less complexity and fewer project interconnections.

If two projects have a large number of interfaces connecting them, consider combining the work into one larger project, or analyze the project definitions to explore possible changes that might afford more independence. If a program has a dozen projects and 200 interfaces, there is almost certainly a better breakdown with fewer cross-dependencies. Large numbers of interfaces among projects make programs difficult to track and control, and increase risk. As your understanding of the program comes into better focus through interface analysis, consider alternatives for project definition that could increase the autonomy of the project teams. On multistage programs, monitor the number of interfaces you are managing, and as planning begins for future phases of work, explore alternatives that may offer a logically simpler program breakdown.

Use your Straw-man milestone program timeline and interface table issues to initiate a project-level planning update cycle to address shortcomings and other problems you have found. Provide a summary of your findings to all project leaders, along with specific guidance and advice for adjusting their project-level plans. Request that the project teams update their plans to minimize open interfaces, unresolved interface problems, and issues for the program as a whole.

Developing a Tin-Man Program Plan

After each project team has revised its plans to reflect suggested changes and resolve problems, update the master interface table and your program-level timeline using any modified or new interface definitions. Close out all resolved interfaces by getting formal signoff from the leader of the supplier project and any leaders of the customer projects. Verify that each defined interface has a specified due date, a clear description including measurable completion criteria, and unambiguous agreement from the leaders of all projects involved.

At this stage, most identified interfaces will have clear specifications defined by the supplier project with agreement from one or more customer projects. After only a single cycle of planning adjustments, though, there are generally quite a few remaining timing problems. There are usually many cases where project teams are still looking for inputs before the corresponding outputs are scheduled. There will also be at least a few interfaces where the input specifications requested and the output specifications planned remain incompatible. Reconciling such cases usually involves participation by the program manager or staff.

In some cases, rearranging the sequence of work in the supplier project can resolve timing problems. One principle that may help is scheduling work based on the "weighted shortest job first" (WJSF) principle. WJSF has each team look at the urgency of need for each task it needs to schedule, and use a combination of the weighting and duration estimates for the work to rearrange the workflow to minimize delay. In cases where overall program progress and specific project timelines are impeded by queuing problems, resequencing the work within projects causing the logjams could provide a way to resolve open interfaces.

There may be program-level options for resolving interface differences if they involve staffing, resources, or other project constraints. You may be able to provide additional money or contributors for schedule compression of the supplier project to pull a timing difference into alignment. Adding staff to the supplier project team or providing funding for external expertise may help to achieve results that would otherwise be unrealistic. There may be an acceptable off-the-shelf alternative for some inputs needed by customer projects available from outside the program that could (perhaps at an increased cost) fulfill their needs. At the program level there may be viable options for resolving interfaces based on shifting priorities or reallocating resources among the various projects. Seek ways to optimize the program plans and solve interface problems creatively by modifying constraints or using program-level reserves.

There may also be issues that surface as interface issues that reveal program scoping issues. Sometimes customer projects may request input for their part of the overall program deliverable that exceed what any supplier project can reasonably deliver. If there are specification differences between projects that relate to feasibility, resolving them may require discussions with key stakeholders and adjustments to overall program scope. Scope changes to the program during the planning of large, complex programs are not uncommon, because until the details of the work start to come into focus the boundary between what is possible and what is not can be quite fuzzy.

Not all interface discrepancies will yield to program-level assistance, however. Some interface differences can be resolved only through program-directed changes, changes that may be resisted by one or more of the project leaders involved. Sometimes it may not be possible to keep all the parties engaged with an interface equally happy. There will be situations where the program manager must make decisions that best serve the program. This may involve compromise on the part of all parties, moving everyone to an intermediate position to align the inputs with the outputs. Some situations may require shifts in the responsibilities and sequencing of project-level work. Strive to find solutions that minimize disruption in cases where the program goals are in conflict with what appear to be the most logical project tactics, but keep a steady focus on the bigger picture and seek commitments and agreements that support your overall objectives.

Track the progress of interface and planning discussions, and update your master interface table to reflect the status of interface issues as they are resolved. As you proceed, also capture the status of all remaining interface issues. Use the supplier project dates for each interface to revise your milestone chart and program-level timeline. Based on the bottom-up project-level plans and your program milestone timeline, assess the staffing, funding, and other resource requirements for the program plan as it evolves. Assess the effects of any holidays, staff vacations, and other times where people will be unavailable to the program. Document any issues where the program plans call for more people, funding, or other resources than will be available.

Every program interface is also a potential program risk. Review the master interface table to assess each linkage for a lack of clarity, or for uncertainty because of novelty, innovation, timing, or other sources of concern. Identify any interfaces where the description appears less than entirely credible or the linkage represents something likely to keep you up at night during the program.

Prepare for a final "clean-up" planning cycle, using data from your Tin-man milestone program schedule and master interface table. Develop a summary of the overall status of remaining issues. Include specific information on any expected problems with resources or calendar timing and high-risk program interfaces. Consult with project leaders to discuss how they plan to handle residual problems in their project-level schedules. Ask each project team to update its plans to close any open interfaces so you can finalize the program plans.

Creating a Gold-Man Program Baseline Plan

By the time the project teams have completed fine-tuning their plans, most interface definitions will be either resolved or very close to resolution. Verify that all the reconciled interfaces in your master program interface list have formal commitments from all project leaders involved, especially that the commitment from the leader of the supplier project is credible. Develop a plan for reconciling all remaining open interfaces. Update the master interface table with the status of all interfaces, and include information on actions underway to deal with any unresolved issues.

Adjust your program-level milestone schedule using information from the updated project schedules. The resulting Gold-man program plan will provide a solid overall approach for your program based on realistic, bottom-up planning data.

Compare your program plan at this stage with the overall objectives for this phase of the work and your program roadmap. Ideally, your overall plans will align well with stakeholder goals. If you find significant differences that cannot be resolved through planning, document the program goals that are unrealistic and summarize the reasons why.

Document your program plans in preparation for setting program and project baselines. Make note of the following:

- Program milestone timeline
- Issues remaining related to current program goals
- Master interface table
- Project planning detail documents

PROGRAM WORKFLOW RISKS

Before setting the program baseline, identify and assess program risks that emerge from your plans. The process for managing program risks mirrors the process used in most other environments:

- Establish a framework and plan for managing risks.
- Identify risks.
- Assess risks.
- Develop risk responses and establish risk reserves.
- Track, monitor, and review risks as you proceed.

Chapter 2 explored the sources for program risks, including risks related to the program's projects, risks inherent to the program itself, and risks from above and outside the program. Chapter 2 also outlined planning for program risk management and establishing a framework for risk management. Identifying risks is a key part of program management planning. Discovering risks related to scope management was covered in Chapter 3, and finding risks arising from staffing and organizational decisions will be discussed in Chapter 5. That said, the primary focus for identification of program risks—as well as the assessment of their consequences and development of responses—is program planning, the topic of this chapter. As part of your overall program planning efforts, allocate sufficient time for understanding and managing program risks.

Project-Based Program Risks

Program risk management begins with effective project risk management. Ensure that the leaders responsible for the projects in the program apply good project risk management principles in planning and executing their responsibilities. As the risk plans for the program's projects come together, review the exposures noted by the project leaders. Project plans are a fertile source of program risks, because all of the projects are correlated, so be thorough. Even risks that may appear to be relatively minor at the project level may represent significant program-level risk if the same exposures are found in many of the projects.

At the program level, review all the project-level risk registers thoroughly to see what exposures have been captured. One purpose of the review is to ensure that the leaders of each project have done a thorough job of listing the risks inherent in their work. Check that all defined interfaces are listed as risks in the customer projects depending on external inputs. Also look for inclusion of risks related to activities in each project involving integration with other project results. Generally look to see that each project risk register appears to encompass risks typical for this type of work.

Not every project-level risk will also need to be managed as a program-level risk, but some will, which is yet another reason to review all the risks captured at the project level. Determining which project risks to "promote" to the program risk register begins with setting a threshold for potential program impact. The project-level risk register will list an assessment of both impact (or loss) and probability (likelihood), but thresholds are best set using primarily impact, because probabilities are often underestimated, and at the program level it is always best to plan based on the worst-case scenario.

The primary consideration for setting thresholds will be the overall risk tolerance of your program sponsor and key stakeholders. Some programs involve a lot of risk, so significant levels of program risk may be acceptable. Other programs, especially those undertaken on a contract basis, will be quite risk averse. Set the threshold for listing project risks on the program risk register as a specific amount or percentage of stated program goals, in alignment with your management's risk appetite. For risks involving schedule slippage, a risk-averse program might choose a threshold of a 1-week or greater potential program delay when selecting project-level risks to include in the program risk register. A program embracing higher levels of risk might choose a threshold of 10 percent (or perhaps even higher) of the current program phase's budget for including project risks having financial impact.

Build a program risk register similar to that used at the project level, and populate it with risks "promoted" from the program's projects. Include project-level risks in your program risk register whenever they are:

- "Showstopper" project risks that could threaten the overall program
- Items listed on your master interface table
- Project risks with potential impact exceeding a defined program threshold
- Risks involving resources shared by several projects
- Risks involving significant technical complexity, innovation, or new processes
- Significant activities delegated to outsourced or distributed teams
- Risks identified in several projects representing substantial aggregate program impact
- Projects that are risky overall

Program-Level Risks

You will discover additional risks for your program risk register during program planning. Some program-level risks are due to size and scale. If a program is substantially larger than any recent past work completed successfully, probe for potential failure modes that relate to the magnitude of the work, the duration, the number of contributors, the overall budget, or other factors.

Programs also involve at least some novelty and innovation. Consider any sources of risk originating from overall complexity, "bleeding-edge" program deliverables, new processes, novel configurations, updated technology, development methods, or hardware, and other potential exposures that may not have been captured as project-level risks.

Programs are made up of more than just projects. As you assemble your plans, consider potential program problems with operations or other parts of your organizational infrastructure that you will depend on. Consider potential risk sources related to administration, office and IT support, and other "white space" aspects of program work.

As part of your planning, spend some time with the program staff (or PMO) to brainstorm risks. Consider risks related to potential program staff commitment conflicts, loss of key program staff, queuing for program resources, potential program communication problems, and loss of motivation (particularly on long-duration programs). Review the lessons learned and results of earlier programs that are similar, and note as risks any past problems that may occur on the present program. Use scenario analysis to review the program roadmap and timeline, looking for possible problems and issues.

As your planning proceeds, accumulate the program-level risks you discover in your program risk register.

Risks from Above or External to the Program

There are also additional program risks that are a consequence of decisions and objectives above the program, and even more risks can arise from outside the program.

Major programs carry strategic risks that originate with organizational decisions and objectives. Programs, especially big ones, are often initiated with assumptions based on suppositions and broad goals. Some of these assumptions may be credible and reliable, but others may be wishful thinking or guesswork. Program work often begins before much (if any) detailed planning and analysis has been done, so there may be a good deal of legitimate doubt about whether what is expected is even possible. List as program risks any assumptions that appear to be unsupported speculations. If your program is initiated with unrealistic expectations regarding benefits, return on investment (ROI), or value to be delivered, note any potential shortfalls that might occur as risks. If program budgets, staffing, or other resources appear to be inadequate, include risks showing the potential im-pact based on more credible estimates. If there seems to be a chance that your budget could be cut as the program runs, document the potential fund-ing or resource reductions as a risk. As you validate program objectives and proceed with planning, include potentially problematic program constraints or assumptions that are out of your control in your program risk register.

Programs also may be subject to long-term contracts or other legal constraints that carry uncertainty and exposure. List any potential problems involving external contracts or other binding agreements in your program risk register.

External changes are always potential risks for programs, especially those with long timelines. Customer and stakeholder requirements may shift over time and create problems. Note any specific concerns about the durability of scoping expectations as risks. For programs responsible for managing products or services in a marketplace, the actions of competitors or the introduction of substitutes will be risks. Accumulate any potential developments that you are concerned about that could affect the value of your deliverables on your risk register as well. Other changes that can im-pact programs include changes to standards, rules, or regulations. Survey what is planned in the near future by external standards organizations or governments that might affect your program, and list them as risks, too.

Identifying Program Workflow Risks

Many risks will be detected during program planning, including those orig-inating in the program's projects, inherent to the program overall, and from outside the program. Program risk identification is an ongoing responsi-bility, and it is an important part of program reviews and planning of each phase, iteration, release, or stage of the work. As you transition to future work at the close of one planning horizon, a host of new risks will come into focus. Those associated with planning can include the following:

- All cross-project interfaces
- Work involving unprecedented size or scale
- Risks that recur in multiple projects

- Uncertain program timing estimates or excessively aggressive deadlines
- Project teams with limited or questionable experience
- Dependencies involving uncertain inputs, parts, components, information, regulations, standards, or other requirements originating outside the program
- Project activities requiring invention, investigation, or innovation
- Unreliable program planning assumptions
- Conflicts concerning program objectives between key stakeholders
- Significant program goals that appear likely to change
- All program risks not associated with a specific project (including "white space" or overall program exposures)
- Program constraints inconsistent with overall objectives
- Potential shifts in management or program governance

Assessing and Managing Program Risks

A program risk register starts with a list of risks, including those identified in scoping (discussed in Chapter 3), planning (such as those above), and staffing (discussed in Chapter 5). Assessment is based on a combination of impact and probability (as with project risk management), which is used to sort and prioritize the list. Most program risks with impact estimates that are substantial relative to the program's goals warrant attention, especially if the likelihood of occurrence is high. Always assess program risk probabilities conservatively, using estimates on the high end of what you think the range of likelihood will be. Underestimating probabilities for program risks is common, because people tend to estimate the chances of adverse consequences (especially those they hope to avoid) to be much lower than is realistic. Also, in most cases there will be very little experience with the listed program risks to guide probability estimates.

When analyzing program risks, also consider correlation. Risks in a program, like activities, are interrelated. When you trace risks back to root causes you are likely to discover that multiple risks you have collected share common triggers, and in some cases you will find domino effects where once a particular risk happens it will almost certainly be followed by others. Effective program planning includes thorough consideration of potential problems and failure modes, and making adjustments to address them.

Strive to prevent major program risks where possible. Seek effective actions to avoid, mitigate, or transfer the consequences of risks that can reduce program exposure. For risks where the response tactics you come up with can be cost justified, work with the project team (or teams) involved to adjust plans and implement the necessary actions. Because of the complex interrelationships with program work, some risk responses may result in unintended consequences. Reassess the situation in cases where you implement plan changes to verify that you have not created any new risks.

It will not be possible to do much about some listed risks because their root causes are out of your control. While you will probably need to accept these risks, it does not mean that you should ignore them. Even when you cannot specifically address a risk, including it in your risk register will keep it visible and make a difference. When people understand the risks a program faces, including the pain, consequences, and the cost of dealing with some of the largest ones, they will work differently. They will proceed with their work in ways that will avoid the worst of the problems. Also, because they will be aware of the potential for trouble, when a risk does occur they will detect and report it promptly.

Managing program risks also involves recovery planning. For the most significant risks you are unable to prevent, develop contingency plans outlining the steps to take to bring the program back on track. Determine what to do, and allocate sufficient resources and dedicated staff to get it done. For all major risks that remain on your risk register, define the trigger event that reveals it has occurred, and delegate responsibility to an owner on the program staff who will monitor for the event, initiate the recovery process, and monitor status for the risk.

Recovery planning should not be limited to risk situations listed on your program risk register. Programs are large and complex, and represent unique challenges that carry risk that is difficult to uncover even with the best planning. Dealing with unknown program risk starts with establishing program-level funding reserves to deal with both known program risks and unexpected eventualities that you have not anticipated. A reasonable program budget reserve needs to cover the sum of the expected costs (financial impact multiplied by estimated probabilities) for the risks in your program risk register and appropriate provision for your contingency and recovery plans (again, weighted with probability estimates), plus a margin for expenses associated with unknown risk. The size of the reserve to cover unknown risk is generally based on past experiences with similar program work. This starts with a review of the magnitude and frequency of earlier unexpected problems. For program work having little precedent, a reserve amounting to roughly 10 percent of the current program phase budget would likely prove to be an adequate initial target.

Establishing program-level schedule reserve is another effective tactic for managing unknown program risk. It is good practice to establish targets supported by credible plans for key program completion dates that are earlier than your committed deadlines. Having a buffer you can use for unexpected recovery work is essential on large programs where schedule slippage will be unacceptable. Good practice for schedule reserve sets a target dates where your confidence in on-time completion is at least 50 percent, based either on Monte Carlo schedule simulation analysis or program staff estimates.

Another type of generic risk recovery strategy relies on establishing some slack in staffing. Committing all of the available time for every program contributor will result in a very brittle program plan. Anything that goes wrong will cause slippage, cascade effects, and additional problems, because recovery efforts will have to depend on resources already fully dedicated to other work. Programs must have at least some spare staffing resources to tap when problems occur to keep other work on schedule. Setting aside some uncommitted staff resources for this can facilitate successful recovery from even significant unanticipated problems. Reserve staffing is often implemented using generalists on the program staff who have wide understanding of the program and broad knowledge and experience.

Effective program risk management begins with thorough project risk management, and it builds on that foundation to understand and deal with the uncertainties and potential difficulties inherent in the complex work required. Program risk management for the COMPASS program at Hewlett-

Packard (discussed in Chapter 2) was a central part of program planning for each stage of the work. It was a main focus of release planning, and there was a monthly risk management meeting to keep on top of key program risks. The program risk register generally had about thirty items listed on it, a mix of significant scoping items, cross-project interface dependencies, and issues related to changes. (At any given time the program risks being managed at the project level were typically in the hundreds.) Risk management for the COMPASS program will be discussed in more detail in Chapter 6.

HIERARCHICAL PLAN BASELINES AND PLAN DOCUMENTATION

Following iterative project and program planning, risk assessment and further plan adjustments, and revising scope to reflect any shifts necessitated by planned risk responses, you are ready to set a program baseline for the current phase of work.

Prepare for Program Baselining

Perform an overall program plan inspection looking for inconsistencies, oversights, overly aggressive estimates, resource conflicts, and other defects. Review the actual funding and effort required for similar past program efforts to verify that your program has similar levels of committed resources. Contrast the timing and results delivered by earlier programs (program phases) with your objectives. If your plans call for results that are in excess of previous outcomes, consider revising your scope, estimates, or deadlines to make your program plans more realistic.

Also compare the results of your planning with your stated goals for the program and stakeholder expectations. If there are important program objectives that are out of sync with the results of your plans, consult with your program sponsor and develop a strategy for resolving the inconsistencies. If you are unable to align program realities with prevailing expectations, you will need to find a way to change the expectations. This is particularly true for programs planned using stage-gates for integrated big-bang delivery, but it applies as well to programs having shorter, iteration-based objectives.

When the gaps between stated program goals and what is feasible are substantial, consider your options. Your planning efforts will provide a great deal of information on what can be accomplished, as well as explanations for why some requested deliverables might be unattainable. You may find alternatives that revise your program roadmap and phase plans to deliver program outputs with greater frequency, focusing on providing the most important results sooner. There may be options for adjusting the scope to deliver a superior result based on technology or work methods unknown to your stakeholders. Working with knowledgeable program staff and project leaders, there may be dozens of possible program variations worthy of consideration.

Programs vary significantly in scale and complexity, but it is always useful to prepare your information for presentation to sponsors, management, and key stakeholders in layers of detail, starting with a very clear high-level summary. Assemble all of your detail documents, such as the program milestone or release timeline, the master interface table, program resource analysis, and all the project-level information. Use your planning data to develop a short executive summary of your program plan describing the overall approach, key dates, significant risks, and any outstanding issues you need to address. Plan to begin program baseline discussions with a concise overview. Diving immediately into enormous volumes of planning detail tends to be more annoying than helpful, so focus initially on the headlines and most essential information.

In addition to summary information, plan to bring along details to support any discussions that may require them. Include the following:

- The program roadmap
- Your high-level program milestone chart for the current program phase or release
- A short description of all the projects in the program showing the roles for each

- A summary of significant interim deliverables, interfaces, and dates
- Program staffing, resource, and budget summaries
- Significant program risks and issues
- When necessary, proposals for potential program adjustments

If your plans align with overall program objectives, discussions to set the program baseline will be brief and straightforward. If you need to negotiate program changes, however, you also need to prepare presentation materials to justify any required adjustments. Develop a clear summary describing any expected program results that are inconsistent with realistic plans, and provide specific evidence showing why the goals cannot be met. Plan to rely on your knowledge, experience, and expertise when laying out the case for changes, and remember that knowledge is power.

It is always best when reporting a problem to come armed with potential solutions, so develop several high-level descriptions of credible, plan-based alternatives. Focus your summary on the business case for what your program could produce and the value that you can realistically deliver. Try to avoid debates about cost and timing, and instead focus primarily on the difference between plan-based costs and initial assumptions about budgets and other constraints. Program initiation is often based more on hopes and dreams rather than any credible analysis, and arguments demanding unrealistic results with inadequate resources (or time) are never productive. Also, in most cases, the power balance between a program leader and key stakeholders for major programs is very lopsided, so this is a debate that you will rarely be able to win. Focusing discussions on what is possible and on the beneficial results you can actually deliver will yield much more satisfactory results.

Schedule sufficient time to discuss your baseline with your sponsor and any other key stakeholders who need to approve it. In preparation for the meeting, particularly if you expect to propose changes to program objectives, rehearse your presentation with someone on your program staff, and solicit criticism. Refine what you plan to say to support your message, and structure your presentations to emphasize your strengths: your experience and skills, knowledge and background, and enthusiasm for the program.

Set the Program Baseline

Meet to discuss your program with those who oversee the work: your governance body, your sponsor, and others as needed. Open your meeting with a brief summary of your planning results for the current phase or release of program work. Describe what you will be able to deliver and when. Also provide a summary of significant risks and issues that you face. If you are proposing any shifts to program goals, use high-level, fact-based explanations that demonstrate why the changes are necessary and build consensus for the needed changes.

Invite questions as you proceed and be open in your responses, even when dealing with pointed questions or criticism. Setting a program baseline is not a competition, it is a collaboration. Strive to keep everyone's attention on the program's value and how everyone will benefit from establishing and delivering achievable program results. A force-fit, unrealistic baseline imposed by high-level stakeholders will be a loss for everyone. Managers will not get what they have demanded. You will be responsible for a failed program, and program contributors will be demotivated and depressed because they are part of a doomed effort.

When proposing program changes, provide compelling evidence showing why the initial goals cannot be supported by a credible plan. Build a business case for one or more alternatives for program objectives that will be possible. Seek agreement for program modification using fact-based, principled negotiation. Use program planning data to gain stakeholder agreement and support. Begin discussions with changes that you believe will deliver the most value and benefits. Present compelling, plan-based options to focus your discussions on collaborative problem solving. Engage everyone in resolving program issues and rational decision making. Seek the best alternatives for aligning program goals with credible plans.

Following a discussion of your program plans, request approval for a specific baseline for the current phase or release of program work. Define deliverables, funding, and timing for the program that are consistent with realistic plans.

In some cases, you may be unable to secure approval for necessary changes and find yourself compelled to accept a program baseline that is not achievable. If you find yourself in this predicament, document your concerns and do the best that you can with the established goals. Because programs often have a succession of phases, this sort of problem may be self-correcting, because a program is more of a marathon than a sprint. When setting the baseline for the next phase following one where there were problems, shortfalls, and issues, negotiations tend to go much more in the favor of the program leader.

Document the Program Baseline

After securing approval for the program baseline from your program governance body, sponsor, and other key stakeholders, document the results for use in monitoring and controlling the work. Publish the final versions of documents for the current program phase and communicate the plans and commitments to your program staff and all project leaders. Freeze scoping for current program work and store all finalized program planning documents online in your program management information system. Set up baseline schedules in the tools you will use for both program and project tracking, and begin monitoring and reporting on program interfaces and other status. Begin disciplined control of all changes using your scope and overall change control processes.

An Example Hierarchical Program Plan

For the COMPASS program at Hewlett-Packard, plans were maintained at three levels: for the overall program, for each deployment wave release, and for the functional projects supporting each wave. Each type of plan had appropriate detail that corresponded to how and where the plan was used, but all plans were synchronized throughout the program's duration.

The Overall Program Plan

The COMPASS program was responsible for quarterly release waves focused on implementing the system in three to six new countries and making ongoing improvements. Each release wave lasted approximately 8 to

9 months from initial requirements gathering through completion of each release, and at any given time activities were underway simultaneously for four to five waves. The program used Primavera TeamPlay for the high-level multiple release wave plan. This plan included sufficient detail to identify timing conflicts resulting from the overlapping deployment waves. For planning meetings, communications with program stakeholders, and other discussions requiring high-level program information, we periodically created extract versions of the plan. The extracts used Microsoft Excel or PowerPoint to facilitate distribution and interpretation. A somewhat simplified example of the high-level plan is in Figure 4-9.

The multi-wave extract of the plan was used to decorate large expanses of wall space in the meeting room for the periodic planning summits. Throughout the program, we created evolving versions of this chart, dropping completed waves and adding new ones in a moving time window that extended approximately 1 year into the future. These high-level views were frequently updated and maintained in the program management information system also online, where all program contributors could easily view them.

The Program Release Wave Plan

One level down from the overall program plan were plans containing a more detailed view for each deployment wave. The first version of this plan was constructed for the program's pilot. That plan was implemented in Microsoft Project, and it contained roughly 1,000 activities—nearly all of them involving information technology development work. The density of this schedule made it generally incomprehensible, so it was not terribly useful. In addition to the issue of the overwhelming quantity of information included, it had an additional deficiency—it failed to include most non-IT activities.

We adopted a more successful planning approach for the subsequent deployment waves. To better address key activities across all the program's functions and to make the overall release wave plan easier to read, we developed a format that grouped key decision points and milestones shared by all parts of the program at the top of the plan, under the heading "Wave Key Milestones."

We identified milestones 2 to 3 weeks apart, and arranged them in sequence. The remainder of the plan clustered summary-level activities for

Figure 4-9 A portion of a program-level multiple release wave plan.

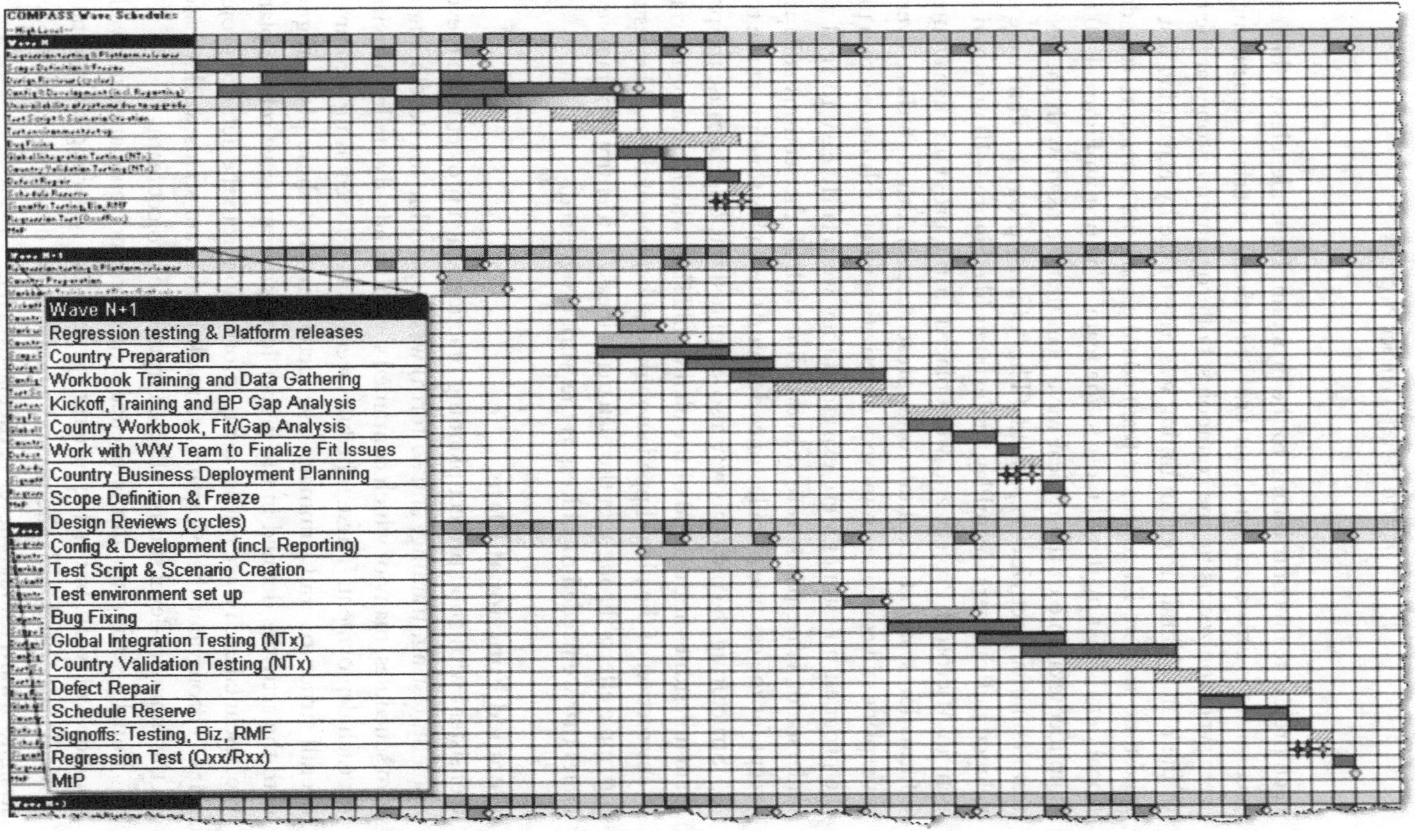

The following legend labels appear within the figure:

COMPASS Wave Schedules

Wave N+1
Regression testing & Platform releases
Country Preparation
Workbook Training and Data Gathering
Kickoff, Training and BP Gap Analysis
Country Workbook, Fit/Gap Analysis
Work with WW Team to Finalize Fit Issues
Country Business Deployment Planning
Scope Definition & Freeze
Design Reviews (cycles)
Config & Development (incl. Reporting)
Test Script & Scenario Creation
Test environment set up
Bug Fixing
Global Integration Testing (NTx)
Country Validation Testing (NTx)
Defect Repair
Schedule Reserve
Signoffs: Testing, Biz, RMF
Regression Test (Qxx/Rxx)
MtP

177

each project team contributing to the program. Dependencies within each section were linked as usual, but cross-functional interface dependencies were synchronized using the common set of program milestones at the top of the plan. Overall program timing was easy to see by expanding just the milestone section. Each project team could expand its portion to see additional details that mattered most to the team. The plan in Figure 4-10 is a simplified example of the typical wave plan that we used, with the testing team's summary activities expanded. (The "official" program plans were developed in Primavera TeamPlay, but extracts like Figure 4-10 mirrored the plan in Microsoft Project and were placed in the program management information system to facilitate widespread access.) Although these overall wave plans still contained hundreds of activities, when only one section plus the program milestones were expanded they were fairly easy to read and understand. Wave plans were stored online with all the sections collapsed except for the cascade of milestones defining the wave's timeline at the top.

Structuring the plan this way also simplified tracking, because the program milestones at the head of the plan would shift whenever any interface in any section of the plan slipped enough to affect one of them. The resulting ripple effects throughout the plan made it easy to identify program-level issues that we needed to address as the work progressed.

Detailed Functional Plans

Consistent with good project planning practices, each project team (development, testing, training, and so forth) was responsible for developing its own schedules, many of which contained several hundred detailed activities for each deployment. These schedules were all developed using a common overall structure, and summary-level activities from these plans aligned with the activities defined in the higher-level program wave release plans. We baselined each wave release using information from the detailed project plans. Throughout the program, we tracked program status weekly based on the summary-level status collected from each project team.

Initially setting up all the needed structures and templates involved a good deal of work, but as the program proceeded, reporting on the status of work associated with the several simultaneous deployment waves was straightforward (though never particularly easy).

Figure 4-10 A portion of a single wave release plan.

ID	WBS	Task Name	Duration	Start	Finish	% Complete
1	1	**Wave N Key Milestones**	**199 d**	**Jul 4**	**Apr 6**	**0%**
2	1.1	Wave N Participants finalized	0 d	Jul 4	Jul 4	100%
3	1.2	Wave N Participant Configurations Documented	0 d	Sep 5	Sep 5	100%
4	1.3	Wave N Requirements Complete	0 d	Oct 10	Oct 10	100%
5	1.4	Wave N Scope frozen	0 d	Oct 31	Oct 31	100%
6	1.5	Wave N Scope changes prohibited	0 d	Nov 21	Nov 21	100%
7	1.6	Wave N Design Complete	0 d	Dec 22	Dec 22	100%
8	1.7	Wave N Construction Complete	0 d	Jan 16	Jan 16	100%
9	1.8	Wave N System Tests Complete	0 d	Feb 6	Feb 6	0%
10	1.9	Wave N Participant Tests Complete	0 d	Feb 20	Feb 20	0%
11	1.10	Wave N sign off and release	0 d	Mar 9	Mar 9	0%
12	1.11	End	0 d	Apr 6	Apr 6	0%
13	2	**Program Staff activities for Wave N**	**191 d**	**Jul 4**	**Mar 27**	**76%**
34	3	**Business Process activities for Wave N**	**194 d**	**Jul 4**	**Mar 30**	**71%**
76	4	**Participant activities for Wave N**	**199 d**	**Jul 4**	**Apr 6**	**67%**
121	5	**System Development activities for Wave N**	**179 d**	**Jul 4**	**Mar 9**	**79%**
153	6	**Output development for Wave N**	**180 d**	**Jul 4**	**Mar 10**	**77%**
170	7	**Finance activities for Wave N**	**180 d**	**Jul 4**	**Mar 10**	**80%**
179	8	**Testing activities for Wave N**	**95 d**	**Nov 1**	**Mar 13**	**62%**
180	8.1	Develop Wave N test plans	20 d	Nov 1	Nov 28	100%
181	8.2	Communicate participant testing requirements	20 d	Nov 1	Nov 28	100%
182	8.3	Develop Wave N test scenarios	15 d	Nov 29	Dec 19	100%
183	8.4	All test data loaded	16 d	Dec 23	Jan 13	100%
184	8.5	Test Plans for Wave N validated	16 d	Dec 23	Jan 13	100%
185	8.6	Conduct system tests	12 d	Jan 17	Feb 1	0%
186	8.7	Conduct Participant tests	13 d	Feb 2	Feb 20	0%
187	8.8	Retest, following defect correction	28 d	Feb 2	Mar 13	0%
188	9	**Training activities for Wave N**	**110 d**	**Nov 22**	**Apr 24**	**33%**
199	10	**Support activities for Wave N**	**140 d**	**Nov 1**	**May 15**	**39%**
213	11	**Release activities for Wave N**	**17 d**	**Feb 7**	**Mar 1**	**0%**

179

KEY IDEAS FOR PROGRAM PLANNING AND ORGANIZING

- Define a life cycle and formats for planning documents appropriate for the program and to be used consistently by all projects.
- Develop plans for initial program work and establish a schedule for program planning reviews at least twice a year to extend and update plans.
- Select program software tools that can adequately support planning and execution for the work, and ensure that all projects in the program use the same tools in a consistent way.
- Define projects for each program phase, release, or iteration that mirror the components of your deliverables and have leaders with sufficient experience.
- Use a multiple cycle planning process to develop coherent project plans that align with an overall program plan.
- Focus program-level planning on defining the specifications and timing of cross-project interfaces.
- Diligently identify program-level risks, develop effective responses or recovery plans for the most significant ones, and frequently review and update the program risk register.
- Document all program, subprogram, and project plans, and store them where program contributors can access and use them.
- Set a realistic baseline for each program phase, release, or iteration, based on credible, bottom-up plans.

Program
Leadership

Of all the things I've done, the most vital is coordinating the talents of those who work for us and pointing them towards a certain goal.

—Walt Disney

Programs are complex because of their system-based deliverables and the network of interrelationships intrinsic to the workflow, as discussed in the two previous chapters. They are also complex because of the hierarchies and sheer numbers of people required to do the work in major undertakings. Getting a large community of people heading in the same direction starts with a clear definition and vision of what is to be accomplished. Establishing structures and processes that maintain alignment within a large hierarchy of individuals is vital to successful program management.

Overcoming the challenges of leading a large, diverse team of people starts at the top, with the establishment of effective governance for the program as a whole. It also depends on processes for managing the expectations—often conflicting expectations—of key stakeholders.

At the program level, you will need a staff of skilled and competent contributors who can assume responsibility for organizing and leading the work and for performing the functions of a program management office (PMO) (whether or not that terminology is used).

Major programs rely on a hierarchy of teams and leaders. Organizing all the contributors into aligned project teams that can operate smoothly is crucial to good program management. Successful program managers adopt leadership styles consistent with geographically remote and diverse teams, establish effective communications processes, and work to keep everyone who has a program role engaged and motivated.

Managing large-scale staffing and a significant budget carries a good deal of risk, so good program management also depends on identifying, assessing, and managing program resource risks.

PROGRAM GOVERNANCE AND STAKEHOLDER EXPECTATIONS

As discussed in Chapter 2, initiating a large program is a big deal, and it requires considerable high-level support and attention. In the absence of this support, a major program could never overcome the significant organizational inertia required to get going. Effective governance and stakeholder cohesion are never a given, however. Enthusiasm—even while it lasts—is never a substitute for thorough oversight and competent management.

Good program governance begins with appropriate sponsorship, which for large programs tends to be complicated. The larger the program, the more likely that its inception depends on a single, powerful, often visionary, individual. Some programs are sufficiently urgent or important to justify the ongoing operational involvement of the person or small team of people who get the ball rolling, but in most cases the responsibility for program work is delegated to a governance body that oversees the efforts as they proceed. Day-to-day management responsibilities are often further delegated to program staff, key stakeholders, or others as part of defining program roles and responsibilities. However these oversight responsibilities are initiated and staffed, they form the basis for program governance.

Good program governance includes clear definition of the program's overall objectives, processes, roles, and responsibilities. Governance also involves establishing the support, funding, and staff needed for the work. Governance for a large program is generally delegated to some sort of permanent committee composed of individuals who have sufficient authority and power to support the program and to sustain its ongoing progress. Governance committees go by many different names based on the type of program, such as *steering committee, management review board, release management team, portfolio management board, system control committee, division management board*, and myriad other terms. Whatever it might be called, the governance body is charged with ensuring a good start, ongoing control, and ultimate program success. At the inception of a new program, resolve issues such as who will sit on the governance committee, how often and where it plans to meet (monthly is not uncommon, and teleconferences are often necessary for global programs), and the topics that will be on the agenda for its periodic meetings.

Goals and Objectives

Effective program governance keeps a steady eye on both the organizational strategies and the specifics of the program. The initial business case for a major program begins with defining a problem (or set of problems) to be solved or an opportunity to pursue. The specifics of what the program will deliver must align with the motivations for taking on the program, and good governance focuses on ensuring that the goals and objectives will meet the stated need. Program documents such as the program charter and roadmap may originate with the governance body, but even if they originate elsewhere the governance body will need to approve them, based on a thorough review. You should secure support for your program's stated objectives, both initially and on a regular basis throughout the program. Document your objectives, including a clear description of what is to be delivered, how it will be evaluated, and why the expected results are important to the organization.

As discussed in Chapter 2, managing the needs and expectations of key stakeholders is essential to program success. Some key stakeholders will inevitably participate in program governance, and exert their influence on program goals as members of the body. Others may be involved more peripherally, but their priorities and needs still matter. As the program proceeds, provide thorough status information to your stakeholders on all program deliverables currently in development, plans for the next stages of work, and any significant scope changes being considered. Long-duration programs will experience drift, both in what the program is producing and in the current needs of key stakeholders, so frequent, effective communications that keep plans and expectations in sync are crucial to overall program success.

Effective program leaders also must manage any goal conflicts, significant revisions to program objectives, and differences in program priorities that arise throughout the program (discussed in Chapter 6).

Process Definition and Alignment

Effective program management depends on consistent, well-defined processes. Setting up the processes for defining program deliverables and for program planning, discussed in Chapters 3 and 4, may be accomplished by the governance body directly or delegated by them to others, but in any case will be at least subject to review and approval by the committee as part of program initiation. The role of program governance in establishing effective processes varies considerably, but there are several governance-related processes that are always part of effective program management. The main processes related to governance are the following: making program decisions, managing overall program scope, performing periodic program reviews, handling escalations to individuals in the organization with higher authority, and establishing requirements for high-level communications and reporting.

Problem Escalation and Decision Processes

Large undertakings periodically encounter unexpected difficulties requiring high-level attention. There are also many predictable events such as approvals, review sign-offs, and other decisions that need prompt attention. Processes that provide for decisive action at appropriate management levels are a key part of program governance.

An effective process for basic program decision making begins with establishing clear, unambiguous statements outlining the questions to be answered or the issues to be addressed. For recurring decisions, such as those associated with phase gates, new stages of work, financial commitments tied to fiscal periods, or other predictable events, specifically define the program decision criteria that must be considered, the inputs required, and the expected timing—for both the start and the resolution of each decision. Whenever relevant, define the priorities, weightings, and other quantitative aspects of the decision process. Significant decisions require participation of the program sponsor(s) and key stakeholders. For each anticipated decision, determine all the participants who need to participate and describe their roles in the process. As part of program initiation, have all the people who are involved in overall decision making review the planned processes and secure their commitment to participate at the times when decisions are scheduled.

Adopt a process for decisions that is objective and based to the largest extent possible on verifiable facts. Define measurable criteria for decisions that relate to program goals, and establish priorities showing the relative importance of each defined criterion. For example, with a decision to approve the next stage of funding or to move into the next phase of program work, establish minimum thresholds for performance and benefits delivered in earlier phases, credible estimates for both expected results and work planned, and other program metrics.

Adopt a process for decisions that includes all key stakeholders who will be affected by the decision. Decision processes that strive for consensus (or at least some level of cooperative buy-in) from all important players serve programs much better than those that rely primarily on a small cabal of decision makers who drive program decisions with minimal input from the people their decisions will be inflicted upon. Decisions also need to be timely, so define a process that solicits and acknowledges a wide range of inputs, but avoid open-ended attempts to hear everything from everybody.

Define a process for assessing the inputs gathered, using an objective context to analyze the situation and possible options. Establish a clear process for prioritizing alternatives and determining what appears to be the best decision. For example, at the close of a program phase, options could include proceeding as planned, proceeding with one of several proposed modifications to previously planned objectives, or, in some cases, deciding to terminate the program. Prioritizing the possible decisions using weighted criteria established in advance results in a rank-ordered list for consideration by those charged with making the decisions.

Program-level decisions are rarely simple, because much of the information they require pertains to future work about which there is significant uncertainty. For some decisions, Monte Carlo or other simulation tools can assist in determining which options are most likely to serve the program best. Generally, the most straightforward process for developing a consensus starts with a review of the possible outcomes by the key stakeholders, focusing on the provisional decision outcome that rises to the top of the sorted list following an objective analysis of the alternatives. Define a decision process that collects inputs from people on the governance body (and others involved), assembling what they think about the proposed decision.

If there is general consensus for the provisional outcome, review it for possible problems. If there are none, adopt it as the final decision. If there are any significant stakeholder objections to the "best" result, or if there are valid problems with the provisional decision, refocus the discussion on the next alternative, seeking a consensus decision for the program. Adopt a decision process that has a strict, inflexible deadline, and makes a final choice within the time set that is both the choice that appears to be best for the program as a whole and the choice that has as much consensus as possible. In general, it is better to make program decisions without undue delay, even if you suspect that you may need to revisit them later. Waiting for more information or hoping to increase overall buy-in is rarely justified.

Specify in your process how to communicate program decisions, including the rationale whenever it is in conflict with the expectations of any key program stakeholders. Implement decisions promptly, but monitor for results. Always be prepared to revisit and adjust program decisions whenever they lead to unintended adverse consequences.

When documenting the overall process for program decision making, also address how you will manage problem escalations arising within the program. Prompt escalation to program leadership (or perhaps even the governance body) is necessary whenever situations arise within the program that cannot be resolved by the people at the source of the trouble. An effective escalation process describes how you plan to deal with significant problems requiring outside assistance, and defines the responsibilities of those in authority who will need to act. As with the overall decision process, it is best to handle escalations objectively and with broad involvement of those involved.

As a general matter, even on very large programs, escalations should be rare; it is always quickest to resolve problems locally whenever possible. However, when issues that could threaten the program as a whole lie outside the control of the people who detect them, you must escalate promptly. Problems can progress from serious to disastrous to fatal very quickly on major programs. For escalations, set criteria for action, including thresholds for slippage, cost, or other program consequences that will trigger the use of the process. Establish a process that outlines the information required and sets expectations for timely response. Also describe the criteria for escalating higher within the program when necessary, and identify both who among your key stakeholders or governance body will be involved and who will manage the escalation process.

A good escalation process generally begins with submission of problem information to the program management team (or PMO). Such information may be part of normal project or program status collection, but for urgent situations, flags may be raised sooner than this. However the issue comes to the attention of program leadership, if it could affect the program as a whole it requires prompt attention. The basic information needed for escalation includes a description of the situation, actions taken so far to understand and resolve the issue, ideas for response, and individuals (if known) who have the authority to take action. Establish a format for program escalations that makes collecting the needed information as thorough and simple as possible. Provide space to summarize any proposals that the team having the problem has devised, including responses requiring more authority than they have. Estimate both the costs and timing for the responses proposed and the consequences to the program if the problem persists.

Define an escalation process that quickly verifies the information and augments it with any additional related problem descriptions, other possible responses, or additional data available at the program level. If the program team has sufficient authority to resolve the problem, move to resolve it. If the problem exceeds what the program team can accomplish, escalate it without delay to individuals higher in the organization who can deal with it. Whether acting at the program level or escalating to parties above the program, track the escalated issue with other active program issues, set a due date for resolution (or at least action), and name the owner of the issue who will be responsible for its resolution. Set expectations with your management and key stakeholders that escalations may occur at any time, and secure their commitment early in the program for prompt response when problem escalations arise.

As with other decisions, use objective analysis and develop as broad a consensus as possible when acting to resolve escalated problems. Review potential resolutions before taking action to test them for unintended consequences (solving one problem while creating a new, larger one will not help the program). Also communicate proposed actions in response to escalated problems and listen to the feedback of the stakeholders, project teams, and others who are involved.

If you can find a credible, effective response that is consistent with the program as currently defined, implement it. If there seems to be no response that will deal with the issue without a significant program modification, use the change management processes defined for the program before acting to determine the best response.

Conclude the definition for your escalation process with monitoring the results of the actions taken, and continue to seek resolution through further escalations whenever the responses taken are not sufficiently effective. Continue tracking and communicating progress until the escalated issue is fully resolved. Further guidance on handling program escalations is provided in Chapter 6.

Program Scope Processes

Governance processes also must address managing program scope. The overall processes can vary considerably, from highly prescriptive, formal roadmap and requirements and tracking systems to more flexible structures supporting a more agile, evolving approach. Document the process you intend to use for the program, and ensure that it will serve the needs of your work as you proceed.

For programs having multiple releases or phases of deliverables, the process needs to operate at two levels: defining and managing scope and changes at the roadmap/major deliverable level, and defining and managing changes and scope within the sets of projects that release specific results. As discussed in Chapter 3, the high-level scoping process tends to be relatively open to evolving requirements as the program proceeds through a succession of deliverables, and the process used to manage scope within each release tends to be more closed and resistant to changes. Establish program scoping processes aligned with the goals of your governance body, and gain its explicit support for how you plan to manage scope as the program progresses.

Documenting the overall scoping control process for a program should summarize the requirements collection and documentation, the criteria for prioritizing and baselining scope for program deliverables (both overall and phase by phase), archiving requirements for program scope information, the process for making changes at the various levels of program deliverable definition, and the roles and responsibilities for the individuals involved in the process steps. Controlling program scope is discussed in Chapter 6.

Program Review Processes

Programs generally have durations that exceed a reasonable planning horizon. Because of this, as discussed in Chapter 4, programs require periodic reviews to assess progress, evaluate processes, and validate detailed plans for upcoming work.

Adopt a process for conducting program reviews, and plan them at least semiannually. Include topics and events in the review agenda that support teamwork and other leadership goals, such as the following:

- Reviewing the program vision and overall objectives
- Reassessing stakeholder expectations
- Formally recognizing significant program accomplishments
- Analyzing lessons learned from earlier work and planning adjustments to remove barriers, resolve problems and frustrations, and improve program processes
- Reinforcing relationships, trust, and overall teamwork

Build the strongest case you can for a face-to-face review meeting, and determine who should participate. Plan to include all program contributors who would benefit from participation, such as the program staff (or PMO), key stakeholders, selected project leaders, and any others who could make the review more thorough and effective. It can also be helpful to involve one or more members of your governance body at the start or end of your program review meetings. Work to secure the necessary funding from your program governance body for the reviews, including money for travel so that geographically remote contributors will be able to participate in person.

Conducting program reviews is discussed further in Chapter 6.

High-Level Communications and Reporting Processes

One additional area where high-level processes are needed involves communication and information management. Communication processes provide the glue that holds everything together, especially for programs having very large staffs.

At the start of a program, define formats and frequencies for reporting and to be used for periodic status and other formal reporting, at the project level, program level, and at any levels in between. Most routine status reporting should be set up weekly, with exceptions for program work requiring updates either more frequently (as with urgent issue management) or less often. Also define the formats for any planned presentations, such as those associated with project reviews and for meetings with your governance body.

Also set expectations for reporting on significant risks, with a format for isolating major program exposures pertaining to upcoming work. Plan to review and update your program risk register on a regular schedule, such as monthly.

Also work to define a structure for a program management information system such as the one outlined in Chapter 4 to store current and archived program plans, scoping data, and other program information needed by program contributors.

In addition to formal reporting and information archiving, communications also involves program websites for general public information, training and documentation related to program work and methods, and potentially many other types of useful communications. In general, it is always best to err on the side of too much communicating rather than too little. Further guidance on communications is provided later in this chapter and in Chapter 6.

Program Roles and Responsibilities

Effective governance also relies on clear definition of who will be responsible for what on the program. Stakeholders for the work include all the individuals who can affect the program and all who will be affected by it. Key stakeholders include those on the governance board, the program leader and staff (or PMO), leaders of the current projects within the program, and any other individuals who have involvement with program funding, decisions, inputs, or direction. Establish a central roster or database at the start of your program to capture the names, contact information, and other information about these people, and keep it up to date throughout the program. Along with the contact data, also identify everyone's place in the program organization and define each person's role in the program and contribution to the work. Include a sufficiently detailed description of what is expected from all contributors and how their work will be assessed and evaluated.

One or more hierarchical organization charts may be needed for very large programs to keep everyone straight, and some programs find it helpful to also establish a structured database for their program roster. It is best to keep this information online within your program management information system, where anyone who may need to contact a program contributor can readily access it.

At any given time, there may be many other individuals who are (or could be) affected by your program. Although their roles at any given time may be peripheral, you should endeavor to identify and track at least a representative sample of the users, customers, and others who will ultimately be responsible for realizing the program's value (or, alternatively, could interfere with what you want to accomplish). Particularly on lengthy programs, reach out periodically to reconfirm program assumptions about stakeholders who will be on the receiving end of what your program produces. Some useful techniques include surveys, focus groups, user interviews, and other methods associated with market research. Also consider involving representative users in ongoing tests and evaluations of program deliverables. Assign roles in key projects or at the program level to individuals who can at least represent the perspectives of typical users, customers, or others who need to cooperate with (or at least not oppose) what the program plans to do. Using agile techniques, such as frequent deployment of incremental change and making "product owners" part of the development efforts can be very effective in avoiding obstacles to the smooth delivery and successful acceptance of what your program produces.

Establishing a centralized repository of stakeholder data contributes significantly to effective program governance. Keep your program stakeholder information current and work to ensure that all stakeholders and contributors are sufficiently in the loop to maintain program cohesion, coordination, and cooperation.

Program Funding, Staffing, and Support

Program governance also involves providing program resources. Initially, this requires start-up funding; allocation of staff to the program and all projects; commitment of space, equipment, and other assets needed for program work; and approval of any travel, services, contracting, or other necessary program expenses. At the start of most programs, resources tend to be adequate, with any shortfalls in initial funding or staffing promptly identified and addressed.

The real challenges for governance in this area tend to be in the later stages of work. Establish governance processes to track changes and align funding with ongoing overall program expectations. Establish budget oversight procedures to ensure that any proposed program changes will be considered only in light of their effect on the overall staffing, budgets, and resources committed to the program. Approving changes that increase program scope or effort must be linked to corresponding increases in program resources that will be sufficient to support the revised objectives. Conversely, whenever program funding cuts are contemplated (a tactic common during the later portions of fiscal years for underperforming organizations), good governance policies must revisit current program objectives and adjust expectations to accommodate any reduced budgets, staffing, or other cutbacks.

Also, long-duration programs face a challenge because the program goals are established, in at least some detail, far into the future, but funding for the work is generally only committed for the current fiscal year. As the end of each year approaches, programs generally must compete for funding during the annual budgeting process with other programs, projects, and organization priorities. Engage your program governance body in proactive management of this, and keep plan-based budget requirements up to date and synchronized with your program roadmaps and other scoping documents. Periodically review your progress, objectives, and overall budget projections for work in future years as part of managing your relationships with your sponsors and key stakeholders, especially any stakeholders who have influence on your next year's staffing and budget. Never assume that current allocations will be automatically renewed as you transition into a new fiscal year. Strive to keep both your resource requirements and the benefits and results you are delivering visible to all in positions of funding authority, especially as you approach the closing days of accounting periods.

THE PROGRAM MANAGEMENT OFFICE

Program management offices have become a hot topic in recent years, and with good reason. Organizations that aspire to better project management often turn to PMOs as a key part of their strategy for improvement. A PMO is generally a small team of individuals with solid project management expertise who take on the responsibility for increasing and maintaining overall effectiveness and the success of project work in an organization.

Such teams may or may not be called a PMO, and different organizations tend to define their responsibilities to best align with their current perceived needs. These days teams established to support organizational project and program management goals go by a variety of names, most including the term *project* or *program* (adding the term *management* or not) in their title along with alternative descriptors to *office* such as *center of excellence, group, consulting team, competency center, compliance support, initiative*, or many other variations on these themes.

Types of PMOs

Whether it is formally called a PMO, the staff reporting to a program leader is one type of PMO. In addition to the program staff, the environment for some programs may also involve other teams in the organization sharing PMO-type responsibilities. However such teams (or combinations of teams) may be set up or identified, they tend to be responsible for one or more of the primary PMO functions: execution, auditing, and enabling.

Execution: Execution is always the main focus of a program staff team, because the team is charged with the program's overall control and success. Program execution is a major theme of earlier chapters of this book, and the role of the program staff in execution will be discussed in more detail in Chapter 6. For very large undertakings, the program staff is actively involved in planning at all levels, tracking overall progress, managing changes and escalations, and maintaining general control of program work. This is the function where a program manager and staff tend to have the most authority and undisputed responsibility.

Auditing: PMOs also focus on establishing and monitoring processes and addressing operational problems. As was discussed in Chapter 4, consistent processes for planning and running the projects composing a major program are critical to overall control and success. PMOs with auditing responsibility also track the status of troubled project work. Sometimes these PMOs intervene and get involved with measures to address issues. Other times they just report on projects using a "watch list" or similar document and leave resolution of the problems to others. Either way, such visibility tends to create the attention that projects and programs making insufficient progress require to get back on track.

Without standards for tools and common formats for plans, documents, forms, templates, and general communications, programs can come to a standstill under an unmanageable jumble of inconsistent and confusing information. In some program environments, the establishment of common methods and the power to enforce compliance are exclusively in the hands of the program staff. In others it may be shared with PMO teams set up elsewhere, sometimes higher in the organization. Having a team external to the program acting as "process police" to ensure that all rules are strictly followed can actually be beneficial to a program. If others establish process standards, it will not be necessary (or at least not as urgent) for the program staff to do it. External standards also help to ensure that other projects and programs operate consistently, and contributors coming to the program from other parts of the organization will already be familiar with how things need to be done. Overall, mandatory standards related to quality, security, safety, information storage, work methods, and other aspects of the work can greatly enhance your ability to understand and control a program. Aligning your program with standards established (and enforced) by this type of PMO can boost your overall productivity and help you avoid many types of problems. Also, being able to rely on others to be the "bad cop" when there are problems may allow you to delegate to them punitive actions that are needed to keep the program on track while preserving good relationships with your project teams and program contributors.

Working under restrictions mandated by people outside your program can have a downside, however. Some compliance requirements may represent overkill for your program work, especially if they originate from a team that believes that in the realm of process, "If some is good, more must be better." If you find that your program is subject to requirements that are not useful, or that consume effort that could be more productively applied to other work, seek to modify them. Review the processes that you are working under, and whenever possible endeavor to minimize unproductive process overhead and eliminate any practices that could make things more difficult.

In areas where your program team is empowered to define and enforce the processes to be used, apply the same criteria. Look for and mandate practices and methods that will support the program and enhance your control and progress, and avoid or eliminate processes that deliver insufficient benefits to justify their application, monitoring, and enforcement. As the program proceeds, review your progress to identify inefficiencies that you can remedy and problems that could be avoided by improving processes or adopting better, more consistent methods.

Enabling: The third broad function addressed by PMOs aims to enhance the knowledge, skills, and project management effectiveness of individuals and teams. The program staff might provide this for itself, but in many cases, as with auditing, there may be an external group with some or most of the responsibility for this.

Developing project and program management skills among a large community of program contributors enhances the effectiveness and cohesion of the overall team. It provides a basis for consistent and efficient work on and among teams, and provides a common vocabulary and foundation for unambiguous communication.

Training in project management methods originates from a wide variety of sources. Universities and colleges, professional organizations such as the Project Management Institute (PMI), consulting firms, training organizations both inside and outside of the organization, and many others offer a great deal of useful education on project management. Providers of such services also produce written materials, such as papers, articles, and books aimed at building project management expertise.

Ensuring that what people learn will be appropriate to the environment and effective is a PMO function. Effective guidance for project leaders and others responsible for program work is also a function of others in the organization who are responsible for learning and education in general, part of a "center of excellence" team, or others engaged in employee development. Sorting through what is available and recommending learning or reference resources that will be useful is a very powerful tool for building organizational project and program management maturity.

In addition to locating offerings and facilitating access to education and reference materials, the program staff may also get involved in teaching, mentoring, and providing specific information to program contributors. This often involves creating process documentation, job aids related to project management or to methods used for program work, and written materials concerning technologies or equipment important to the program.

Whether or not the program staff is involved in the general education and development of program contributors, it certainly is necessary for the program team to provide feedback and guidance in specific instances, such as problem resolution. It is also common for program staff to provide help when needed for infrequent activities such as project startup workshops or post-project analyses.

In some ways, enabling PMO activities can be seen as a counterbalance to auditing activities. Whenever it is necessary to "pull rank" and compel project leaders or other program contributors to do something that they would prefer not to do (or to do in a different way), engaging in activities that help the leaders and teams to learn something new or improve their skills can be an effective way to bring things back into friendlier territory. Establishing a reputation for program staff expertise and helpfulness can do a great deal to increase cohesion across the program team, so it is always a good idea to look for situations where people are struggling due to skill gaps or for other reasons that can be addressed by building competencies.

The program staff, however talented and hard-working they may be, cannot be everywhere. The more capable and flexible the program contributors are, the more successful the program will be.

Responsibilities of the PMO

On significant programs, the program staff often takes responsibility, at least initially, for a wide range of activities, such as the following:

- Defining program life cycles, checkpoints, and decision criteria
- Managing the program scoping backlog and processes for overall change control
- Establishing a program management information system and providing for its security, access, and maintenance
- Selecting and setting up structures and templates for planning and scheduling tools
- Providing help with planning, agenda building, and facilitating project start-up workshops
- Providing formats and templates for routine program reporting
- Identifying and resolving cross-project interrelationships and interfaces
- Setting communication standards and providing telecommunication infrastructure
- Reviewing plans and providing quality checks for program documents
- Reporting on troubled projects and programs and providing assistance with issue management and problem escalations
- Defining and managing the collection, analysis, and archiving of program metrics
- Providing guidance and assistance with decision making, conflict management, performance problems, contract issues, and other project responsibilities that can have an impact on the program

- Managing expectations and relationships with key stakeholders, program sponsors, management, customers, and other parties external to the program
- Assisting with planning, facilitating, and following up on project and program reviews
- Facilitating post-project retrospective analyses and assessing lessons learned
- Documenting and improving project and program processes
- Managing program budgets and financials
- Dealing with program and organizational changes

Example of a PMO

The COMPASS program at Hewlett-Packard, a large information technology program discussed in earlier chapters, provides an interesting example of an execution-type PMO. The program organization at a high level is summarized in Figure 5-1. The program staff included a good number of contributors, but only a few were part of the small team that reported to the IT program director responsible for the overall program plans (shown in the gray blocks in the figure). Others involved in IT work reported directly to other managers, as in a typical matrix organization.

The primary responsibilities for the program staff members reporting to the IT director were the following:

- Overall program planning, deployment wave planning, and alignment of detailed functional plans
- Program scope management
- Program-level communications and training
- Program information management
- Program processes and lessons learned
- Program risk management
- Overall testing and deployment control

For most of the program's 5-year duration, I served as the program planner. I was responsible for several of these functions and contributed to all of them. Planning functions for the program's overlapping deployment

Figure 5-1 High-level organization chart for the COMPASS program participants.

waves required the full-time efforts of three program staff members, two who focused on the execution of alternating releases (among the four or five actively in progress at any given time). My primary role was in coordinating the overlapping activities, tracking program risks, managing (and enforcing) the scoping for each release, and managing general communications and information. As with many modern projects and programs, the core IT program staff members had no direct control over the large number of IT contributors who were ultimately responsible for program development work.

The overall IT staffing for the program represented about a third of the roughly 200 program contributors at any given time, with many others on the business side. Coordinating those efforts was the responsibility of the business program director, who worked to manage the efforts of these contributors, nearly all of whom reported to other parts of the organization and were located in many different countries. Managing all of this was daunting, but the COMPASS program had a supportive steering committee and management that provided effective governance. We were also successful in establishing a strong management matrix early on that effectively converted most of the managers responsible for key program functions into de facto "solid-line" members of the program staff for the duration of the work.

Regardless of their actual reporting relationships, all the key program leaders were included on the COMPASS organization charts, were involved in planning and tracking, and attended program staff and review meetings. No distinction was made on the program team based on management reporting relationships, and we put a great deal of effort into ensuring that the primary loyalty of each team member remained with the program, not elsewhere.

Because the COMPASS program team was distributed worldwide, there were people on the extended program staff located across many time zones. We conducted face-to-face planning summits about every 6 months throughout the program to foster trust and loyalty. These program reviews were rigorously planned, multiday meetings during which we did a great deal of planning and decision making. All program staff members and a good number of other contributors who were responsible for significant program deliverables participated in these semiannual sessions, and over time scores of people attended one or more of the meetings.

These periodic face-to-face summits substantially benefited the COMPASS program. In addition to the analysis, decisions, and plans created during these summits, the team building that resulted from putting faces to names helped establish the camaraderie, trust, and respect the program needed to work through difficulties, conflicts, and problems. Sharing meals, networking informally, and attending events (such as a legendary bocce outing) ensured that the program seldom encountered problems common with "virtual teams."

For routine interactions, the program team scheduled weekly 60- to 90-minute conference calls to provide overall program continuity. Starting times for these meetings varied during the program to accommodate geographically remote participants. We distributed detailed meeting agendas in advance, and following each meeting we promptly distributed meeting notes to all program staff. We also posted the meeting minutes on our program management information system, where all program contributors could see what was discussed. Standard agenda items included the status of the deployment waves that were active at any given time, with additional topics added to address significant current program issues. Meetings were kept on point, and they frequently ended early. For the most part, everyone involved attended regularly and with little complaint.

Over the several years required to complete this program, the program staff succeeded in developing and using effective processes for managing scope and timing at all levels of the program. Many program contributors provided "lessons learned" following each deployment wave for improving the scoping process. Because of the improvements, we successfully delivered substantially more functionality using fewer contributors in the later waves. Hierarchical decomposition and synchronization of plans made it possible (though never easy) to control the hundreds of interdependencies and myriad activities necessary to keep the overlapping wave schedules on track (and, for the most part, out of one another's way). Program management processes that over time were fine-tuned to our needs were essential to the COMPASS program's accomplishments.

Effective process management was necessary, but in retrospect the largest factor in the program's success was the investment the program team made, early and often, in building strong team relationships and trust as the work progressed. While this was generally true across the whole program, it was especially important among the members of the program staff. Everyone on the extended program team placed the needs of the program well above the specific details of his or her designated role. There were never any issues of coverage when people had to be absent from the program. Each individual's broad involvement in multiple aspects of the program was instrumental in uncovering risks and future problems. Because all members of the program staff were aware of the whole program, individuals could spot potential complications from their perspectives that would not have been visible to others. Blurring of roles was also common during times of stress (which were frequent). For example, when collecting configuration requirements simultaneously from a half-dozen countries to start a new wave, freezing scope for the next wave in the face of an avalanche of new change requests, and dealing with the late stages of release testing for the current wave, it mattered little what each contributor's assigned roles was. Each person pitched in to get things done. Trusting people, providing frequent, truthful, and timely status, and investing heavily in team building created the atmosphere of "one for all and all for one" that established the foundation for a successful program.

HIERARCHIES OF TEAMS AND LEADERS

Large, multi-project programs have hierarchies for scope (discussed in Chapter 3). They also have hierarchies for plans (described in Chapter 4) that at the lowest level tend to mirror the corresponding level of the scoping hierarchy. Each of the project plans in the planning hierarchy aligns with one of the program's project teams. Similar to the hierarchies for scope and plans, the program staff and project teams form a third program management hierarchy.

When documenting the organizational chart view of this hierarchy, check that it makes logical sense, and that the leaders at each identified level appear to have the skills, knowledge, and expertise that they need to manage their portion of the program work. Analysis of the staffing hierarchy and resources often reveals additional program adjustments to consider that will make the overall work easier to manage.

A program organizational chart may have several layers, such as the three-level generic example in Figure 5-2.

How many layers and how many projects (or subprograms or other divisions) are in each layer is a function of scoping, planning, and other factors (such as geography, discipline, technology, or organization alignment). A staffing breakdown that lacks balance or has too many items on any particular branch may be problematic; it is good practice to analyze such an organizational chart using guidelines similar to those applied to a project work breakdown structures. Seek a breakdown that has a limited number of items on each branch (most people can only remember and effectively deal with about seven items at a time, so strive for no more than this). Consider reorganizing the reporting relationships whenever there are

Figure 5-2 Example of a program's organizational chart.

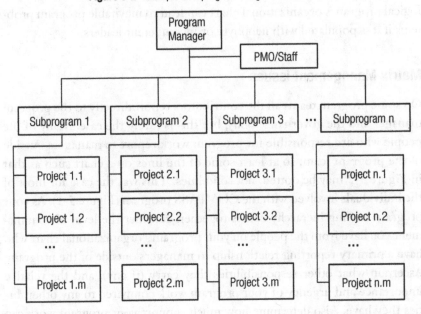

too many subordinate teams reporting into any given part of the chart, or if the portion of the work (and staff) represented on a single branch overwhelms the rest of the chart. Also verify that the projects at the lowest level of the organization chart are staffed at a level consistent with project management practice, with about a dozen contributors. The point of decomposing a program into smaller projects is to apply project management processes successfully, so ensure that the project teams the program depends on are structured appropriately.

As the program's organizational chart takes shape, assess the experience and skills of the individuals who are assigned to each of the project teams and at all intermediate levels. While it may be fine to assign a successful project leader to a subprogram coordination role if you plan to provide ongoing mentoring and guidance, it is unwise to have too many leadership roles in a program assigned to individuals with little relevant experience. Even asking project leaders to take on a team as little as 20 percent larger than those they have led in the past can be risky. The best-looking, most logical program's organizational chart can lead to inevitable program problems if it is populated with neophyte or incompetent leaders.

Matrix Management Issues

On some program teams all the contributors report directly to the program manager and the governance body, but this is rarely the case. Many of the people who are responsible for program work report to managers outside of the program team, so at least some of the lines on a chart such as that in Figure 5-2 may be dotted, not solid lines. This was the case for most of the individuals involved with the COMPASS program (Figure 5-1). As your program staffing hierarchy comes together, consider the level of commitment you have from the people on your program's organizational chart who have a primary reporting relationship to managers outside of the program. Ascertain what other responsibilities they carry (if any), and the relative importance and urgency of your program work compared to any other duties they have. Also determine how much support your program work can expect from the managers of these contributors. If you detect any potential problems in securing meaningful commitments for the work outlined in your program plans, seek to resolve them.

In some cases there may be opportunities to use your influence to engage higher-level managers with sufficient authority to raise the priority of your program to effectively deal with conflicts. You may also be able to work collaboratively in planning and early program effort to increase the involvement of external managers with your program to secure more robust support.

In other cases, there may not be much you can do about some identified contributors and teams that have only a tenuous link to your program. If it seems that your objectives could be at risk because of too little authority or influence, investigate other staffing alternatives that might prove to be more dependable. Consider involving others within your organization, adding new staff to your program team and developing their skills and expertise to meet your needs, or contracting talent from outside the organization. If you find an option that serves the program better, propose it and secure the needed funding or approval of other program changes to your plans to make it happen.

Project Team Interactions

As discussed in Chapter 4, decomposing complex system deliverables into components provides a good starting point for program planning. As the interfaces and cross-dependencies in the project plans come into focus, issues often surface that reveal deficiencies and unnecessary complexities in the initial scope breakdown. Program planning can uncover the need to adjust the overall system design to deal more effectively with problems, imbalances, and other issues. As you assess the teams of contributors who will carry out the work, additional issues may appear. As you create rosters for project staff and consider how the teams will operate, you may find situations where components and plans for closely related portions of the program are expected to be staffed by teams that are many time zones apart. In cases such as this, it is prudent to adjust either the scoping or staffing decisions to minimize communication and coordination problems. There may be numerous other situations where project teams will face significant organizational, geographical, cultural, language, or other obstacles that will increase program challenges and risk. In general, it is wisest to staff closely related program work with teams that are located near to one another, and to delegate work to geographically remote project teams only when the distributed team can operate autonomously most of the time.

For programs employing agile methods and short iteration cycles, separation of project teams can make program integration and overall progress difficult. Even working in heavily matrixed environments can become problematic. As the program's organizational chart takes shape, carefully consider the need for frequent, effective interactions between the project teams. In general, high program complexity does not mix well with geographically distant project teams.

Changes to the program scoping and planning to reduce the need for frequent project team interactions is especially good practice, but this may not always be feasible. Sometimes work on closely related parts of the program must be delegated to remote teams. In such cases, the program needs to carry additional overhead to provide the "glue" and the ongoing effort needed to overcome the challenges. A program team using agile methods to implement a "Scrum of Scrums" provides as example of this. When teams are located in close proximity, a single individual can usually fulfill the "product owner" role for several teams of developers. But when teams are distant geographically each team requires someone local to play this role, because Scrum depends on frequent, robust interaction between the developers and an individual who can adequately represent the customer. This either requires adding another product owner or a "product owner proxy" who can take on this role for geographically remote teams. In addition to the additional contributor role, all the individuals having product owner responsibility need to check in with each other regularly to stay in sync, and for efforts involving more than a small number of Scrum teams it is good practice to add a product owner coordinator to facilitate and keep track of these interactions.

Similarly, Scrum also requires a Scrum master for each team (or at least a Scrum master proxy who can assume the role for each developer team). A program manager (who may or may not carry that title) leading a "Scrum of Scrums" is generally responsible for coordinating the Scrum masters, but additional individuals and meetings (at least daily Scrum master check-in meetings) are necessary. Even people experienced with scaling agile methods for large programs tend to put an upper limit of about 100 total contributors for such undertakings, which is about where the overhead for agile team interactions begins to exceed what can be reasonably be effectively coordinated.

Whether you choose to compartmentalize program work to minimize the need for frequent interactions between geographically remote teams or to add staff responsible for coordination (including loss of sleep from frequently staying up late or getting up early to dial into meetings with distant teams and the effort needed to provide up-to-date documentation current for work), make any organizational adjustments necessary to ensure that program work can proceed effectively.

Shared Project Resources

Scarce resources are another program staffing challenge. As you assess the skills and specific resources each project team has identified, look for specialized skills or other needs that are or could be in short supply. If several teams need the only available expert or specialist at the same time, consider options for adjusting schedules, teams, or deliverables to minimize queuing and delays. (And always investigate other demands on contributors having unique skills that could further restrict availability.) Investigate the possibility of obtaining contract staff with the needed expertise (and gain approval for the needed funding). If there is sufficient time, propose having other program contributors develop the scarce skills, to provide both more capacity and a backup. On lengthy programs, always pursue development opportunities that could provide additional contributors who are capable of assuming responsibility for critical activities requiring specialized expertise for future phases of the work.

You may also find that you require test gear, equipment, or other facilities that could cause program bottlenecks due to short supply. If so, identify the constraint as early as possible in program planning and secure sufficient funds for additional assets or upgraded infrastructure in your program budget to meet the need. If this proves infeasible, adjust your program plans to accommodate the resources you have.

In cases where there are potential resource conflicts due to sharing organization resources outside your program, use your program's priority whenever possible to ensure that you are able to gain access when you need it, ahead of the other work. If there is a possibility that other programs will take precedence over your program and cause your work to queue, either seek alternative ways to do the work or adjust your plans and risks accordingly to reflect the potential for conflict.

Turnover of Staffing on Long-Duration Programs

On long-duration programs, staffing will change. Inevitably, some people who are there in the beginning will leave, so plans based on current contributors for work several years down the road are unrealistic. Turnover is not uncommon, even on shorter programs.

As program work begins, involve people in overall planning and assisting in program work even for tasks where others have primary responsibility. Identify roles within the program that would cause a slowdown or bring the program to a halt if the individual responsible were unavailable. Assess the overall program team—including program staff, project leaders, and other key contributors—for potential overlap and redundancy. If there are other program contributors who could assume responsibility for critical work, or might be able to do so with training or mentoring, identify them and begin necessary preparations. Even if you do manage to hold on to key contributors and experience minimal turnover, building capabilities to spread the work around and offer roles with greater variety will serve your program well, build motivation, and enhance teamwork.

Non-Project Program Work

Managing a program involves all the projects needed for the work, but it does not stop there. The staffing hierarchy for most programs also includes other individuals whose efforts contribute to the overall program objectives but not as part of one of the projects. Some teams you depend on may be involved in ongoing functions such as support, operations, or other parts of your organizational infrastructure. Whether this is an explicit part of the program's organizational chart alongside the defined projects or whether it is part of the "white space," good program management includes these functions and contributors when assessing the resource needs and constraints.

Determine the specific dependencies your program will have on non-project resources, and analyze the timing for any commitments you will depend on. If you detect issues, work to resolve them through adjusting priorities, program expectations, or reassigning the dependencies to others who are dedicated to program work. (And always ensure that whatever tactics you adopt are both feasible and adequately funded.)

PROGRAM LEADERSHIP

Managing large, complex programs requires considerable authority and power. What types of power are available and who wields them vary from program to program, but running a lengthy program with insufficient authority adds risk and inefficiency and can result in program failure. How you use the power you have also matters. Using authority poorly can hurt your program.

Types of Organizational Power

There are many types of power inherent in the work environment, and all are relevant to program management. These include the following:

- Expert power
- Informational power
- Reward power
- Referent power
- Legitimate or coercive power

Project and program leaders have a good deal of the first four of these, but they may or may not have much legitimate power. The amount of legitimate power available may not matter a great deal. This is because using it in a program environment ("Do it because I told you to do it"), especially if done too often, can be counterproductive and demotivating. It is always best to play to your strengths and use power to enhance program commitments and cooperation rather than erode it.

Expert power is based on what you know how to do. Program leaders typically have a good deal of this type of power, and this is probably the main reason why they were selected to manage the program in the first place. Expert power is particularly useful when dealing with sponsors, managers, and key stakeholders who have more organizational authority than you do, because it is the one area where you tend to hold the upper hand. It can also be effective when dealing with program contributors, but here it

211

tends to be limited to matters involving the program as a whole and expertise for organizing and effectively managing complex undertakings. Your expertise in project and program management can be a considerable source of power and authority, for both those above the program and those within the program team.

Your technical expertise and knowledge of specifics relevant to program work may also be useful, but many, if not most, program contributors probably have considerably more expertise in their specific fields than you have. On very large programs depending on many kinds of expertise, it is not possible (and not necessary) for the program leader to be expert in all relevant areas. Even among the program staff, however, you still may be perceived as a generalist with creative problem-solving talent who can provide valuable insight and perspective useful to program specialists who possess deep knowledge in specific fields. (Some cynics joke that PhD stands for "piled higher and deeper." All too often, an excess of narrow expertise becomes an impediment to problem solving.)

Informational power is about what you know. This is another source of considerable power for program managers, because once you are up and running, there should be little that you do not know, or can't easily find out, about the program. You are in fact probably the world's foremost authority on your program. You will also be responsible for the program documents, reports, presentations, and program management information system, so you will be seen as the primary source for needed information throughout the program. It can be very useful periodically to remind people involved with your program of this as you progress (as long as you do it diplomatically).

Reward power is about what you can do for others. As a program leader, you may have limited ability to grant significant rewards, such as salary increases or significant bonuses. Despite this, all project and program leaders possess a great deal of this type of power. You can always praise people, thank them for their contributions, nominate individuals and teams for rewards, and do many other things that will be appreciated. While the size of a reward can make a difference, even apparently trivial recognition can yield substantial results. Program managers who frequently offer positive feedback and effectively use opportunities to thank people thoughtfully will improve trust, cooperation, and team cohesion. Always include the managers in any communications praising program contributors, particularly when the individuals involved report to managers outside of your program.

Using reward power to express gratitude can be quite effective in building trust and personal relationships with program contributors. Maintaining respectful personal relationships with those working on your program can be especially valuable during times of stress, when you need all the friends you can get.

Referent power is about who you know. For large programs with important sponsors and stakeholders, this sort of power can be very useful when working in matrix organizations and with people who are managed by others. While you may not have any authority over some of your program contributors, there may be powerful individuals interested in your program who do have influence over them. Overuse of referent power can be counterproductive, but subtle reminders about who might be disappointed by a lack of cooperation or follow through for program work can be very effective.

Legitimate power is about your position in the organization. This tends to be the kind of power in organizations most people think of first, because it is associated with being "the boss." Legitimate power confers formal authority attached to a named position (generally some type of manager). This sort of formal authority implies the power to coerce. Some program leaders have extensive legitimate power, and as program manager they have many contributors who directly report to them. Other program leaders have little (or even no) legitimate authority, because all or most of the program staff reports directly to others, having only a dotted-line reporting relationship to the program.

While having this kind of authority can be useful when you need to move quickly to deal with urgent situations or "pull rank" to get a result in support of program imperatives, even program managers who possess legitimate power use it sparingly. Coercing, threatening, and punishing people can be effective tactics in the short term for getting things done, but ultimately program management is about the long run. The cost of overusing command-and-control power can carry a high cost to future program work, in demotivation, malicious compliance, resentment, and perhaps even excessive staff turnover. Not having much formal power is usually less of an impediment to effective program management than many program leaders think it is.

Leadership Styles

Your organizational power defines what you can do. Your leadership style relates to how you go about doing it. Figure 5-3 shows a range of possibilities, from the autocratic on the left side to consensus-based behavior on the right. Because many program leaders lack the formal authority to make commands stick, their actions generally rely on the tactics toward the right side of the figure. Even program managers with a great deal of legitimate authority find that collaborative decisions work best over the course of a long-duration program.

Different situations call for different strategies. In emergencies when quick action is required, program leaders may have to make an autonomous decision based on minimal consultation with others (and hope it is accepted in cases where they have little legitimate authority). Conversely, when con-

Figure 5-3 How program actions are determined.

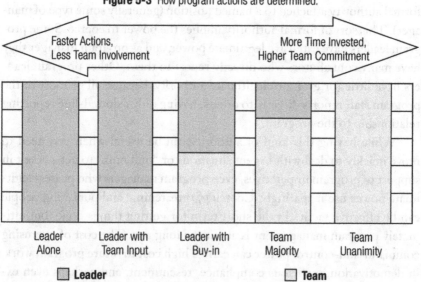

Faster Actions, Less Team Involvement			More Time Invested, Higher Team Commitment	
Leader Alone	Leader with Team Input	Leader with Buy-in	Team Majority	Team Unanimity

■ Leader   □ Team

fronting highly complex decisions even the most autocratic dictators and military leaders will collect extensive input before taking action. Such decisions are common on large, complicated programs, so carving out the time to involve key members of the program team is generally a wise investment. Not only does this increase the number and quality of options considered, it also creates buy-in for the decisions made that will enhance teamwork and overall program cohesion. Even in cases where the program manager has extensive authority and is fully empowered to make solo decisions, failure to consult others can contribute to resentment and a loss of motivation. Using program team consensus to at least guide all significant decisions can significantly augment your overall program control.

Over time, the leadership style that works best will vary. When initiating a new program or following significant changes, especially changes that bring new contributors into the program, you may find it necessary to be more autocratic and strongly guide discussions and decisions. Later, when all involved in the program understand what is going on, consensus decisions (or delegation, even for overall program decisions) may be more appropriate. Programs employing agile methods involving extensive collaboration will always endeavor to fully engage all key stakeholders in decisions, and overall cohesion for any type of program will benefit from ongoing, meaningful contributor involvement.

Striving for consensus does take more time and effort, and it may appear to surrender control needed for program management. In practice, though, the time invested in collaborative planning and decision making often saves enough time by avoiding debates, complaints, and other conflicts to more than compensate. In fact, program leaders who strive for consensus retain significant control because they generally facilitate and guide the discussions and exchanges. There is almost always ample opportunity to influence decisions to ensure that they best support the program.

Good program managers also tend to favor asking questions and active listening over telling people what to do. Both tactics can ultimately get you to the same result, but asking questions shows your interest in what others think and paraphrasing responses demonstrates that you are listening. By asking open-ended (not "yes or no") questions you often learn important things about your program that you would not hear otherwise, or only discover much later. Even better, by using questions to guide discussions, you can often make it appear that the team members you are speaking with have come up with a conclusion on their own that matches what you had in mind.

Overall, effective program leaders tend to operate with as much collaboration and consensus as possible, balancing program constraints and timing with the need for staff buy-in and cooperation.

Working Together

Large technical programs tend to have compartmentalized "silos" of expertise that are most comfortable working independently. This can be efficient because it minimizes interruptions, but for successfully developing complicated program deliverables it is rarely effective. When Boeing started the program to create the 777 passenger jet in the early 1990s, the program team members realized that they faced challenges of unprecedented complexity. To avoid many of the types of problems caused by the "throw stuff over the wall" tactics used for designing earlier aircraft, they initiated what they dubbed "Working Together." As described in Karl Sabbagh's *Twenty-First-Century Jet*, the concepts of Working Together and extensive use of design-build teams pulled the disparate parts of the overall program team together in unprecedented ways. There was initial resistance, as engineering and other teams wanted to solve their own problems and avoid admitting when they ran into problems. Over time, however, the phrase *Working Together* became ubiquitous and was broadly embraced by everyone involved. It became common to raise issues promptly and reach out for help. Ron Ostrowski, a senior engineer, explained, "It's OK. It's almost like 'Celebrate our problems,' get them out in the open so we can go to work on them."

"Working Together" was on banners, hats, posters, and T-shirts. It became the name of the initial 777 built, and was even extended to all the contractors and customers involved in the program. Over the course of the work, it made a difference in part because it really did foster a proactive approach to problem solving and enhanced program teamwork. It also made a difference simply because people believed it would do so, which proved self-fulfilling.

Alan Mulally, who ultimately served as Boeing's program leader for the 777 (and recently retired as president and CEO of the Ford Motor Company), said about the openness required for Working Together, "If your idea didn't work out, share it. Share it early. Share it with the people that have a shared destiny in it, that are affected by your decision, and then let's just keep working together." The philosophy permeated meetings, reviews, conversations, and the program as a whole. It was instrumental in quickly resolving the many complex technical problems that arose as the program progressed to its successful conclusion.

PROGRAM COMMUNICATIONS

Communications are crucial to any project. On large, complex programs, failure to communicate well can quickly result in chaos and disaster. Program communications include both formal and informal interactions. They also involve a wide range of tactics, from "same time, same place" face-to-face dealings to "different time, different place" exchanges. Good program management uses many types and modes of communication, at whatever frequency best serves the work.

Modes of Program Communication

Communication on programs uses many methods, to accommodate a wide range of timing and locations. For most human interactions, the most effective methods are face-to-face, with all parties at the same place at the same time. Programs having geographically remote teams in multiple time zones cannot be limited to this, however. For some interactions, "same time, different place" methods are effective. For communicating complex information, asynchronous methods using written communications are necessary. In general, all "different time" communication methods are useful for contributors in any location. For any given program, any or all of the communication modes in Table 5-1 may be appropriate.

Table 5.1 Communication methods.

	Same Place	Different Place
Same time	• Conversations • Status meetings • Presentations and broadcasts • Networking • Team-building activities • Celebrations	• Telephone calls • Teleconferences • Videoconferences • Web-based meetings • Instant, text, and social messaging • Network collaboration tools
Different time	• Voicemail • Email • Social media • Meeting minutes • Program reports • Memos • Newsletters • Audio recordings • Video recordings	• Program Management Information System • Web sites • Cloud services • Yellow sticky notes • Documents and databases • Interoffice mail • Postal and express mail • FAX

For projects and programs it is nearly always better to overcommunicate than to communicate too little, because people can more easily disregard information they do not need than intuit information they do not have. This can be overdone, but within reason it is most prudent to err on the side of communicating more than you think contributors need, rather than less.

Additional communication effort is especially relevant when dealing with significant program information. Plan to use multiple modes to convey critical program communications. Follow up important telephone conversations and meetings with written summaries of key topics. When distributing complicated written documents, schedule time for discussion of significant items to verify understanding and coherence. Also, strive to ensure that all program communications convey consistent messages. Keeping a large, diverse, distributed program team in sync is possible only when all contributors have the same information.

Determine what communications will be useful to the program, and define a fixed frequency for all periodic program reports, status, minutes, and other messages. Assign responsibility for all routine, scheduled program communications, delegating the tasks to a willing owner on the program staff, or do it yourself. Investigate technical options for program communications. Make use of the best methods available, and obtain the budget, services, and infrastructure needed to support them.

Do not limit your communication planning to the program level; review the communication plans for project work, and coordinate schedules for items such as status reports to enhance their usefulness, keep them consistent, and minimize the effort needed to sustain them.

Put particular effort into planning communications with your program sponsors, key stakeholders, and governance board. Determine what they require, and devise methods and formats to ensure that you keep them current. Communication of complicated program information to management can be tricky. Plan to use graphics, clear summaries, and follow-up to ensure clear understanding of program status, accomplishments, and challenges.

Formal and Informal Program Communications

Many of the methods listed in Table 5-1 are examples of formal communication, such as reports, structured meetings, presentations, and archived program documents. Others are informal, and for project and program work these ad-hoc communications can be at least as important as formal communication. Potential problems, new risks, and other program information often surface earliest by way of conversations, emails, and other spontaneous interactions. Ongoing program team cohesion and cooperation depends heavily on these interactions.

Successful program leaders invest the time to ensure frequent, unstructured exchanges with and among program contributors. Even on large geographically distributed program teams, where there may be little opportunity to speak with people face-to-face, there will be at least the occasional chance to meet in person. Never pass up opportunities to meet with remote program staff, key stakeholders, or contributors, and challenge yourself to connect with people by telephone in between. On very large teams, schedule time around formal meetings and presentations for questions, networking, and general discussions, taking full advantage of these interactions to build trust and enhance interpersonal relationships.

Do not hesitate to phone geographically remote program contributors, even at times when there may be no urgent business, but strive to do so when it is convenient for them and they are awake, alert, and have time to speak. Many program leaders set aside time on their calendars at least once a week for "managing by wandering around" (MBWA), which can be quite an effective method for enhancing program teamwork and cohesion. While MBWA is best done in person and with no particular objective, you can also make it part of regularly scheduled one-on-one meetings, telephone calls for status collection, or other program discussions. Asking questions about interests, family members, or other nonbusiness matters adds a personal touch and helps build ongoing cooperation, particularly if the conversations are brief and focus on topics of mutual interest.

Informal communications can also be added to program-wide events and communications. When making presentations or conducting monthly teleconference events for the program as a whole, include time for general discussions, inquiries, and news of general interest concerning program team members (births, weddings, awards, or other noteworthy events or extracurricular accomplishments). When you do hold periodic face-to-face program meetings (such as start-up workshops and program reviews), include time for social activities, such as dinners or recreational outings. Get to know your team so you can avoid activities likely to be seen as impositions. Take advantage of chances to reinforce team relationships through events of mutual interest that will enhance relationships and cohesion throughout your program.

Social media technologies also provide excellent opportunities these days for informal program interactions. Judicious use of social media, instant messaging, and other electronic communication can build trust and increase interpersonal connections, but beware of overuse. Excessive or ill-timed messaging can reduce productivity, be annoying, and result in "social not working."

When working with large teams of people, especially teams that are global and may have frequent changes in staffing, effective formal and informal program communications provide a primary foundation for successful program management. Effective program communication is part of overall program information management, and its role in program execution and control will be discussed further in Chapter 6.

PROGRAM STAFF MOTIVATION

Programs are difficult to manage for many reasons, including complexity, size, and scale. They can only succeed when the people working on them care enough about them to contribute, work through the inevitable challenges and difficulties, and retain their motivation. A flawless plan for a perfect program deliverable is of no use without a motivated team of people who will do the work.

For some programs, staff motivation starts and remains high because contributors accept and believe in the importance and priority of the work; they deeply care about the program's vision and goals. This is not true of all program contributors, however. Widely dispersed teams may have only a tenuous connection to the work as a whole. Contract workers may care about little beyond the money involved. On lengthy programs, people may eventually become bored and lose interest. The size and scale of a program can both enhance and inhibit staff motivation. Effective program leaders work throughout a program to maintain engagement and minimize demotivating factors.

Program motivation starts with aligning individual contributors' goals with overall program goals. For programs that are aiming to solve significant problems or create exciting new products, services or offerings that people care deeply about, this might be easy. Some contributors will align their own goals with aspirational program objectives and engage enthusiastically. Others may not personally care much about overall program goals, but there may be aspects of the program that do matter to them, such as opportunities to work with individuals and leaders they admire and respect, or chances to develop new skills or gain experience that will benefit them in the future. Others may see the program as an interesting challenge, or want to get involved with high-priority work for reasons of job security. Ultimately, everyone is most motivated by WIIFM ("What's in it for me?"). Good program leaders spend time to understand what the people important to the program would like to do, and strive to align their program responsibilities with this as much as possible whenever delegating work.

Assigning ownership of program work is also motivating. As program plans take shape, ensure that project leaders and others in key program roles are clearly documented as responsible owners, by name, for all planned program work. Build commitment to program efforts by engaging the owners of program tasks in planning, analyzing, estimating, identifying risks, and determining methods for execution. Incorporate contributor input into overall program plans to reinforce each owner's involvement and secure their buy-in.

You will increase motivation and secure more overall participation by recognizing and using what you and the program have to offer in exchange for reliable commitments to the program. Determine what people care about, and employ what you have available to offer people in return for their contributions to the program. Reciprocal exchanges are the basis for most human interactions, and program management is no exception. Programs are large and generally have a great deal to offer, so offer things that individuals value (and then deliver them) in exchange for the commitments you require.

Establish an environment of respect and fairness across the program. Be quick to praise people and recognize accomplishments publicly, but handle criticism, personal performance problems, and other negative feedback privately. Freely offer recognition and, when appropriate, rewards throughout your program. Devise rewards that will be valued by program teams and individuals, and find opportunities to recognize good performance. Never underestimate the power of intermittent positive reinforcement.

Pause to celebrate success periodically throughout the program. Following project reviews or after significant program milestones, hold an event (or events, for global teams) to gather people to congratulate and thank them. Consider public rewards and tangible recognition, but avoid doing this so often that it becomes expected or ineffective. Favor team rewards over individual rewards, and even if you are unable to recognize everyone at once, endeavor to rotate the attention to all parts of the program team over time. Periodic celebrations and reviews that re-engage program contributors can be a very effective way to "recharge the batteries" for parts of the program team that otherwise might become bored, distracted, or uninterested in long-duration undertakings.

Also work to minimize program behaviors that can demotivate contributors. Be proactive and prompt in dealing with program problems and issues. Particularly with major escalations having significant program impact, focus your efforts on resolving the problems, not in identifying scapegoats or "blamestorming."

As the program progresses, monitor the work for excessive change or ineffective processes that result in needless overhead. Strive to anticipate organizational shifts or other factors that could disrupt program efforts and work to minimize their impact. Streamline meetings and cancel or at least shorten any that add little value to the program. Review the utility of program reports and documents, and revise or eliminate any that are not sufficiently useful to justify their effort. Overall, strive to find and remove ineffective program processes, activities, and effort.

Throughout the program, create an environment of *authenticity* (where people are encouraged to say what they mean) and *integrity* (where people deliver on what they say that they will do), especially among the program leaders. Motivating a large program team is only possible when people believe they can rely on the statements and commitments of others.

PROGRAM STAFFING AND OTHER RESOURCE RISKS

Initiating a new program requires planning for program risk management, as discussed in Chapter 2. Managing program risks starts with identifying potential problems, issues, and uncertainties. Chapter 3 explored identifying risks associated with program scope management. Chapter 4 summarized the overall program risk management process and focused on exposures associated with program planning and workflow. Risks arising from staffing and organizational structure also require scrutiny, and may include the following:

- Uncertain program funding and staffing for future fiscal periods not yet committed
- Essential program work requiring unique or scarce skills, knowledge, or experience
- Expert staff, infrastructure, equipment, or other specific resources shared by multiple projects
- Potential conflicts or issues arising from matrix management
- Insufficient reserve for program funding or staffing
- Inadequate governance or overall support
- Program work delegated to other companies on a contract basis
- Program staff that is dispersed over large distances and multiple time zones
- Potential communication problems related to language, culture, work functions, organization boundaries, or other differences
- Staffing that has been assumed in planning but not yet assigned
- Work involving unprecedented numbers of contributors
- Uncertain program effort or cost estimates
- Significant "learning curve" requirements for developing new skills or working with new equipment or technology
- Program dependencies involving decisions, approvals, or other management actions likely to be delayed
- Potential changes in program sponsorship, interest, or organizational priority

Accumulate program-level risks identified in each stage of your resource and staffing planning, and assess and manage them with the other risks in your program risk register.

KEY IDEAS FOR PROGRAM LEADERSHIP

- Plan for ongoing management of interactions with your governance body, program sponsors, and key stakeholders.
- Confirm program processes, communications requirements, funding, and overall processes.
- Set up program staff and PMO functions for support of program work.
- Clearly define all program roles, responsibilities, and reporting relationships, and store the information where it is available to all program contributors.
- Revise planned program work to minimize potential problems associated with matrix, distributed, and cross-functional teams.
- Maximize your influence through use of influence and effective leadership.
- Communicate frequently, clearly, and using a wide range of methods.
- Identify and manage staffing-related and other risks related to program resources.

CHAPTER 6

Program Execution and Control

In preparing for battle, I have always found that plans are useless but planning is indispensable.
    —Dwight D. Eisenhower

Program management depends on plans, and the earlier chapters of this book have explored several aspects of the overall planning process. Plans are imperfect, and for major programs they tend to be deficient in many ways, because analysis can supply, at best, only a partial picture in the face of complexity. Even if you do an outstanding job of program planning, you will inevitably encounter surprises, problems, and other issues. It is also true, however, that with systematic analysis you will encounter fewer unexpected events than you would with less planning. Lowering the stress, even a little bit, can make a good deal of difference when leading a major program.

In addition, thorough program plans provide a solid foundation for understanding. You will never be able to adequately anticipate everything that a program will encounter, but a robust planning process provides a basis for execution that makes replanning, adjusting, and course correction much easier, faster, and more effective. While your plan will probably never mirror exactly what actually unfolds, a robust planning process builds confidence that the work is possible, prepares you with a deep understanding of the challenges and risks ahead, and arms you with the information you need to navigate the twists and turns ahead.

Program goals tend to shift over time, particularly for long-duration efforts, so maintaining control starts with keeping in alignment with the evolving expectations of your key stakeholders and your governance body. Program control requires measurements that provide data on program work and on how the program is progressing. Measuring program progress, monitoring status, and adjusting program plans are essential to successfully delivering results in each program phase, release, or iteration. Effective program communication and access to up-to-date thorough data are essential throughout a program.

Following each stage of program work, program reviews examine past progress and prepare for future work. As a program proceeds, managing program scope depends on a disciplined, benefits-oriented change control process. Because ensuring that what the program created will deliver value often requires organizational change, program execution must also work to modify business processes and people's behavior to ensure acceptance of program results and overall success. Managing program work requires a good deal of ongoing effort, and there are rarely any dull moments.

SPONSOR AND STAKEHOLDER EXPECTATIONS MANAGEMENT

On large programs, there are many stakeholders. In addition to the considerable challenge of maintaining alignment with expectations that will inevitably diverge (and may not have been in perfect agreement to begin with), you also need to deal with changes as the roles of specific individuals shift, the focus of you program evolves, and the people involved with your program come and go.

Stakeholder Relationships

For obvious reasons, managing the expectations of the most influential and powerful stakeholders tends to be a high priority for most programs. This generally begins with the individuals who initiated the program and those who are part of your governance body. As program work progresses, be disciplined about communicating with key stakeholders. Schedule periodic program update presentations for the people your program depends on, and verify that they continue to be supportive, engaged, and in alignment with other program stakeholders. Establishing governance and sponsor engagement was a key topic in Chapter 2 (on program initiation), and stakeholder involvement in planning was a key topic in both Chapter 3 (on deliverables) and Chapter 5 (on leadership).

As your program progresses, focus attention on communicating with your key stakeholders and listening to what they say when engaged in all of the topics this chapter covers: status reporting, controlling scope, program reviews and planning for future phases, managing organizational changes, and other program execution activities.

Stakeholder Communications

Influential program stakeholders tend to be busy people, so it's vital to provide messages that are clear, short, and unambiguous. Tailor your messages to include a short summary at the start that focuses on what is most important to each individual key stakeholder. When providing formal project information to high-level managers, always carefully reread what you have written before you send it. Review your messages from the perspective of the recipient, and rewrite any parts that could be confusing or misinterpreted. Clarify technical information using graphs, diagrams, and simple descriptions for stakeholders who may not be directly involved with your program. Don't use acronyms, technical jargon, idioms, or any other language that might interfere with understanding, and provide explanations and definitions for any potentially unfamiliar concepts that you must communicate.

Always send program reports or other information you have committed to provide to stakeholders when they are expected, even when you are very busy or have unpleasant news. Whenever things are not progressing as planned, it will not help to hide the situation or delay letting people know. It is best to be honest and open in describing program status, to explain how you plan to deal with any difficulties, and to provide explicit proposals or requests for any actions you need from your stakeholders.

Communicate with key program stakeholders regularly. Focus your conversations on program progress, and take advantage of every chance you have for reinforcing your relationship with each manager, sponsor, customer, or member of your governance body using informal communications.

Stakeholder Expectations

Whenever contemplating program changes, involve key stakeholders in discussions and decisions, and inform all stakeholders of any shifts in your program roadmap, current baseline, or future plans. Involve stakeholders in the discussions of future program scope during program reviews. Manage program issues and escalations as they arise, and inform your key stakeholders of status and progress toward resolution—especially if the resolution could modify the current program baseline or deliverables.

As program work continues, some stakeholder requirements may drift or even change significantly. Whenever stakeholder expectation issues or disagreements arise, deal with the situation as you would handle a stakeholder conflict at program initiation. Listen to all the stakeholders, solicit their requests and preferences, and then endeavor to reach a consensus using a combination of principled negotiation and reliance on the decisions and direction of your governance body and your most influential and powerful stakeholders.

The expectations of all stakeholders matter, but on major, long-duration programs there will inevitably be situations where some stakeholders may need to settle for less than they want, or have to wait longer for results than they would prefer.

New Stakeholder Engagement

Not all stakeholders are involved at the beginning of a program, particularly on lengthy undertakings. As time goes on, some stakeholders are replaced by new people. Other individuals with a stake in the work emerge as the program progresses into new phases or geographies, or evolves in other ways.

Whenever new stakeholders emerge, promptly set up a meeting to introduce yourself. Also introduce new stakeholders to your governance body and processes, program sponsors and managers, and other key stakeholders. Review your vision, roadmap, and overall objectives you are pursuing, and describe the overall value expected from program deliverables. Discuss your program progress to date and the current plans. Provide all new stakeholders with access to your program information archive and copies of program documents and reports you have distributed to other stakeholders.

Explore the needs and interests of the new stakeholders so that you understand what they expect from the program. Answer candidly any questions they ask about your program. Where applicable, describe how your program results and plans align with their needs and expectations.

Also make note of any requirements that new stakeholders have that lie outside of your presently committed program scope. If they are simple additions, work with your new stakeholders to document them and submit them as potential changes, either to be considered for current work (but generally only if they are both very small and involve significant, demonstrable benefits), or for inclusion in scope in future program phases. If any new stakeholder's needs appear to be in conflict with the wishes of existing program stakeholders, begin discussions to resolve the differences. In general, strive to harmonize the perspectives of new stakeholders with the program as a whole, accentuating the areas of alignment and what you intend to deliver with the program as it is currently set up. Strive to gain support for queuing the new stakeholders' desired modifications as potential inclusions in the scoping for future program work. Align new stakeholders' expectations with the overall program goals, involving your governance body, sponsors and managers, and other key stakeholders as necessary.

PROGRAM METRICS

Major programs proceed gradually, phase by phase, over a long arc of time. Control and reporting are always difficult, but defining a set of appropriate measures makes it possible to set realistic goals, assess progress, and motivate efforts toward success. As with projects, most key program metrics are associated with planning and progress reporting.

One key use of program metrics is to test program goals and objectives for feasibility and to detect situations requiring adjustments to scoping, timing, funding, or other program parameters. Without adequate understanding of available resource capacities, credible estimates for the work, and sufficiently defined scoping requirements, program goals are generally little more than wishful thinking. As an example, a few metrics that might be used to evaluate program scale and provide data for negotiating adjustments include the following:

- Program deliverable benefits and value estimates
- Staffing and skills assessments
- System complexity measures
- Number of projects within the program
- Cost and headcount estimates
- Duration estimates for program phases, releases, or iterations
- Project cross-dependencies and interfaces
- Risk impact estimates

A second role for program metrics is evaluating progress. Program tracking depends on metrics to identify delays, cost overruns, and other problems. Overall program control depends on accurate, timely information and a credible baseline of expectations to measure them against.

Metrics are essential to good program decision making. Faced with complicated choices, credible program data can help differentiate options that will serve the program from options that could cause trouble. Metrics provide data that identify underperforming program processes and guide adjustments to fix them. Measurement of work also affects team behavior, so selecting metrics carefully can be an excellent way to motivate and coordinate the efforts of program contributors.

A set of metrics that are well defined, used effectively, and aligned with program objectives will significantly improve your chances of maintaining overall program control, so deciding what you will measure (and how and when) is fundamental to good program management.

Types of Program Metrics

Program metrics may be used to assist in controlling programs. To make this work, you need to use the three following types of metrics, each of which contributes to overall program management:

- **Predictive program metrics:** These measures are derived from planning, and include estimates, forecasts, and other program projections. Predictive metrics are used to validate program assumptions and goals and to provide baselines for program tracking.
- **Diagnostic program metrics:** These are real-time measures of current program status. They are used to detect variances from plans, identify impending risks and issues, solve problems, make decisions, and guide other program actions.
- **Retrospective program metrics:** Post-execution program measures assess the performance of completed processes and often align with corresponding predictive measures. They are useful for improving the accuracy of planning and estimating processes, and provide data for identifying process performance issues, chronic problems, and adverse trends.

Selecting Program Metrics

While all three types can be useful for program control, it is all too easy to define superfluous program metrics that entail a great deal of overhead but yield only intermittent value. Effective program management relies on selecting a compact set of measures that provide useful perspective on program performance and actionable indicators for guiding program efforts to make them more efficient and successful.

While it is theoretically possible to track all project activities at the program level, doing so on a major program entails a great deal of work and generates an avalanche of often impenetrable data. An example of this affected the 1960s space program at NASA, as described in *Angle of Attack* by Mike Gray: "At any one moment, the computer was trying to keep track of some 30,000 separate activities, and a single biweekly report on the spacecraft generated forty boxes of printout. Nobody even had time to glance at it." As you define your system of metrics and consider how you will track program work, use care in deciding what to measure, and ensure that the data will be both useful and used.

Programs are complex, so you need to define at least a few metrics; determining which ones requires judgement, experience, and some patience. At the start of a major program it is generally better to err on the side of collecting slightly more data than you think you might need.

As you proceed, it is usually easier to stop collecting data when you discover they are not beneficial than it is to initiate the collection of new information, especially for the diagnostic metrics that you will collect frequently throughout the program. As program work begins, and during planning for subsequent phases, releases, or iterations, you can assess the utility of the metrics you are collecting and fine-tune your metrics to better monitor and control your program.

Predictive Program Metrics

Many specific predictive metrics for the program as a whole emerge during program initiation, and relate to the topics covered in Chapter 2. You could consider the following measures:

- Total number of program phases (or releases, or iterations)
- Complexity (and overlap) measures for the program roadmap
- Number of discrete program deliverables
- Total number of pending program scope (and change) requests, items in the program burn-down list, or quantity of pending requirements in some other program-level scoping backlog repository
- Overall expected value of program deliverables and benefits
- Program return on investment (ROI): payback, net present value (NPV), internal rate of return (IRR), or other financial projections
- Maximum number of projects executing in parallel
- Overall total program budget
- Size of program management office (PMO) staff
- Number of program contributors
- Portion of program work to be outsourced

- Number of identified program-level risks
- Overall program risk assessment

Predictive metrics for each program phase (or release, or iteration) relate to the program planning topics in Chapters 3, 4, and 5, and might include the following:

- Program deliverable system assessments (system diagram blocks, flowchart densities, component counts, architecture analysis, function or feature points, or other complexity metrics)
- Scoping requests (or changes) included in program phase from scoping backlog
- Maximum number of concurrent projects
- Total number of projects in the program phase
- Project cross-dependencies (defined interfaces) in the program phase
- External project dependencies in the program phase
- Planned program phase duration
- Total program phase schedule exposure (based on worst-case project duration analysis)
- Established program phase schedule reserve
- Program phase budget
- Total cost estimates for the program phase
- Total cost exposure (aggregated worst-case cost estimates)
- Established program phase budget reserve
- Total effort estimates for the program phase
- Number of program contributors (based on full-time equivalents)
- Estimated contributor turnover
- Number of geographically separate sites
- Total number of identified risks for the program phase

Most of these predictive metrics will naturally emerge from project and program planning or from extrapolations of data collected during earlier program phases.

Diagnostic Program Metrics

Because diagnostic metrics relate to current work, they mainly relate to a single program phase (or release, or iteration). Some examples are the following:

- Delayed cross-project interfaces
- Interface closure index (defined below in Table 6-1)
- Cumulative program phase slip (or acceleration)
- Program phase schedule reserve consumed (and remaining)
- Current program-level escalations
- Projects underway
- Current number of program contributors
- Unplanned project effort or cost for the phase
- Cumulative project costs to date for the phase
- Program phase budget reserve consumed (and remaining)
- Cumulative project effort to date for the phase
- Earned value management (EVM) metrics: planned value (PV), actual cost (AC), earned value (EV), and similar measures (for the program phase as a whole)
- Results of deliverable tests, inspections, reviews, and walk-throughs
- Deliverable quality control statistics
- Number of current open program-level issues (including escalations)
- Program-level risks encountered (and avoided) in the program phase
- Current program communication metrics (such as volumes of email, voicemail, and other formal communication)

Diagnostic metrics provide much of the information that you need for assessing program status and creating program reports. Some of these metrics may be easily established and used. Others require more up-front effort and ongoing effort to deploy. The metrics involving EVM may or may not provide a cost-effective way to monitor program work. If the methods underpinning these metrics are mandated (as they may be for many defense or construction programs), they will provide a useful ongoing indicator of progress that can highlight issues with cost, schedule, or both. The overhead associated with these measures at the project level is substantial, though, so it is not always useful to invest in a full implementation of EVM for all the projects composing a program where the methods are not required.

What may be useful, however, is to transplant the EVM tracking concepts from the project level (using activity-cost loaded work breakdown structure) to the program level (focusing on a program phase and its included projects). At the program level you will generally have partitioned your overall budget to cover each of the projects, and will also probably be tracking resource consumption for each project as it runs. Further allocating parts of each project's budget to the work falling between program milestones (or between cross-project interfaces) permits at least a high-level approximation of the basic EVM metrics. This, combined with the collection of key completion dates for project events affecting the program, will enable you to calculate cost variances, schedule variances, and other compound EVM metrics for the program phase as a whole. For major programs, even such an approximation may provide valuable insight into control and execution issues. Such metrics may allow you to spot potential program budget problems much earlier than other tracking methods.

Retrospective Program Metrics

Like predictive program metrics, some retrospective metrics relate to a specific phase and others relate to the program as whole. Here are some retrospective metrics relating to a program phase:

- Unidentified cross-project interfaces discovered during the program phase
- Total program phase slip (or acceleration)
- Number of program-level escalations in the program phase
- Projects completed (categorized as early, on time, or late)
- Program value delivered by program phase
- Number (and magnitude) of scope requests actually delivered in the program phase
- Deliverable scoping dropped during the program phase

- Actual program phase duration (and variance from plans)
- Overall program phase cost (and variance from plans)
- Overall program phase effort (and variance from plans)
- Number of program contributors
- Unplanned program phase overtime
- Staff turnover during the phase
- Program-level issues opened and closed in the phase
- Program-level risks encountered in the program phase
- Program-level risks identified and risks retired during the program phase
- Overall program phase communication metrics (such as volumes of email and voicemail)
- Total number of unanticipated program-level meetings

Here are some retrospective metrics relating to the overall program level that might be useful at program closure:

- Total number of program phases (or releases, or iterations)
- Total number of projects successfully completed
- Number and magnitude of changes made to the program roadmap
- Volume and magnitude of program baseline changes made
- Program deliverables successfully deployed
- Scoping items from the overall backlog delivered
- Overall measured value of benefits from program deliverables
- Actual program ROI: payback, NPV, IRR, or other financial measures
- Total overall program budget (and variance to plans)
- Actual overall program duration (and variance to plans)
- Program staffing statistics (including turnover)
- Costs for program work outsourced

Many retrospective metrics align with predictive metrics and provide a basis for validating the accuracy of the estimates and forecasts made in program planning. They help in identifying both the planning processes that are working well and those that require attention and improvement.

Measurement Definition and Baselines

Predictive metrics are assessed at the start of work (or a phase of work), and are used to establish a baseline. Retrospective metrics are evaluated at the end, and are used to assess results and process performance. However, most of the effort in managing program metrics goes into the diagnostic measures, because they are assessed repeatedly as the work proceeds to provide the data needed for progress reporting.

Diagnostic data are collected from a large number of people on a major program, so defining these metrics well and getting buy-in for their use are crucial to their accuracy and usefulness. Defining each metric clearly helps ensure that each person in a large community of contributors provides consistent information. For each prospective diagnostic metric you plan to use, specify the following:

- Its name and a clear description
- The main purpose of the measure and how it will be used
- How the measurement is to be made and how the data will be collected
- Who will provide the data
- How the data will be verified or audited, if necessary
- The frequency for data collection (most diagnostic metrics are weekly)
- Units of measure to be used, when relevant (such as days, euros, or effort-months)
- Potential issues with collection of accurate data

Additional information may be needed to further clarify some metrics, such as how the metric will be baselined and interpreted or the tools to be used. An example definition for a diagnostic program metric intended to provide early indication of delay is documented in Table 6-1.

Before committing to using a metric, discuss it thoroughly with each program contributor who will be involved. Strive for agreement on the definition, on how the measurements will be collected and used, and on what the data will mean. Obtain willing commitments from all involved in advance to supply accurate data.

241

Table 6-1 Program metric definition: Interface closure index.

Description and purpose	Calculation of progress in fulfilling cross-project dependencies for program reporting.
Calculation	(Number of interfaces completed) / (Total number of interfaces) / (Percent of program phase timeline consumed)
Reported by	Project leaders
Frequency	Weekly
Data	Completed interfaces, current date
Baseline target range	0.95 to 1.1 (higher is better)
Tools used	Program interface table and scheduling tool
Potential barriers	Front-loading the program phase with extra interfaces; prematurely reporting completion of cross-project dependencies

Implementing Metrics

As your set of program metrics takes shape, review it to verify that it will provide what you will need to understand and control your program. Consider the effect of the metrics overall on the behavior of program contributors and overall program cohesion. Determine how you plan to use the metrics positively to identify and solve problems, recognize accomplishments, and reward contributor performance.

Before adopting a set of diagnostic metrics for program control, verify a baseline or expected range for each. For metrics that are already in use, baselines will likely be well established and based on recent history. For metrics that are new, or for existing measures that will be deployed in a different environment, you will need to establish an expected range. The baselines for most diagnostic metrics will relate to corresponding predictive metrics such as the estimates generated in program planning.

"Gaming" Program Metrics

No set of program metrics is foolproof. Most metrics, and in particular project and program metrics, are not difficult to undermine. "Gaming" of metrics, or reporting inaccurate data, happens for a variety of reasons. Minimizing this begins with understanding the reasons why program contributors submit erroneous data:

- Metrics are used for criticism or punishment.
- Measurements may include personally embarrassing or private information that might be reported publicly.
- Reporting of adverse results is discouraged (regardless of facts).
- Metrics are misaligned with systems for rewards and recognition.
- Inaccurate information is tolerated.
- Metrics are poorly defined.

Dealing with these causes starts with clear definition and a commitment to using measurements to solve problems and improve the program overall. If program contributors know that reporting bad news will be valued and generate helpful responses for moving past the current issues, they will do so willingly and promptly. If program teams suspect that they will suffer consequences when things are not going as planned, or that no one really cares, accurate data will be hard to come by. Programs are highly subject to cascade effects, and small problems can quickly develop into big ones, so anything you can do to ensure timely, accurate, and useful information will help keep you out of trouble.

One of the most effective ways to avoid having people game program metrics is easy: ask them not to do it. When people agree to provide accurate information, they will generally follow through. You can also help ensure a steady flow of useful data by always thanking program contributors for their status updates, even in cases where the information they provide is far from what you were hoping for.

PROGRAM STATUS TRACKING

Monitoring program status is a program staff (or PMO) responsibility for most programs. The primary focus of this should be on tracking cross-project interfaces, managing issues escalations, and monitoring program risks.

Program Status Collection

On major programs, there may be so much potential status information at any one time that reviewing and trying to understand it all may be nearly impossible. Monitoring just the most critical data may be a daunting task. Most program tracking is centralized in the hands of an individual or team or people at the program level who are responsible for managing program plans. Especially if some project teams are geographically remote, using email or an online tracking application can be effective in assembling substantial amounts of status information. The frequency for collecting program status will generally be weekly, but depending on the program and the projects in it, even shorter cycles may be required. Repercussions of program issues can propagate quickly, so most programs evaluate overall status at least weekly.

When collecting program status data, do your best to make the process as simple as possible. If using email to survey progress, consider distributing a short survey containing a line for each input you need from specific contributors, and customize it to request data for just the current, overdue, and immediately upcoming events. The more complicated you make the process, the less successful you will be in quickly obtaining the program data you need.

The main focus of each status cycle relates to the program milestones and cross-project interfaces. Based on the overall plans and interface tracking tables, each project in the program should have only a modest number of interconnections to other projects and deliverables due to the program staff. Automating a collection system or creating an extract (using a small table or spreadsheet) is an effective way to gather pertinent data from project teams while keeping the process as straightforward as possible. By keeping the focus on tracking interfaces, you will limit the overhead required but still be able to keep the overall program's progress visible. For each current interface or milestone, collect information such as completion dates, revised completion dates, cost or other resource variances, and any known issues that could affect the program.

Whatever method you employ for collecting the hard data (metrics, facts, and figures), also provide space for people to include additional soft data (early warnings of trouble, current challenges, staffing productivity or other resource issues, upcoming risks, rumors, and other anecdotal information).

Plan to follow up on any status that seems incomplete, inconsistent with earlier or other project status, or otherwise erroneous. To learn more about what is happening, also follow up on any of the anecdotal information that could cause larger program problems.

Once you have assembled status data from all current projects, analyze the data to identify any variances from the program's current phase baseline. Identify all significant differences, and remember that even small adverse discrepancies can be harbingers of bigger problems or lead to unintended consequences that could derail your program.

Program timing problems tend to be both the most common and most damaging, so consider corrective program actions to minimize them. For slippage that you cannot remedy, determine the amount of delay to other work and identify the program consequences. Initiate issue tracking for each significant situation you discover.

Also identify any reported project resource variances. You may be able to use program-level resources to address project staffing, funding, or other kinds of shortfalls, but consider the level of program reserve available and what you have already used. If you see a trend due to systematic underestimation or you have nearly exhausted your program reserves, document this as a program issue. Identify any additional issues or variances as you review your overall status, especially issues that relate to program deliverables and committed scoping.

Track all significant status variances as program issues, and plan to escalate situations where you will need external help. If an issue appears to require unavoidable changes to the overall scope, timing, or budget of the program's baseline, document the proposed changes and initiate the process for considering them. Managing program baseline changes is discussed later in this chapter.

Program Issues and Escalations

As discussed in Chapter 4, program problem and issue management does not differ much from project issue management. However, it focuses on significant situations that affect the program as a whole, not on every issue that arises in every project.

Most program issues become evident either during routine program status collection or through escalation to the program level of issues that originate in one of the projects. Threshold criteria for initiating program issues include significant (or likely) schedule slippage, budget overruns, staffing issues, deliverable complications, and stakeholder problems.

Program issues require prompt, effective attention to prevent them from growing more serious or even threatening the entire program. Many project-level issues escalated to the program level can be resolved using program-level staff or resources, and it is always best to deal with program issues within the program whenever possible.

Program issue management uses a table, database, or other list to track issue descriptions, named owners, target resolution dates, status, and other relevant data for each issue. Issues require attention at the program staff level at least weekly, and issue review is generally a recurring agenda item at the regular program staff meeting. If issues can be resolved at the program level, do so promptly.

Resolving some program issues will require actions exceeding the authority available within the program. After you have (quickly) exhausted all of your options for dealing with an intractable program issue and determine that you need to seek higher-level assistance, plan to escalate without delay.

Escalation of problems to higher-level managers, your governance body, or influential stakeholders should occur rarely for most programs, and should be used as a last resort following robust efforts for resolution. Escalating issues too frequently will erode management's confidence in your abilities and will annoy the people you report to, but when facing issues representing severe program consequences that you cannot resolve locally, do not delay. Use your process to communicate your situation to those who will need to participate promptly. Include a summary of the situation, any previous attempts at resolution, any suggestions you have developed for response, a target time for closure, and the names of individuals you believe would be able to act. Also describe the consequences to the program should the problem persist.

If an acceptable proposed resolution is consistent with the program phase as it is currently defined, strive to implement it with the assistance of the high-level individual or team you have escalated the problem to. In any case, work closely with those involved in addressing the problem. Should an issue require actions that would modify the program, use your program change management processes to guide your response.

After determining how to resolve an escalated issue and taking action, track the results to ensure that the problem has been taken care of and that there are no significant unintended consequences. If further actions appear necessary, continue working to solve the problem. Monitor the situation until the escalated issue has been fully resolved.

It is not uncommon for program escalation actions to upset contributors or stakeholders. Turning over key program decisions to people outside the program team may take the work in a different direction from what program contributors would prefer. If necessary, strive to rebuild relationships, trust, and overall program cohesion following an escalation.

Program Risk Management

Major programs entail a great deal of risk, much of which only surfaces as the work proceeds. Because of this, it is prudent to reassess program risk on a regular basis. How often this is needed will vary with the program, but it is a common to update the status of the program risk register either monthly or quarterly. Every day on a program you will see and learn new things, and impending risks that were not apparent earlier will emerge.

Reviewing risks begins with scanning the current risks and plans to see if any assessments or planned responses require updating. Some risks listed may no longer be relevant, because either they will have occurred or they relate to work that is now completed. New risks related to program changes or recently identified must be added to the risk register and evaluated. After updating the entries, you can sort the risk list and then devise or validate your risk responses for the highest priority program risks.

An effective and robust risk management update process was an important factor in the success of the Hewlett-Packard COMPASS program. From the start, the program's risk management process was well defined and documented. The program held a monthly program risk review meeting involving the program staff (with additional key contributors as needed), typically eight to twelve participants who participated via teleconference. Twice each year the risk meeting was held as a part of face-to-face planning summits, where a larger group of at least twenty people participated in identifying and reviewing exposures related to the next phases of the program. The focus of each risk planning meeting was a detailed update of the program risk register. Risks that were no longer of concern were retired, and new risks were added based on evolving program plans and external changes. During each meeting we reprioritized the listed program risks, and then for key risks we reviewed or established risk responses and contingency plans for recovery.

Significant new complex risks often required more attention beyond what could be completed during the meeting. For these, risk response planning was initiated and then delegated to a risk owner responsible for fleshing out an adequate strategy. The risk register was revised after each monthly meeting and distributed to the program staff and all the project leaders. Updated and past versions of the risk register were also available on the program's web-based knowledge management system to all contributors. Many problems were avoided by methodically considering program risks and keeping them visible. The process contributed substantially to keeping the program on track.

PROGRAM REPORTING AND INFORMATION MANAGEMENT

All projects and programs require effective information management. This includes both the information that you provide to program contributors and the information you store for their use. Maintaining control of significant programs requires disciplined focus on managing information, because both too little and too much information can cause problems and impede progress.

Ongoing Program Communications

As discussed in Chapter 5, program communications are a significant part of program leadership and staff management. Poor communication in a complex program environment is a formula for disaster. Effective program communication involves both planned formal interactions and frequent, more casual informal exchanges. With the amount of information that a typical program entails, it is certainly possible to overdo communication, but program problems are more commonly a result of communicating too little.

There are many types of formal program communications, including the following:

- Reports and email
- Status collection
- Meeting minutes
- Website updates
- Training and presentations
- Scheduled meetings

Good program management depends on scheduling these interactions, meetings, and messages appropriately, and setting them up so that expectations, formats, and the information conveyed are both understandable and useful.

A very large construction program in San Francisco provides a good example of the growing connection between good program practices and agile methods. While productivity in many fields has improved remarkably in recent years, in construction work it has lagged. In response to this, the program team members responsible for this construction effort have adopted a number of lean/agile practices for their work, many based on Toyota Production System methods. Applying these methods to construction programs promises to yield superior cost management, productivity, and results. This construction effort has adopted a strategy of integrated delivery, where all of the categories of contributors—architects, engineers, tradespeople, and others—are involved for the entire effort, not just for a short portion of the overall timeline, as would be more traditional. In addition, all functions are co-located at one site adjacent to the construction, enhancing communication and overall team cohesion. Daily stand-up meetings for sharing status keep everyone abreast of progress, issues, and upcoming work, and have prevented numerous situations from developing into serious problems. Also, the program teams spend considerable time in a large, communal meeting space dedicated to the program. The "Big Room" has the overall timeline for the construction program laid out around the room's perimeter, showing all the key program milestones and events. The walls beneath the timeline are used for posting documents, diagrams, and status information for easy access and to keep all involved and up to date.

Chapter 5 discussed some considerations for establishing and planning for formal communications. As a program runs, it may be appropriate to modify the schedules or specifics of formal communications, but uninterrupted regular communications on an established schedule are the minimum needed to keep contributors engaged and on track. Some program leaders are tempted in times of stress or crisis to skip routine communications, but this is dangerous. While focusing on recovery or escalation is necessary at times, maintaining normal communications must remain a high priority. Missing status cycles or standard reporting sends a message that it is unimportant, and may result in contributors using your behavior as an excuse to ignore their communication responsibilities. Even worse, when you focus on one aspect of a program, you pay less attention to others. While concentrating on resolving difficulties for part of the work, you may miss new problems arising elsewhere that could cascade into much deeper trouble.

Treat formal communications as a contract with your program teams, and strive to hold up your end so that others will do so too. What you don't know about your program will nearly always hurt you.

Informal communications are generally not planned, but are also crucial to effective understanding of complex program work. They include the following:

- Face-to-face conversations and informal phone calls
- General networking and interactions
- Social media and instant messaging
- Management by wandering around (MBWA)

Informal communications are the basis for interpersonal relationships, trust, and teamwork. Additionally, casual interactions are often the best early warning system you have, because it is very common to learn of an impending problem or a new issue during a conversation long before it would have surfaced as part of a formal status report. Informal communications can be overdone, however, so be aware of what people are comfortable with and minimize interruptions that could interfere with productivity and program progress.

Good program management uses many types and modes of both formal and informal communication, at whatever frequency best serves the work.

A Program Communications Example

On the COMPASS program at Hewlett-Packard we invested a good deal of effort in program communications throughout the work. In addition to informal communications among the program staff and between the staff and contributors, significant effort went into formal communications. This included monthly program-wide broadcast events, several weekly status bulletins, periodic special reports, training, websites, and other program communications.

"All-Hands" Monthly Conference Calls

With roughly 200 program contributors from various functions located around the world, it was not possible to hold regularly scheduled, in-person meetings that included everybody. To make up for this, we scheduled "virtual" program team meetings via teleconference. These meetings were well attended and helped to keep the program work synchronized. For the convenience of the global program team, we scheduled each "All-Hands" teleconference twice, once early in the morning California time and another about 10 hours later the same day. Members of the program leadership team (typically two or three people) summarized the status of current waves and plans for future work during these 2-hour phone conferences. Each month 100 or more contributors participated in these calls. The presentation materials discussed on the calls were distributed in advance and were also available on the program knowledge management information archive. Current materials were stored online with previous All-Hands materials for future reference and for review by contributors new to the program. Each COMPASS All-Hands meeting started with a one-way broadcast focused on program status and news, but ample time was reserved at the end for questions from the participants and open discussion.

Program Reports

Weekly meetings (such as the program staff meeting and other cross-functional meetings) always produced meeting minutes that were emailed to appropriate distribution lists and posted to our knowledge management system. In addition, the release managers published and emailed a weekly status report for each wave in progress that provided the definitive source for up-to-date information concerning each release. Monthly risk reviews, periodic scoping change reports, and other program-level documents were similarly distributed and archived.

Program Training

One early program focus was on establishing high-level training for program contributors and future end users to ensure a sufficiently thorough understanding of the intended COMPASS solution. This was needed to identify gaps in the solution and any significant issues that would need to be addressed in the scheduled release waves. The training included orientation to the modules of the commercial SAP application modules involved, as well as specific COMPASS functions. The initial training was delivered by the central program team for each region, but training responsibilities were soon delegated to experienced business team members in the regions as the work progressed.

There were also dedicated training teams that developed much more detailed and practical end-user training for each wave. Training was delivered near to each release date for new users in the countries involved, with assistance from other trainers worldwide. For each wave, the functional training team also summarized all new program functionality that was being deployed and provided the details to previously installed users in their quarterly training bulletins.

Training for the technical development team included both overall training for new program contributors (including a high-level version called "COMPASS for Dummies") and quarterly knowledge transfer sessions for support team members.

In addition, each functional team in the program conducted both overall introductory training and ongoing updates for their specific portions of the program as the system evolved over the life of the program.

Program Website

We also maintained a comprehensive program website in addition to the detailed program knowledge management archive that supported the program staff and contributors. The general site provided a high-level summary of program status and upcoming objectives for people working on the program or outside of it. It provided "headline" versions of overall progress and contained links that pointed to more detailed and specialized information stored elsewhere online. The high-level external orientation of the website served as a good source of overall information, and was used by both casual users and people involved with program governance. Keeping it up to date was a good investment, because it allowed most people to quickly find answers to their questions without undue delay or disruption of program staff.

Program Management Information Systems

As outlined in Chapter 4, a well-organized program management information system is a significant asset for complex programs. As your work proceeds, monitor the questions and sources of confusion that arise, and consider structural changes to your information archive that might aid in avoiding them in the future.

Organize program information to make access easy and logical for the program contributors, even if perhaps the format and structure might not be ideal for your personal needs. There are more program contributors than leaders, and if the people doing most of the work are unable to quickly locate the information they need, they will either do without it (and probably make mistakes) or have to request it from someone on the program team (which is both time-consuming and inefficient).

Setting up the archive for program information to best serve a given program may not be simple, but if you pay attention and make adjustments to improve it as you proceed, managing complex programs will become a good deal less difficult.

A Program Information System Example

The COMPASS program established a program management information system that proved very useful and effective. The program's information system was online in a knowledge management system that provided program contributors worldwide with around-the-clock access. We provided all program contributors with "write" access to all areas of the main workspace, and anyone could read and update program information whenever they wished. Version control automatically archived all earlier versions of program files that were updated, and retained them so they could be referenced as historic project records or recovered whenever it proved to be necessary. The only overall restriction we set up for the knowledge management system was that we disabled "delete" access for most users to prevent inadvertent data loss.

We defined the structure of the file space to reflect the overall program structure. There were areas that contained overall program and release-specific information and areas that were set up to house information particular to the functional and regional teams staffing the program. The goal of this organization was to ensure that information would be stored where people would be most likely to look for it so that they would need little assistance in finding what they needed.

One exception to the principle allowing anyone to update anything in the repository was the program plan of record (POR). This was a high-level document that we established in a partitioned workspace where everyone could read it, but only a small number of people on the program staff could update it. The POR tracked a summary of the scope for all past and planned future wave releases, and we kept it synchronized with all program scope decisions. The POR provided a thorough summary of both the program's overall achievements and its planned deliverables.

The main partition of the program management information system contained information organized into areas for overall program information, program function details, change requests and status, process documentation, and program retrospective analyses.

Overall Program Information

We maintained general program-level information in a number of folders set up for program plans, information specific to each release wave, program staff information, and other matters of interest to all program contributors. These folders served as the central program management information system archive for the COMPASS program.

Program Function Details

In addition to the general program folders, we also established sections in the knowledge management system to be used by each of the functional and regional teams. This team-specific information was centrally maintained and available to everybody, using broad guidelines for structure to aid in navigating the information. While each team maintained its functional plans and status information independently, because this information was all in one place and consistent we could easily assemble weekly program progress reports directly from each team's data. This was not the ideal structure for the program management staff, but it simplified access for the far more numerous project-level contributors and encouraged centralized storage of the information. Some functional teams established elaborate substructures in the program management information system. For example, the testing team set up a system that relied on detailed information posted by participants during each release wave's testing to support largely automated status reporting.

Change Requests and Status

Change requests came from many sources, but all program change requests were listed, stored (after verifying their contents), and organized in one place. We used a single online list within the knowledge management system to track all submissions, many hundreds over the course of the program. The list contained the names of individuals who were responsible for the changes, status information (including the release wave containing each change that made it into scope), links that pointed at the change request documents for each proposed change, and other information. The list could be sorted, filtered, exported, and printed by any contributor. We used the list to support the complex wave-by-wave prioritizing, analysis, and scoping decisions throughout the program.

Process Documentation

We also centrally maintained all key program process descriptions in the knowledge management system. Whenever we determined the need to change a process, we thoroughly discussed it with all the affected teams and individuals, worked with key stakeholders to improve it, documented the revised process, communicated the change, and promptly updated the on-line process descriptions.

Program Retrospective Analyses

At the end of every release wave (and sometimes within a wave following resolution of particularly bumpy issues), we conducted a "lessons learned" analysis by soliciting written feedback from all program contributors. We distributed a form with a number of high-level categories (Program Management, Program Organization, Communications, Tools and Deliverables, and Other Areas for Improvement) to contributors for documenting feedback, and then held teleconference meetings to refine, augment, and prioritize this information. We "mind-mapped" the inputs into categories and worked to determine principal root causes. We used the analysis to prioritize the results and developed proposals for presentation to the program staff. For each release wave, we committed, in advance, to take action on the top three opportunities for improvement and then tracked progress on each of them. We also archived all the retrospective survey information for later reference and to help in identifying longer-term trends.

CONTROLLING PROGRAM SCOPE

Managing program scoping is one of the most challenging aspects of major programs. As discussed on Chapter 3, one approach that makes it more straightforward is to adopt a two-level process that makes defining scope for a phase or release as a whole an open process that focuses on the big picture, but tightly controls scope within the phase. Adopting this sort of scoping process can make a program manager's job easier and programs more successful.

Multiphase programs can benefit greatly by leveraging the methods of agile management. Although the sizes of the "time boxes" are generally longer, programs generally proceed by doing detailed scoping for the immediately upcoming set of projects in the overall roadmap, defining only general high-level requirements for subsequent program deliverables. Similar to agile management methods such as Scrum, the scoping within a phase or release is changed only infrequently, to enable the plans to successfully deliver the next increment of value predictably and on time.

An effective scoping process uses stakeholder inputs, guidance from the governance body, and other inputs to determine scope for the next program phase or release on a frequency that makes sense for the overall program and in line with the roadmap. The primary goal of program scope management is to define a set of requirements that maximizes utility and value for the program stakeholders.

Once the scope for the next phase, release, or iteration of the program is established, scope management focus shifts to a process that restricts further changes so the projects can be defined, planned, and managed to deliver the committed scope on a reliable schedule. The primary objective of a program change management process is to review all proposed changes and defer all but the most urgent and unambiguously high-value proposals to a queue or backlog containing all the items to be considered for future program work. An effective change management process does not give even the most worthy changes a free ride. For every change that is accepted, some lower-priority requirements must be dropped and bounced back to the queue for later reconsideration. An effective program change management process operates as a zero-sum game—for any change that adds to scope, some aspect of the current scope will be dropped to make room for it. Scrupulously limiting scope protects the overall program phase baseline.

The process flowchart in Figure 6-1 is fairly typical for program scope and change management, and is based on the process used to manage overall program scope and wave release changes for the COMPASS program described earlier. The phase-defining scoping portion of the process is on the left side of the figure, with the tighter scope-controlling, change part of the process on the right.

Program Scoping

Program scoping starts as part of program initiation. For programs that deliver results in phases, releases, or iterations, the overall exercise is repeated periodically to begin each new cycle. Inputs to the program scoping process can originate from a variety of sources. Some come from outside the program, and may originate with organizational requirements, related programs, external standards, or changes to technologies, applications, or equipment used for program work. Requirements also arise within the program from decisions regarding how to structure the work and prioritize the timing of program deliverables.

Program scope management establishes a clearly documented program POR, tracking completed deliverables, deliverables under development, and commitments for future deliverables. Setting the POR for each program phase begins with a review of the overall backlog of scoping items. All proposed requirements, regardless of source, should be documented in a format consistent with the program change request form. Change request

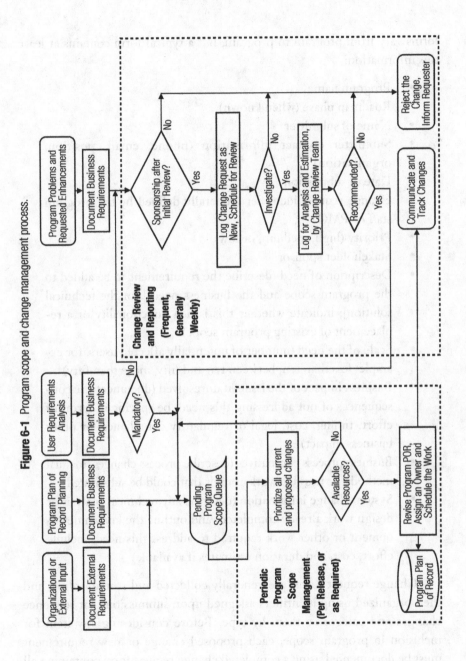

Figure 6-1 Program scope and change management process.

forms vary from program to program, but a typical form contains at least this information:

- Program name
- Roadmap phase (when known)
- Name of submitter
- Submitter contact information (phone, email, position, organization)
- Date of submission
- Change request identifier (generally defined by the program staff or PMO)
- Priority (high, medium, or low)
- Stakeholder sponsor
- Description of need (describe the requirement to be added to the program scope and the business need [not the technical solution]; indicate whether this is new functionality or a replacement of existing program scope)
- Scale of the need (number of potentially affected users, for example: less than ten, between ten and fifty, more than fifty)
- Business impact of the issue, if unresolved (document the consequences of not addressing this need; be specific in terms of effort, timing, cost, legal or regulatory compliance, or other business impact)
- Business process alternatives (describe process changes, manual methods, or possible workarounds that could be substituted)
- System change information (describe any technical analysis or design work already completed, and outline the known development or other work required to address this need; include effort, cost, and duration estimates if available)

Change request forms are generally collected and stored online, and then organized using identifiers assigned upon submission that sequence changes and categorize them by type. Before considering any item for inclusion in program scope, each proposed change or new requirement must be documented using a completed change request form containing all needed information. Each request also requires a credible analysis of the required effort and a description of the expected impact on the program and on other work.

Program scoping cycles vary and are synchronized with releases—quarterly, monthly, or on whatever cycle works best for the program. In emergencies, program POR and scope updates may be escalated and scheduled at any time.

Routine scoping decisions are the responsibility of the program manager and staff, along with other contributors who may participate by invitation. Escalated POR changes may require additional approval by additional levels of management.

Prior to setting the POR for an upcoming release, new phase, or iteration, review all pending change requests and other submitted requirements for consistency and completeness. Any change requests missing information or having any outstanding issues will be excluded from consideration in the current cycle.

The POR begins with a review of the current scope. All work, both ongoing current efforts and proposed new work included in the program scoping queue, is prioritized (by consensus of the program staff and key stakeholders) based on business value and urgency. All new potential scoping items must be either assessed as mandatory or be recommended by the program staff. Each item listed for consideration is prioritized by the program staff and invited stakeholders using an iterative process.

Status indicators are assigned to each request to establish the relative priority for each scope item under consideration. The ranking process is iterative, using data collected from the participants to sort the items according to priority. The initial ordering begins with individual inputs indicating which items are most important. (Using status indicators of "In," In?" "Likely," "Maybe," "Maybe?" "Not yet," and "Out" facilitate the tracking of status and provide an easy way to sort the list.) Over the course of discussions and several meetings, a general (though rarely universal) consensus for rank ordering will emerge.

Begin defining the program plan of record by determining the overall staffing capacity available for the phase, release, or iteration. Set a limit based on current committed staffing, historical productivity information, contributor plans, and other program data. Plan to establish a cutoff for program scoping that leaves at least a small amount of slack for dealing with problems, underestimates of effort, and contingency (10 percent is typical). Set scoping for your program phase by listing the highest priority program components in your POR and deducting the corresponding effort and staff required from your program resource capacity. As you add items to the POR, your remaining uncommitted staffing decreases. The scoping process concludes when you reach your established resource limit. Before closing the process, review the POR to verify that the scoping is coherent and that it includes all related items needed to deliver credible benefits and value. Also assess specific skills needed for the work and adjust if needed to align with any unique expertise you depend on, or scarce or shared staffing that you may have problems securing. Compare the lowest priority items that made it into the POR with the highest priority items that did not. There may be opportunities to increase the value you can deliver by accepting several small items that failed to make the cut in place of one or more larger ones that did.

All scoping items that are not included in the program POR will remain on the scoping queue for reconsideration in a future program cycle. In rare cases it may be possible to expand the POR to include a deferred requirement if a requestor offers to provide sufficient incremental resources to adequately staff and fund the work. Accepting additional items into the POR on this basis should always be entirely at the discretion of the program staff.

Make final adjustments and secure the support for the overall POR from your program stakeholders, governance body, and management. Formally set the program phase POR by documenting it for distribution and storage in your program information system. Update the status of all change requests that are now part of a program phase POR. Also communicate all changes that will have consequences for other programs (both the items in the POR and any that were anticipated but were not included) to the leaders of those programs.

Program Change Review Process

Once the program POR is documented, managing further changes shifts to the much more limiting program change review process. All program change requests, regardless of source, must be documented using a change request form. As with any scope input proposal, the program staff members responsible for managing the queue of pending requests review each form for completeness and clarity. The ongoing change review process is managed by a program change team. Permanent members of the change team are the program leader and a change team facilitator, with other members of the program staff and additional stakeholders invited to participate as needed. The change team meets regularly (generally weekly) to review and consider urgent changes.

Each change submitted that proposes to modify the current program phase POR must be initially reviewed by the change team facilitator. To be considered as a change to current program work, each submitted change must include compelling details describing the specifics of the change, a description of relevant alternatives or workarounds, and the business impact (in effort, cost, timing, or other consequences) of not making the change. If the business impact or other required information is incomplete or not credible, the change team facilitator returns the change request form to the submitter for update before further consideration.

While all complete change requests submitted are listed in the program scoping queue, the change team reviews only those recommended for immediate attention by the change team facilitator. All change requests requesting prompt attention must also originate from an appropriate stakeholder. For example, a change affecting a specific development team requires sponsorship by the individual project leader (or other management) responsible for that team. Each vetted change request begins its review by being categorized as discretionary (an enhancement, a response to an issue or problem having a workaround, or other non-mandatory shift) or nondiscretionary (solving a serious problem, related to a significant program issue, based on a legal or standards requirement, or necessitated by other program mandates).

Once all needed change request information is complete, the change team facilitator schedules it for consideration at the next change team meeting. The facilitator distributes the meeting agenda and all new change requests to the team before each meeting. Depending on the changes to be discussed, additional attendees might be invited to specific change team meetings. Additional attendees who can add value or needed perspective may be invited by any change team member.

Change team meetings are short, a maximum of 30 minutes, and generally include remote participants via teleconferencing. Meetings should generally be scheduled on the same day and at the same time each week to ensure staff participation.

During the change team meeting, all new change requests must be presented by the requestor, with additional support from others as needed. Based on the change request presentation and discussion, the change team decides whether or not a new change warrants further investigation. If not, the change request is deferred to the program scoping queue for later reconsideration (or, in some cases, might be permanently rejected). The change team facilitator updates the change request status to reflect the decision, updates the change request list, and communicates the decision to the original requester and others involved.

If the change team does approve further investigation, it assigns an owner to analyze and verify the work estimates. The owner is responsible for producing a high-level resource plan and an implementation scenario (training required, process updates, related changes, and other consequences), and for documenting the implications of implementing the change. Each change request approved for further consideration is assigned the status "Analysis" on the program scoping queue.

Once the high-level investigation is complete, a presentation of the results is scheduled for the next change team meeting. The team decides whether enough investigation has been done to make a decision. In cases with insufficient data, change requests are returned to the owner with explicit guidance for any additional required information. If the information available is adequate to support a decision, the change may be recommended or deferred. In either case, the change request and log is updated by the change team facilitator and the original requester notified.

If the change request is recommended, the status on the program scope list changes to "Pending," and it may be considered for scheduling and staffing. Except in extraordinary cases, development effort can only begin on changes following explicit approval by the program leader and overall program management. In rare cases where immediate scope revisions are approved, the current program POR is updated to include the approved change. Such changes to program scope are generally accompanied by dropping some scoping item or items (based on the prioritization used to set the POR) to ensure adequate staffing and other resources needed to complete the approved scoping change.

In most situations, rejected or deferred change requests remain on the program scope queue for later analysis. In unusual circumstances, some requests may be escalated to the next level of management for more immediate reconsideration.

Program Scope Control

Managing the multilevel scoping hierarchy for a complex system deliverable can be a big challenge. A disciplined process can help, but it works well only when all decisions are based on credible assessments of value and realistic estimates for the anticipated effort involved. Formal processes for managing program scope that require detailed tracking and in-depth analysis may appear to entail excessive overhead. Trying to save time by using a more casual scope management process is almost always a false economy. On major programs, the cost of inadequate scope control can soar due to unintended consequences from poorly informed decisions, rework necessitated by inadequate specifications, and frequent failure to meet stakeholder expectations.

Effective program control also requires that most scope decisions made by the program team are final. A process that depends on data (especially credible financial and effort estimates) and avoids decisions driven by emotion or politics provides a foundation for program management that delivers reliable, valuable results. It is particularly important to establish analysis-based criteria for scope change decisions that allow you to generally say no (or at least "not yet") to requested additions and changes. The default disposition for any program change should always be "reject" (or at least "defer"), forcing all changes that are approved to earn their way into program scope by showing credible evidence that what the change is worth exceeds what it costs. Too many programs are derailed by unrealistic scoping expectations—often because of late adjustments to scope that are based more on wishful thinking than good analysis.

"Less Is More"

One counterintuitive aspect of using this process on the Hewlett-Packard COMPASS program was that we discovered we could actually deliver more functionality in a given wave release by putting fewer items into scope in the first place. In early cycles, we sized the scope for each wave based on what we believed was realistic analysis. Over the course of several release cycles, however, we learned that even credible-looking analysis tended to exceed what we could actually deliver, and being overly optimistic with scoping actually resulted in delivering *less* functionality. Unless the work for a given requirement successfully passed regression testing prior to release, we had to drop it. Any requirement with deficiencies, however minor, was excluded from the wave, some just prior to the release window. We learned that we actually were able to deliver more by scheduling less—the effort that was expended working on requirements that were ultimately dropped could be used to ensure that higher priority needs would make it into the release. Figure 6-2 is a graph of a few of the program's waves, showing the fall-off prior to the wave releases.

Figure 6-2 Program scope data for the compass program.

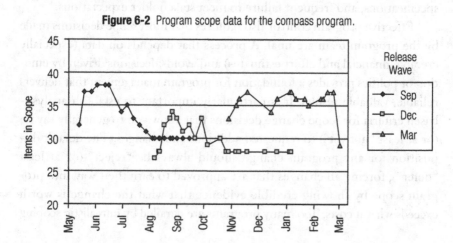

The lesson we took from the data over several successive deployment waves was that being overly aggressive, hoping to accomplish more, was significantly slowing progress. By capping the content of each wave based on more realistic assessments, we were able to deliver nearly all the scope specified for each wave, avoiding the roughly 20 percent fallout we had been seeing. Establishing scope based on history and credible analysis also avoided the overhead of putting items in the plan, then removing them, and then having to return them to the plan for a later wave.

Overall, having an open but fact-driven scoping basis for each wave, coupled with a strict policy limiting changes, substantially improved both productivity and progress. We applied a scope freeze policy for each wave 5 months before each release, based on the scope management portion of our scoping process.

Once the scoping baseline was set, the change review process was used to manage further scope modifications, but with a strict "zero sum" policy for additions that required removal of something comparable in scale for every change that was approved. We ultimately found that we could further improve program predictability and increase customer satisfaction by initiating a strict "scope lock" on each wave at 4 months prior to release, permitting no further additions to scope under any circumstances. This proved to be acceptable because the waves were only 3 months apart, and for the most part it was better to be confident that a requirement could "catch the next train" rather than hoping to be on an earlier release but with a substantial chance of being dropped.

By establishing a clear process and putting teeth into the checkpoints, we saw scoping-related problems on the program drop significantly.

PROGRAM REVIEW

Programs with long durations—especially those exceeding a year—require periodic in-depth reviews. Program reviews revisit most of the information considered during initiation: stakeholder expectations, program roadmaps, assumptions, plans, constraints, budgets, risks, and other program aspects.

Plan the Program Review

Programs vary in how far ahead they are able to plan with any accuracy or precision. For some programs the planning horizon may be very short, because of uncertainties and frequent changes. Such programs tend to adopt more agile, iterative methods and conduct overall reviews approximately monthly. For programs where there is greater stability, reviews might be conducted quarterly or even semiannually. The frequency of program reviews should roughly correspond to the overall program planning horizon, but no program should go longer than about 6 months without revisiting the overall plans.

Program reviews often coincide with significant events:

- Following a major release, program milestone, or checkpoint
- At the end of a fiscal quarter or other important organization date
- After revisions to the program roadmap or baseline
- When adding or releasing program staff
- At a business reorganization

Program reviews, like program startup workshops, work best when you can meet face to face for sufficient time to thoroughly assess the program. Although reviewing plans is the primary reason for a program review, there also are other purposes. The review provides a good opportunity to examine what you have accomplished and make adjustments to any processes or methods that are not working as well as you expect. A program review is also a great opportunity for program contributors who work at different sites to get together; this reinforces team cohesion, relationships, and trust. Reviews are an excellent time to focus on public recognition for significant accomplishments and rewards for the teams that deserve them. Moreover, reviews generate current data for portfolio planning, budgeting, and other organizational needs.

Set up a program review schedule well in advance, and work with your program governance body to get approval, funding, and support for the meetings. Establish expectations that you will be conducting program reviews on a regular basis, with key program staff attending in person, and lasting as long as needed to revalidate program plans and achieve the other goals of a review. Program reviews vary in length, but even for agile programs holding frequent reviews they can take a full day, and major, global programs may benefit from several days.

Define a review process that addresses what you need to cover, such as the following:

- Revisiting overall program vision, objectives, and priorities
- Assessing changes in stakeholder needs, roles, and expectations
- Updating the next steps in the program roadmap
- Revalidating program constraints and assumptions
- Reassessing risk and updating the program risk register
- Revising program schedules, budgets, and staffing
- Assessing program processes and planning needed improvements
- Reinforcing teamwork, relationships, trust, and motivation
- Recognizing significant accomplishments

Conduct the Program Review

Focus a program review on what you will do next, and how you will do it. You learn something new about your program every day, so what you know about it during a review differs significantly from your understanding at its startup or at your last review. Discuss new information and potential changes. Examine recent problems and consider process adjustments to avoid similar future situations. Make any needed changes that the participants of the review are empowered to implement, and capture all proposals and action items for other changes discussed in the review in writing. Add items requiring follow-up to your program issue log, and develop plans for gaining approvals needed to improve your processes and put needed changes into effect.

During the review, focus on scoping and plans for future work. Question assumptions, revise estimates, and update any provisional plans for the upcoming phase of program efforts using what you know now. As you consider the program as a whole, check the plans at each hierarchical level for clarity and validate the coherence of planning between the levels. If significant changes appear to be needed to overall roadmaps, scoping, baselines, or any other program documents, begin to collect justifying information and identify what you will need to obtain buy-in and approval for the modifications.

Program reviews are also a great opportunity for rewarding, recognizing, and thanking contributors for significant program accomplishments. Include social activities on the agenda to reinforce program team cohesion and relationships and to build trust. Allocate at least a little time to having some fun, such as a party or celebration.

Analyze Trends

Overall trend analysis is an additional focus for reviews, especially for long-duration programs. Status data can provide snapshots of how the program is doing, but it is useful once in a while to take a longer view, to work proactively to identify issues with budgets, schedules, or other problems. Trend analysis may reveal problems with estimating or other processes owing to undue optimism, overestimates of productivity, lack of thoroughness in planning, or other factors. Trends and historical data can also help identify a need to revise program roadmaps or baselines to make phase end dates, overall budgets and staffing, the scoping of program deliverables, or other program objectives more credible and realistic.

Follow Up on the Program Review

Another purpose of a program review is to make needed adjustments to your program plans and processes, so thoroughly document all review outcomes. Create a review summary and distribute your findings, proposals, and results to key program stakeholders. It is also often useful to prepare a presentation summarizing the results of a program review and to deliver it to those on the program governance body, key program stakeholders, general management, and people involved with related programs.

If you plan to propose changes that will affect overall roadmaps, program scoping, baselines, budgets, staffing, or any other significant program modifications, develop the information you will need to obtain buy-in and approval. Meet with those who must approve the changes, such as your governance body, sponsor, and key stakeholders. Secure their support, and use your program change control process to track and implement plan revisions or other adjustments that will affect the program's upcoming phases of work (releases, development iterations, stages, or whatever the next effort may be called).

Example of a Program Review

The COMPASS program at Hewlett-Packard scheduled and held reviews every 6 months throughout the program. Before each one, there was a lengthy debate about whether a face-to-face meeting was needed, but each time the program team was able to propose an agenda and generate the data to justify holding a meeting and secure the needed approvals. The meeting places rotated, but most reviews were held in California, because the largest number of participants were there. This made the majority of the meetings logistically simpler and less costly.

The COMPASS program reviews were called "Business and IT Team Summits" because they were expressly intended to involve both the technical and business contributors in the overall review and comprehensive program planning. Each meeting lasted 2 to 3 days, and a typical agenda looked like this (the headings noted here have been generalized):

- Day 1
  - Welcome and agenda review
  - Planned new functions update: plans, timing, and staffing
  - Upcoming software updates
  - Implementation of COMPASS in new countries
  - Testing process changes
- Day 2
  - New services deployment strategy
  - Integration of related systems
  - Plan of record update: sequence, number of countries
  - Dinner and social event

- Day 3
  - ○ Process improvement topics
  - ○ Program risk management update
  - ○ Summit action item review
  - ○ Summit close

For most summits, between fifteen and twenty-five people attended some or all of the sessions. Ground rules included having no computers or other devices in operation except those being used for presentations or capturing information. This ensured that participants focused on meeting business, and it increased the overall productivity. Prior to the meetings, substantial reports were distributed to all participants, usually about a dozen documents, and participants were expected to be familiar with them. Wall-sized versions of the highest level program plans for all current and planned releases in the program plan of record (each similar to Figure 4-9 in Chapter 4) were posted on the walls of the meeting room, and they served both for reference and as scratch pads for changes to release wave plans. By the end of the meeting, each was festooned with yellow sticky notes, arrows, and other jottings reflecting updates and comments. The meetings were quite productive, generating solid, actionable plans for future deployments and significant improvements to program processes. In addition, the summits carved out some time for fun and increased the overall cohesion of the global team members through meals and activities.

MANAGING ORGANIZATIONAL CHANGE

Programs create value through what they deliver, but it is rare for any major undertaking to fully achieve its goals simply by deploying (or changing) a product, service, or result. To succeed, a program must also understand the context of the deliverables and work to shift processes, behaviors, and organizational structures to ensure that the deliverables will be used. This begins with reviewing the status quo and assessing any changes necessary.

Force-field analysis will provide information on factors that will either assist in or hinder making necessary changes. Based on this, program teams can prepare for organizational changes that will support program deliverables. It is often said that people resist change, and often they do. What is always true, however, is that people resist *being* changed. To be successful, program leaders need to effectively figure out how to convince the target users of program deliverables that they *want* to change.

Except for program outputs that are part of fully automated or mechanized systems, all program deliverables must be accepted by people before their benefits can be realized. To achieve this, the first step is to assess the "as is" state currently in place. As program roadmaps and phased scoping come into focus, you can develop an understanding of the users and the environment that are the context for your program and determine what the "to be" state will need to look like (ideally, anyway) to ensure that the program results will be able to deliver the value and expected benefits.

Many useful ideas for managing organizational change originated with Kurt Lewin, an American psychologist from the first half of the 20th century. He was active in group dynamics research, and is perhaps best known for creating a general model for implementing organizational change and for developing force field analysis. Lewin's change model is summarized in Figure 6-3.

Figure 6-3 The Kurt Lewin organizational change model.

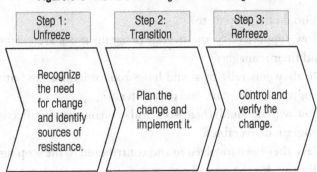

Identify the Needed Change

The first step requires understanding what organizational changes will be needed to support your goals as your program proceeds. As discussed in Chapter 2, initiating a major program requires considerable effort, and the business case tends to include a good deal of credible analysis justifying the major investment to be made. Much of this involves scenarios describing both the current situation and the value associated with achieving the program's results. Key stakeholders involved in funding the effort generally expect substantial benefits and tend to be very supportive of all aspects of the program, including any organizational changes needed. Not all stakeholders fall into this category, however. Some will be the customers and others who are expected to use the results produced by the program.

In reviewing your implementation plans, assess the changes and impact on customer and user stakeholders who will be affected by what you deliver. To gain their cooperation, start with understanding what they currently do and how they do it. If any customers or users will need to adjust to different ways of working and adopt new procedures, new equipment, new technologies, or new systems, persuading them to do so (or better yet, getting them to *want* to do so) must be a big part of your program plans and execution. Uncooperative individuals who can undermine efforts can spell disaster on major programs.

Some of the questions you will need to answer about user and customer stakeholders who are expected to receive and use your program outputs include the following:

- Who do they report to?
- How supportive of the overall program goals are customers and their managers?
- Do they generally trust and have good relationships with the program leader, staff, and overall team?
- How will (or could) their work and environment be affected by program deliverables?
- Have they been involved in and contributed to the scoping and planning for the overall program?

- What could they do to help the program?
- What could they do to impede or hurt the program?

Document what you know about the individuals from whom you will need cooperation and support, particularly any people or groups who appear not entirely enthusiastic about the program, or have little established connection with or trust in the program team. Describe specific challenges and concerns you may encounter with groups and individuals who will need to adopt changes to their business processes, infrastructure, and activities to support your program's results.

Plan for Change

Some changes that appear necessary might be small and straightforward. Others may appear to be nearly impossible. All changes are most easily accomplished through meaningful, thorough engagement in the work required to make the transition. The primary roles for change are the following:

- **Sponsors.** Change sponsorship that is important to programs includes (but may not be limited to) program sponsors and the governance body. Organizational changes generally require support from high-level individuals who will provide resources and communicate their support for the change.
- **Advocates.** Advocates for program changes are often key stakeholders who stand to gain substantial benefits from program results. They are frequently very involved in initiating the program and tend to be active in both developing the program's business case and enlisting sponsorship support for necessary organizational changes.
- **Agents.** Change agents are directly engaged in doing the heavy lifting to put changes into effect. Agents for changes related to program work are often leaders of projects within the program, but also may be on the program staff or operations managers responsible for supporting the program.

- **Targets.** Individuals who are directly affected by program results are the primary focus of change efforts. At least to some extent, target individuals will resist changes, so it is always necessary to plan actions aimed at persuading them to cooperate.

Successfully implementing changes in a business environment relies on a number of factors, summarized in Figure 6-4.

Develop a plan addressing the potential challenges you have outlined involving each of these elements. Document the vision for the program and capture the support you have from high-level sponsors, stakeholders, managers, executives, and others. Post their statements and expectations about the importance of your program on websites, in your program information system, on posters, and in other places where it will be visible to those who need to be persuaded to accept changes. Incorporate high-level quotes in program presentations and reports, and offer to draft memos in the name of program sponsors and influential stakeholders that can be used to encourage cooperation as the program proceeds.

Use your program metrics, especially those related to scope, to document the measurable benefits and value represented by program deliverables.

Figure 6.4 Elements enabling organizational change.

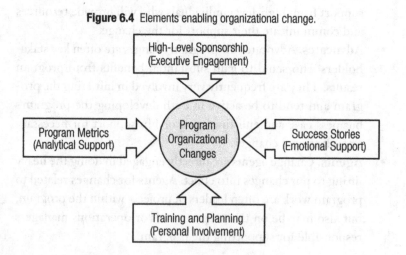

Use the results of pilots, prototype tests, earlier phases of the program, and other previously achieved beneficial outcomes to create compelling success stories to share with those from whom you seek cooperation.

Most important, involve the people who are expected to accept necessary organizational changes in program discussions, meetings, and planning. Listen to what they say, and strive to connect the program's results and benefits with concerns and expectations important to each user or customer stakeholder. Incorporate inputs from all program contributors into what the program is doing and how it is managed. People more readily accept changes that they feel a part of, so try to convert change "targets" into change advocates. Also invest in training for all affected users, customers, and others who will interact with program deliverables, to maximize their understanding of what is pending and provide them with the information they need to become comfortable with changes that may appear intimidating, difficult, or disagreeable.

Force fields, developed by Lewin, help in assessing the net effect of motivations both for and against change, as in Figure 6-5.

Figure 6.5 Force-field analysis for assessing change factors.

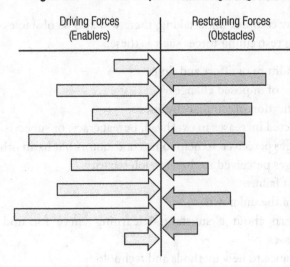

Driving Forces
(Enablers)

Restraining Forces
(Obstacles)

Use force-field analysis to assess what can help or hurt your program. Enablers for change include driving forces such as the following:

- Pain reduction and problem solving
- Pride in helping to accomplish significant results
- Broad inclusion of inputs into plans and deliverables
- Frequent, effective program communication
- High-level, executive attention and support
- Alignment with individual goals; clear connection of program objectives to "What's in it for me?"
- Measurable and meaningful program benefits
- Incentives to encourage adoption of changes (and, possibly, adverse consequences associated with not cooperating)
- Adoption of improved methods (gaining efficiency, effectiveness, productivity, accuracy, quality, and other advantages)
- Ownership and responsibility for program work and results
- Recognition and praise for satisfactory efforts and outcomes
- Job security associated with involvement in a high-priority program
- Access to program resources (including money, people, PMO, equipment, and materials)

As with any complex undertaking, there will also be obstacles and barriers, including restraining forces such as these:

- Expenditure of effort and time
- Dislike of imposed changes
- Modification of familiar routines
- Suspected increases in overhead, bureaucracy, or supervision
- Changes perceived to help some contributors but harm others
- Changes perceived to threaten job security
- Risk of failure
- Fear of the unknown
- Concern about a substantial learning curve for updated processes
- Resistance to new methods and technology

- Lack of meaningful connection to the program
- Threats to existing diversity of cultures or geography

Assess all the positives and negatives for planned changes. Strive to enhance the enablers to increase their effectiveness. Consider what you can do to minimize the obstacles and restraining forces arrayed against the changes required. Develop plans to lower risks, build acceptance, and smooth the adoption of changes. Some organizational change efforts may be best managed as part of individual projects within the program. Others may be effectively accomplished as one of the duties delegated to members of the program staff (or PMO). Still other situations could require a separate dedicated project team within the program, perhaps not even associated with a specific phase, release, or iteration of the work. However you choose to handle the work of implementing needed organizational changes, ensure that you plan it well, staff it adequately with effective and experienced change agents, and include funding to sustain the efforts in your overall program budget.

Implement the Change

In your plans for deployment of program deliverables, include a schedule for needed organization changes. Determine when you need to begin training and communications to establish the foundation for necessary change. Make baseline measurements of the current situation to use in assessing results as you implement the changes. Secure the engagement of sponsors, advocates, and especially of the individuals who will act as change agents, and involve them with sufficient lead time to be effective. Identify all the individuals who will be affected by the change in advance of the deployment, and engage them in conversations, "town halls," formal presentations, and other interactions to prepare for implementation. Consider using incentives or rewards for early target users who adopt changes.

Begin encouragement of change based on your plans and program schedules. Communicate frequently and use measurements and anecdotes highlighting progress to minimize the number of laggards failing to participate. Continue your efforts and monitor progress to ensure that the needed changes are happening. Be persistent and continue to work until you have achieved your change objectives.

A Change Example

With a multiple-phase information technology program such as the COMPASS program at Hewlett-Packard, there was little benefit until the people in each country scheduled for deployment changed their business processes, migrated all of their data, and began operating using the system. For the pilot phase of the program, COMPASS was managed as an IT program, and the only involvement of the business team in the initial country scheduled for deployment was in providing the specific requirements needed to comply with national regulations and to implement other local capabilities needed for the system.

The work was complex, but was finished and tested in time for deployment during the scheduled release window. There were only a few significant technical problems, so the pilot "Wave 0" release was deemed a success. With that, the program rolled forward with plans to implement between three and six countries in follow-on quarterly deployment waves.

As time went on after the pilot release, however, not much was happening. The new system was running, but it had no data and no users, and all the business activity in the initial country remained on the legacy system. Investigating why the implementation was stalled, we learned that hardly anyone understood the new system or its capabilities. In addition, local management was doing almost nothing to encourage people to move day-to-day operations from the existing environment (even though there were pending legal issues that could only be resolved using the new system).

As a consequence of this, we quickly revised the overall structure of the program and focus for planning. While the IT and technical portions of COMPASS were complicated and difficult to manage and did drive the timing and program scope, the business process changes that it represented were in fact even harder. The program team was broadened into a matrix structure, as was summarized in Figure 5-1 in Chapter 5.

Regional and local planning meetings for future wave deployments were started about 8 months before each planned release. Conference calls for planning included all involved country and regional staff. Discussions were not limited to just the specific country requirements. The focus of the calls was broadened to include an introduction to the system as a whole and to initiate conversations about the challenges expected in migrating information from the existing platforms onto COMPASS. As we collected country-specific legal and functional requirements, we also set initial priorities for scoping based on local inputs. Conference call meetings were scheduled as much as possible at convenient times for the country-based personnel, such as 5 a.m. or 9 p.m. California time—not quite so convenient for us—to maximize their cooperation and involvement.

Over the course of about a dozen releases, broad involvement of all system users in planning, testing, and deployment resulted in prompt and successful adoption of the COMPASS system in about fifty countries worldwide.

RECOVERING TROUBLED PROGRAMS

In an ideal world, program execution is expected to go well, maintaining control until all results are successfully achieved. Reality, however, has a way of undermining even the best-laid plans. Complex undertakings are always hard to control, and trouble is never far away.

The initial line of defense for programs in trouble is an effective escalation process, which was discussed earlier (see the subsection Program Issues and Escalations). Even when programs find themselves with severe problems, some situations can be brought into line with outside help from higher levels in the organization.

Programs are larger than projects in many respects. Because of their size, a program failure is a much bigger event than a project failure. Ultimately, some programs will be considered so important that they are not allowed to go under, and will soldier on until someone declares victory and everyone can move on. There are many examples of programs—particularly major, publicly funded construction undertakings—that end with both timing delays and budget overruns that dwarf the original expectations.

The poor track record of such programs is discussed in Chapter 2 from the perspective of Flyvbjerg's article, "Cost Underestimation in Public Works Projects: Error or Lie?" Sometimes adopting an attitude that boils down to "We can't stop now, we're almost done" may very well be the best option. Continuing to throw money, time, and effort at a problem may well be justified in the long run based on the value of what the program will ultimately produce, but this is not the only option.

When it becomes clear that a program will never reach its target destination in line with stakeholder expectations, it is best to cycle back to where it began, assessing the overall undertaking the same way you would for a new program. This analysis will yield one of several decisions: to continue, to terminate, or to pivot. Good program management includes making decisions to cancel or to accept a major shift in program goals as early as possible, not at the end of a long, tortured slog that has consumed enormous amounts of money and effort and continued far longer than necessary.

Reassessing Problem Programs

Early signs of trouble on programs often include one or more of these issues:

- Significant delays in producing program releases or phase deliverables
- Excessive consumption of money, effort, or other resources
- Substantial shortfall in the value, performance, features, or other expected benefits of program deliverables
- Major uncertainties concerning the possibility of producing requested results using available technologies and capabilities

All of these situations relate to major defects in the assumptions that underlie the program, so reassessing the program's business case and potential return on investment is in order. As a program executes, actual performance metrics (or extrapolations based on them) may be substituted in the overall program analysis done initially to investigate whether the program as envisioned continues to make sense.

As discussed earlier in Chapter 2, many programs are initiated using forecasts and estimates (and, far too often, wishful thinking) that may be highly inaccurate. As the data rolls in, program tracking can start to detect whether the differences are small, or large but manageable, or if there are indicators that the program as conceived is fatally flawed. In medicine, the concept of triage separates injured patients into those who will survive (for a time, at least) without attention, those who can survive only with immediate care, and those who are beyond saving. Effective program management must recognize situations analogous to the third group, where continuing cannot deliver results that justify the investment being made, and do it as early as possible.

The basic question to answer when a program is underperforming relative to its objectives should not focus primarily on the variances to plan. The real issue is whether it is progressing in a way that remains a viable business opportunity or an otherwise worthwhile undertaking. Variance to plan can be an indicator of this, but it may also just be showing that you have a flawed plan based on inappropriately optimistic estimates and forecasts. A better test for a program would be an analysis based on credible expenses, realistic timing, and achievable results. With this information you can determine if continuing can be justified based on an updated ROI using realistic costs and benefits. As a program progresses and begins to deliver results and develop historical information about the work, a much more precise picture will come into focus for what can be accomplished.

When the overall business case remains sound even under more credible assumptions, continuing the program by throwing more money at it and pushing out the deadlines could be a justifiable option (assuming the money is available). The ultimate results made the completion of the "Big Dig" in Boston (and the Denver International Airport in Colorado, and the Opera House in Sydney, Australia, as well as many other "failed" programs) worthwhile. In addition, there are often intangible aspects to program deliverables that may be impossible to quantify in strictly monetary terms, including health and safety considerations, civic identity, regulatory and legal requirements, and aesthetics. Decisions to proceed with "runaway" programs are always complicated.

Similarly, some programs will collapse as the magnitude of the required investment coupled with a credible valuation for producible results reveals there is no chance of producing an outcome that justifies the effort. Another factor that can undermine the business case for a lengthy program is a change in user needs or the market for your deliverable, or the introduction of a viable substitute or competitive offering from some other source. Some programs will reach a point where continuing means "throwing good money after bad." Because organizations always have more good project and program ideas than they can fund, prompt termination of unhealthy programs will enable you to shift your focus to better opportunities.

For terminating programs, apply the processes for orderly program closure (discussed in Chapter 7).

The Phoenix Project

A simple dichotomy of either continuing the status quo (at prevailing cost) or pulling the plug is never the whole picture for programs, however. In high-tech product development environments, people often encounter the phenomenon of the "phoenix project." Following the cancellation of a troubled research and development project (frequently following a year or more of frustrating effort and a good deal of expense), a few months may go by. Presently a new project starts up, having a similar objective and sometimes many of the same project team members. The successor project will quickly proceed through planning and early execution, and then produce a new product on schedule and under budget. Upon its introduction, the new product is very successful, beating its sales and revenue forecasts. Although there are often different project leaders responsible for these successive projects, that is rarely the most significant differentiating factor. What really separates the pair of projects is the knowledge base available to the respective teams. The team responsible for the second effort benefits from deep knowledge of what had not worked in the earlier project and where the major risks and problems lay. If you know most of the pitfalls in advance, avoiding them is very easy.

When a program finds itself in trouble, it is always a good idea to diagnose the root causes in some detail before taking action. Some programs progress too slowly due to system decomposition flaws or scoping complexity, as discussed in Chapter 3. Other programs get into trouble because of complications related to workflow between projects, as discussed in Chapter 4. Still other programs struggle because of staffing or organizational issues, as discussed in Chapter 5. Reviewing the overall program may uncover significant issues that could identify root causes and beneficial changes for the work. Process metrics may point to ineffective or inefficient methods or practices that underlie program difficulties.

There may also be cases where the individuals responsible for key program responsibilities are failing to meet their obligations. Reorganizing a troubled program can make a big difference in overall performance. Dealing with skill, knowledge, and experience issues starts with training, mentoring, and providing guidance. Some cases may also require replacing project leaders, program staff, or other contributors with new, more capable people.

Program structure and staffing matters a great deal, but in some cases it may not be the main problem. Some underperforming programs may be aiming at the wrong target. Setting program objectives involves many assumptions about what will ultimately have value (and even what may be feasible). As the work commences, and especially as initial results are produced, these assumptions can be tested. Because programs tend to be structured in phases, releases, or iterations, this feedback can be used to make adjustments that increase the value and benefits possible in future phases of the program. Agile management techniques emphasize the use of short iterations to maximize the learning and enable the team to focus continually on the efforts that will deliver the most value. The principle of "fail early and fail often" captures this well. Knowing what will not work helps in understanding what will, and can ultimately lead to program success.

Incremental adjustments to the program's roadmap, baseline, and phase objectives are an essential part of program reviews. Such modifications over time can effectively provide the control needed to keep most programs out of trouble. Even with diligent management, however, some programs may find themselves deep in the weeds.

When you are managing things well but program results are still not where you need them to be, program cancellation may appear to be the only logical option. Before pulling the plug and giving up, however, it's worth considering if there is a possibility for a phoenix project to rise out of the ashes.

Silicon Valley startups (which are often high-tech programs) overall have a very poor success rate. Historically only about one in ten will ultimately become a successful venture, so it would appear that most who get involved would have to be somewhat crazy. The reason that these startups remain so attractive is that, also historically, the ones that do succeed do spectacularly well. It is also true that failing is rarely the full story. Many startups are excellent places to learn (especially the "what does not work" part). They also provide the information needed for a "pivot," where some part of an effort that has cratered can be used as a foundation for a new undertaking—often one that may have little relationship with the previous one beyond the continuity of some concepts and a few of the same people.

On projects and programs everyone involved learns new things every day. On a major program that gets into trouble, the expense tied up in all of this knowledge may be huge. Simply canceling a program and allowing the intellectual capital to disperse can be spectacularly wasteful. Before deciding to terminate a program, it is good practice to survey the staff to investigate what sort of alternative opportunities might exist that a team of invested, talented people could uncover and exploit.

A pivot for a program that sends it in a new direction will probably require an effort similar to what it took to get the initial program underway. In cases where you discover credible opportunities, visible from a perspective that no one else possesses, the effort will be rewarded. Pivoting a failing program into a trajectory toward a profitable new goal is a much better use of the program team's hard-won knowledge and experience than simply throwing it away.

KEY IDEAS FOR PROGRAM EXECUTION AND CONTROL

- Keep in touch with sponsors and key stakeholders, and strive to align their expectations with program progress.
- Define and use program metrics to understand and control the overall program.
- Track program status diligently and report status on a disciplined, fixed schedule.
- Manage program issues and escalations, and strive for prompt resolution.
- Keep program information up to date and easily available to all program contributors.
- Adopt and use a formal process for program scope control, and strictly limit changes after establishing program deliverable commitments.
- Schedule a program review at least twice a year, to update plans and validate program assumptions. Include program staff and key stakeholders, and conduct the review face to face.
- Regularly monitor program risks, and keep your program risk register updated.
- Plan for and implement organizational changes needed to support program deliverables.
- When programs get into trouble, determine if it is best to shift the roadmap and baselines to reflect more realistic assumptions, cancel the program, or pivot the effort toward a different goal.

KEY IDEAS FOR PROGRAM EXECUTION AND CONTROL

CHAPTER 7

Program Closure

"Begin at the beginning," the King said gravely, "and go on till you come to the end; then stop."

—**Lewis Carroll,** *Alice's Adventures in Wonderland*

Some programs have end points in mind at their start; some are expected to close at some point but are initiated with no defined deadline; and still others are initiated as open-ended efforts that could go on indefinitely. In many ways, programs are similar to partnerships in their range of durations—all the way from partnerships based on a single contract to arrangements expected to be permanent. Like partnerships, however, even programs that might go on forever need a process for closure and termination.

As with most closure processes, the main areas of focus are completing program work, capturing information, and continually improving program management processes.

PROGRAM CLOSURE PROCESS

Program closure involves gaining acceptance of overall program results, finalizing all documents and reports, closing out all program contracts, recognizing accomplishments and rewarding contributors, and capturing what you have learned.

Obtaining Approval to Close the Program

Programs with multiple phases, releases, or iterations tend to have most of their approvals and sign-offs from stakeholders, customers, and others aligned with the delivery of results. Formal approval to close may include such approvals, but it should also focus on obtaining high-level agreement for program termination from the program's governance body, sponsors and key stakeholders, and others in management as appropriate.

Sometimes the process will be implicit, either through a decision to end the program by removing its funding or canceling it, or through reassigning or otherwise removing the program leader, staff, and all assigned contributors. Programs may end through a process not unlike the musical number toward the end of *The Sound of Music*, where the song winds down as one member of the Trapp family after another leaves, and concludes when the youngest exits the stage.

Regardless of the specific circumstances surrounding the end of a program, it is important to review what has been accomplished, as well as any shortfalls or remaining work left undone, with an appropriate manager to ensure an orderly shutdown.

In addition, on closure most programs will require some ongoing support or oversight for program deliverables, so you will also want to pass responsibility to some operational group that can provide adequate coverage after the program terminates. In particular, try to ensure that any pending scoping requirements or requests that remain will be delegated to a responsible party and will receive the future attention that they warrant.

Completing Program Documentation and Reporting

As with approvals, most program data archiving and reporting tends to be tied to a phase, release, or iteration. However, it is also useful to summarize the work as a whole at the time of closure. This will not only provide high-level documentation of the program's accomplishments and acknowledge its contributors, it will also serve as a useful input for future programs.

Construct a final program report beginning with a program summary outlining your most significant accomplishments. Use the report to let everyone involved with the program know unambiguously that it is terminating, and include the information that you have about ongoing support and operations. Also use the report to emphasize the accomplishments of the program team as a whole and to explicitly recognize major individual and team program contributions. The final report should summarize overall program statistics and metrics. And if the program is being terminated before substantial completion of the work expected, provide a summary of what is left undone.

Update your program information archive to include your final report, retrospective program metrics, and all other closure documents. Determine how and where program data should be stored long term if the program archive will not be maintained in its present location, and try to ensure that it is both backed up and migrated to a permanent satisfactory location. If an organization-wide program management office (PMO) exists, work with its staff to capture and retain the knowledge your program generated.

Closing Out Contracts and Program Financials

Complete all program contract paperwork and approve all pending payments. Escalate and resolve any remaining issues with program contracts, and formally terminate all agreements associated with the program.

Also close out all program accounts, and finalize the overall program financials. If there are remaining program funds or budget reserve that can be used by others for ongoing support of program deliverables, transfer the money to them.

Thanking Program Contributors and Celebrating

Be generous with praise, thanks, and recognition throughout the program, but at the end of the program be especially thorough in expressing your gratitude. Thank program contributors, both in person and in writing, and always include the managers of contributors who report to others when sending thank-you memos. Wherever possible, take full advantage of any opportunity to tangibly reward the accomplishments of deserving program staff, teams, and contributors.

Schedule an event at the end of the program to celebrate successes. Even on programs that may be ending with problems, stress the accomplishments that were achieved and strive to end the program positively. On global or distributed program teams, schedule similar events for each location.

Capturing Program Lessons Learned

Programs benefit from frequent post-phase retrospective analysis, program reviews, and process adjustments throughout the work, as discussed in Chapter 6. At the end of the program, it is useful to look back at the entire program to focus on what went well, so you can repeat it on future programs. It is also important to focus on particular program-level issues, problems, and escalations where things did not go well, to aid you in identifying program processes and infrastructure where changes could improve the execution and control of upcoming programs.

Schedule some time near the close of the program with at least the program leader and staff (or PMO) to meet and consider the overall program. A survey prior to the meeting can be a useful way to help people organize their thoughts, and also provide a mechanism for program contributors unable to participate in the meeting (such as those who may already have moved on to other responsibilities). A survey format used on the COMPASS program at Hewlett-Packard that proved useful collected inputs on the following:

- Project management
- Program organization
- Program communications
- Tools and deliverables
- Other areas for improvement

Within each of these categories, people were asked to list items such as what worked well, areas where changes are needed, and recommended improvements.

During the meeting, it's best to focus first on positives before moving on to thoughts about changes and proposed improvements. Begin positively by discussing aspects of the program that went particularly well and program-level practices that people would like to repeat or enhance. As you move on to discussing changes, focus on practices that led to program problems and issues, seeking consensus on what could be modified to make them work better. As you list targets for change, try to uncover the root causes, and encourage brainstorming to flesh out possible improvements.

Discuss the overall list of proposed improvements and select the most promising for recommendation and implementation. Document the results of your lessons learned analysis after the meeting. Distribute a report to the participants and other program contributors, add the summary to your program information archive, and provide copies to your organization-level PMO or others in management who can benefit.

PROGRAM PROCESS IMPROVEMENT

The close of a program is an excellent time to take stock of your overall project and program process maturity. The overall results you have achieved will be a reflection on how effectively you were able to execute the program, and exercises such as an overall post-program retrospective analysis will provide specific recommendations for what you might do differently on a future program to do a better job. If there are particular aspects of program management that need attention, work with your peers, management, and others to address them.

Review the results of your program's lessons learned analysis, and start to work on the highest priority proposed recommendations. If a change proposed is within your control, implement it, and work with others on related programs to propagate the changes widely. Develop a business case or detailed proposal for more elaborate process improvement opportunities, and discuss them with your management. Try to make at least one significant improvement following each program phase, and several more at program closure.

Focus particular attention during program closure on processes that involve high-level managers, key stakeholders, and sponsors. Conversations about changes related to program governance or infrastructure are easier to initiate following a program, both because there will generally be more compelling data to support the recommendations, and it is more likely that you will be able to update high-level program structures and processes before you are engaged in using them.

Following implementation of changes, monitor the updated processes and infrastructure changes to verify that the modifications are having the desired effect and that they are generating no adverse unintended consequences.

KEY IDEAS FOR PROGRAM CLOSURE

- Obtain all needed final approvals and sign-offs for terminating the program.
- Complete all program reports and financial requirements, close out the program contracts, and assess the final program metrics.
- Thoroughly document the program and archive the results for future reference.
- Be generous in your public praise of program contributors and personally thank individuals and teams.
- Learn from each program, capturing practices to repeat and proposals for change that will make subsequent programs more successful.
- Based on your experiences as you close a major program, implement needed governance and infrastructure changes that would be difficult to make during an ongoing program.

CHAPTER **8**

Conclusion

Those who plan do better than those who do not plan, even should they rarely stick to their plan.

—Winston Churchill

Programs are complex, and each one is different. Planning them is inherently imprecise, as it is never possible to anticipate every eventuality. However, regardless of the type, size, or novelty of a program, at least some parts of the work will always rely on established methods and involve efforts that can be understood and planned. The more successful you are in decomposing a program into comprehendible, plannable projects, the easier your program will be to manage. Even an imperfect program plan helps you in controlling a complex program, if it begins to convert an overwhelming number of unknown factors to worry about into a list that is merely very large.

It is also important to keep a focus on the larger context of a program. Takeo Kimura, a technical program manager for Altera Corporation, suggests:

> With programs it's better to be roughly right than precisely wrong. Things change and we need to be nimble and agile. If we aim for precise program schedules, often times we will be wrong. Being roughly right is good enough because we can refine as we go. During the course of a program, there are many opportunities to learn from mistakes. Reflect on your work frequently and take the opportunity to learn right away, benefiting from what you learn immediately.

Program complexity makes planning difficult, so effective program managers strive to minimize complexity. Three main sources of program complexity are system deliverables, workflow dependencies, and the staffing hierarchy. Chapters 1 to 4 focused on ideas for breaking up a program into conceptually more manageable pieces, assessing the results to adjust program plans and expectations to improve their predictability, and using program plans and processes to coherently execute and successfully complete the work.

Successful management of large programs requires attention to each of the primary sources of program complexity.

PROGRAM DELIVERABLE MANAGEMENT

Program scope is often very complex and involves confronting the often conflicting wishes of a community of program stakeholders. Just getting a handle on overall program requirements can be a daunting task, and sorting through the redundancies, inconsistencies, and missing information to assess priorities and lay out a coherent high-level roadmap is a major undertaking.

Specifying a succession of program deliverables, and then applying systems analysis and design techniques to define a hierarchy of subsystems and components, provides perspective and understanding for managing complexity. Chapter 3 also discussed ideas for clearly defining program scope, identifying program scope risks, and using a formal process to control program scope as a program progresses.

PROGRAM PLANNING AND ORGANIZING

Program plans tend to closely overlay defined deliverable components, generally with one project for each defined portion of the program's scope in each phase, release, or iteration. The program's project plans form a complicated hierarchy of interrelated efforts linked by workflow, and create a second source of program complexity. Some of the problems and risks faced in program planning can be minimized by using shorter, more agile program phases composed of simpler projects and less complicated, more frequent deliverables. Techniques for developing a coherent overall program plan were explored in Chapter 4. Understanding interfaces, the dependencies that interconnect projects within the program, is fundamental to building plans for managing and controlling program work. Even catching and defining the most significant cross-project dependencies can help in avoiding unpleasant surprises.

Effective program risk management relies heavily on program planning to assess and respond to project, program, and external uncertainties. Managing potential program problems requires thorough planning, and often involves scoping modifications that minimize risks and help in creating a credible baseline for the overall program.

PROGRAM LEADERSHIP

The program organization chart represents a third complex hierarchy to be managed, alongside the system hierarchy defining program deliverables and the hierarchy of project plans describing the work. The structure for program staffing shares much with the other hierarchies, but it also presents complexity challenges of its own. Aspects of program governance, leadership and skills analysis, and the roles of the program leader and staff were discussed in Chapter 5. Additional topics requiring program-level attention include program communications, distributed and matrix teams, program-level resource risks, and securing ongoing program funding. When reviewing staffing-related plans, you are likely to identify additional opportunities to improve the manageability of the work through updates to program timing, deliverables, and other program goals.

THE PATH FORWARD

Dealing with programs is never easy. One person cannot manage a major program alone; it requires a competent staff. Programs also depend on appropriate formal processes to be successful. Dealing with the challenges of program management is best thought of as a journey, not something that can be mastered all at once.

A good way to start building program management competency and process maturity is to put together a strong program team. Assembling a diverse team of staff members with good general communications and people skills and with a high tolerance for ambiguity represents substantial program-management competence. Developing program planning skills is easier for people who have extensive project management experience. Having a strong background in quality management, business analysis, and market research is beneficial in untangling program scoping complexity. Managing and motivating a large diverse program team is easiest for people who have solid general management experience and a tolerance for interruptions.

Programs are big, and this creates risk. Managing risk on programs begins with a focus on project risk, but it extends well beyond this. Virginia Greiman, professor of megaprojects and planning at Boston University, served as the risk manager for the Boston's Central Artery/Tunnel Project (the "Big Dig"). In her book *Megaproject Management* (p. 310), she suggests:

> Risk management requires a shared vision and mutual cooperation among all stakeholders. A megaproject's organization must be structured to respond quickly to events and to establish open communication and a collaborative environment. All participants must be educated and updated on the underlying assumptions and dynamics of the ever-evolving processes of risk identification, assessment, allocation, response and control.

Effective program management requires ongoing attention to risk, at all levels. Program risks are both intrinsic to the projects and the program itself, and extrinsic to the organization. Successful programs invest substantial effort throughout in identifying and managing risk.

Implementing effective program management is a long-term commitment. You do not need to solve every problem or deal with all program management challenges immediately. To quote James T. Brown from his *Handbook of Program Management* (p. 281), "At the program level, many of the problems you are trying to fix are entrenched in culture, process, and tradition. These problems are not easily or instantaneously fixed; you must continually hammer at them over a period of time before a breakthrough can be achieved."

You can begin by selecting a few ideas to implement, starting with techniques that relate to specific issues that recur or have caused difficulties on recent programs. In particular, focus attention on structuring program work to shorten the time durations of phases, releases, or iterations. Adopting more agile methods having smaller "time boxes" can significantly reduce the overall scale, risk, and complexity you will be dealing with at any given time. Programs, like projects, are mostly about people, so strive to develop solid relationships and deep trust among the program staff, project leaders, and key stakeholders.

Above all, realize that because perfect program management is never possible anyway, working to make things operate more smoothly over time is not just a good strategy for managing complex programs, it is really the best that anyone can achieve.

SELECTED PROGRAM MANAGEMENT BIBLIOGRAPHY

Archibald, Russell. *Managing High-Technology Projects and Programs*, 3rd ed. Wiley, 2003.

Brown, James T. *The Handbook of Program Management: How to Facilitate Project Success with Optimal Program Management*, 2nd ed. McGraw-Hill, 2014.

DeMarco, Tom and Tim Lister. *Peopleware : Productive Projects and Teams*, 3rd ed. Addison-Wesley, 2013.

Englund, Randall, Bob Graham, and Paul Dinsmore. *Creating the Project Office: A Manager's Guide to Leading Organizational Change*. Jossey-Bass, 2003.

Flyvbjerg, Bent, Mette Skamris Holm, and Søren L. Buhl. "Underestimating Costs in Public Works Projects: Error or Lie?" *Journal of the American Planning Association*, Vol. 68, No. 3, pp. 279–295, June 1, 2002.

Gray, Mike. *Angle of Attack: Harrison Storms and the Race to the Moon*. W.W. Norton, 1992.

Greiman, Virginia A. *Megaproject Management: Lessons on Risk and Project Management from the Big Dig*. Wiley, 2013.

Kendrick, Tom. *Identifying and Managing Project Risk*, 3rd ed. AMACOM, 2015.

Kendrick, Tom. *Results Without Authority*, 2nd ed. AMACOM, 2012.

Leffingwell, Dean. *Scaling Software Agility: Best Practices for Large Enterprises*, Addison-Wesley Professional, 2007.

Project Management Institute. *A Guide to the Project Management Body of Knowledge*, 5th ed. Project Management Institute, 2013.

Project Management Institute. *Organization Project Management Maturity Model (OPM3)*, 3rd ed. Project Management Institute, 2014.

Project Management Institute. *The Standard for Program Management*, 3rd ed. Project Management Institute, 2013.

Reinertsen, Don. *Managing the Design Factory*. Free Press, 1997.
Sabbagh, Karl. *Twenty-First-Century Jet: The Making and Marketing of the Boeing 777*. Scribner, 1996.
Senge, Peter. *The Fifth Discipline, The Art and Practice of the Learning Organization*. Doubleday Currency, 1990.

INDEX

function details, 255
high-level organization chart, 201
information management, 254–257
matrix management issues, 206
organizational change, 280–281
organizational charts, 202
overall program information, 255
PMO, 200–204
portfolios, 34
process documentation, 256
program governance, 29–30
program reports, 252
program review, 271–272
program scope and, 266–267
retrospective analyses, 256–257
risk-management, 248
roadmap for, 93
steering committee, 201–202
surveys, 294
training, 252–253
website, 253
workflow risks, 170–171
Humphrey, Watts, 64–65

I

Idioms, 231
IEEE. *See* Institute of Electrical and
   Electronics Engineers
Informational power, 212
Information asymmetry problem, 31
Information management
   communications, 249–251
   HP COMPASS program, 254–257
   reporting in program execution,
      248–256
   systems, 139, 253–254
Inspections, 46, 107, 171, 238
Instant messaging, 251
Institute of Electrical and Electronics
   Engineers (IEEE), 59–60
Integrity, 223
Interfaces
   closure index, 242
   connecting projects, 148
   cross-project, 150–151
   definition form, 151

project plan integration and management,
   146–163
straw-man plan definition forms, 156–159
Internal rate of return (IRR), 43–44, 236,
   240
International Standards Organization (ISO),
   59
Intrinsic risks, 51–53
IRR. *See* Internal rate of return
ISO. *See* International Standards
   Organization
Issues
   matrix management, 206–207
   in program planning, 133–134
   in status tracking, 246–247
   in tin-man plan, 161–162
Iterative program, 152–154

J
Jargon, 231

K
Kano, Noriaki, 85–86
Kano model of needs, 85–86
Kimura, Takeo, 299

L
Leader's Framework for Decision Making, A
   (Snowden and Boone), 15–17
Leadership and staffing, 9
   active listening, 215
   autocratic, 215
   autonomous decisions, 214
   collaboration and consensus, 216
   communications, 217–221
   complexity in, 20
   conclusion, 301
   decision processes in, 214
   funding and support, 194–195
   goals and objectives, 185–186
   hierarchies, 204–211
   key ideas for, 225
   matrix management issues, 206–207
   motivation, 221–223

9 781400 245628